by Jack Dempsey

with Barbara Piattelli Dempsey

Introduction by Joseph Durso

HARPER & ROW, PUBLISHERS

NEW YORK

HAGERSTOWN

SAN FRANCISCO

LONDON

FIRST EDITION

Designed by Sidney Feinberg

Library of Congress Cataloging in Publication Data

Dempsey, Jack, 1895–
  Dempsey.
  Includes index.
  1. Dempsey, Jack, 1895– 2. Boxers (Sports)
—United States—Biography. I. Dempsey, Barbara
Piattelli, joint author. II. Title.
GV1132.D4A29 1977   796.8′3′0924   [B]   76–26220
ISBN 0–06–011054–6

---

77 78 79 80 10 9 8 7 6 5 4 3 2 1

To Deanna
Number Four should have been Number One . . .
Thanks, honey

Contents

Acknowledgments   *ix*

Introduction by Joseph Durso   *xi*

1 · The Move West   1

2 · Manassa's My Home   6

3 · Our Gym Is a Chicken Coop   12

4 · Early Years in the Mines   19

5 · Fighting on the Move   23

6 · Kid Blackie No More   31

7 · Enter Maxine   35

8 · New York—That Wonderful Town   41

9 · I Should Have Warmed Up   52

10 · A Letter from Jack Kearns   60

11 · Off and Running at Last   66

12 · The Ballyhoo Begins   72

13 · Finally, a Following   80

14 • Of Tex Rickard and Jess Willard   87

15 • Signing for the Big Fight   96

16 • Training in Toledo   102

17 • "I Did It! I'm the Champ!"   112

18 • *Daredevil Jack* and the Slacker Trial   122

19 • The First Million-Dollar Gate   134

20 • Dapper Georges Carpentier   145

21 • The Wild Bull of the Pampas   150

22 • Estelle Taylor vs. Doc Kearns   163

23 • We Bomb in New Haven   178

24 • Tunney, the New Champ   188

25 • The Long Count   205

26 • A Friend Dies—A Marriage Ends   221

27 • Hannah Williams   234

28 • In Coast Guard Uniform   251

29 • Deanna   271

30 • Jack Kearns Strikes Again   291

31 • Birthday Party   297

Index   311

Sections of photographs follow pages 112, 144, and 240.

Acknowledgments

We, the authors, both major and minor, would like to thank the following for their help, consideration and time: The Associated Press Wide World Photos; Jack Fletcher and United Press International; *New York Daily News* and Bill Gallo, who cheerfully put up with our ifs, ands and buts; Culver Pictures; Lester Bromberg, who was most helpful post-midnight; Robert Whiteman, who refreshed certain recollections through my old associations with *Liberty* magazine; John O'Neil, Vice President of Mills College for Women, who introduced us to Charlene Ing, who took valuable time out from her studies to diligently sort out the befores and afters of the Slacker Trial indictments; Harry Brand of Twentieth Century Fox, who as publicist and friend provided laughs and fond memories; Will Fowler, a chip off Gene's old block helped with many recollections; Paul Gallico, for his version of our story; Teddy Hayes, who not only was the best trainer a man could have had but proved to be a good friend; Hank Greenspun, publisher of the *Las Vegas Sun*, who refocused the late forties; Jim Jacobs, for allowing us to view the film footage we sometimes lacked; Steve Grundstein, for his patience, time and legal eye; and Elena McGah, for typing what was many times a scramble of a manuscript.

Our sincere gratitude to our editor, Joe Vergara, who, luckily for us, hardly ever shook his head from side to side.

Last, but certainly not least, a special thanks to Joe Durso, who because of a midnight stroll, turned out to be a pretty special friend.

Introduction

When Johnny came marching home from World War I, he marched straight into the era of wonderful nonsense that came to be known as the Roaring Twenties. It was a time of hoopla, hootch, heroes and heavyweights—all spotlighted before a war-weary public on a tumultuous stage.

Part of the people's runaway appetite for action was emotional: the world had been riding a rollercoaster and was not ready to level off. Part was mechanical: great new inventions like the airplane, the motorcar, the motion picture and the radio were bringing events closer together and dramatizing them at the same instant. The results were probably predictable: for a decade or so, until the bottom fell out, life tended to be—well, roaring.

It was a time when society railed at things like "the Bolshevik threat" in Russia, issued ultimatums to the Germans to pay their war reparations, issued warnings that the Allies would occupy the Ruhr Valley if Berlin ignored the ultimatums. Then, having made the world safe again for democracy, people often would rush to get their bets down on a prizefight staged on a river barge because fighting was illegal in the states surrounding the river.

But if people were rushing to embrace causes and crusades, they also were stampeding to break loose from them—especially after the Volstead Act had saddled American society with the "experiment" of Prohibition. As a result, the busiest places in town became the "rum courts," created to hear bootleg cases, and the speakeasies, created to pour the drinks that made life bearable after the courts had recessed for the day.

It was, in fact, a time of style and speed, and passion. When Actors Equity produced an all-star revue at the Metropolitan Opera House in 1921, Alexander Woollcott termed it "a show of strength" and portrayed it in *The New York Times* in these words:

> Here, for instance, was John Barrymore, a pallid, rose-clad Romeo, looking unutterably romantic to the last as the ruthless elevator withdrew him from sight. Here was Laurette Taylor, all loveliness as Ophelia, and Lionel Atwill, looking twice as melancholy and several times as Danish as the usual Hamlet.
>
> It was, in a sense, a night of reunions, for here was Lillian Russell resplendent as Queen Katherine and such old favorites as James T. Powers and Rose Coghlan to show that Equity was no mere enthusiasm of the youngsters. But between those oldtimers and such stars of tomorrow as the Duncan sisters, the audience was all affable impartiality. When these frivolous youngsters did their turn, there was wild applause.

Wild applause. It was the thing that fed the public passion for heroes and heroines in the "era of wonderful nonsense," and most of it was lavished on the stars in the cast—whether the cast performed on the Broadway stage or in the arenas and stadiums where the passion could run loose. And if the wild applause of the Roaring Twenties lingers in echoes today, it lingers over the sporting titans who symbolized the whole mood.

Babe Ruth, joining the New York Yankees and hitting the ball out of sight while attendance doubled in one summer. John McGraw, strutting and goading his New York Giants to four straight pennants. Bill Tilden dominating the men's singles championships six straight years. The Four Horsemen of Notre Dame winning ten straight under Knute Rockne in 1924. Red Grange going from the University of Illinois to the Chicago Bears during his senior year, and then "establishing" professional football by leading the Bears through twenty games before 360,000 customers from coast to coast. And Man O' War finishing first in twenty of the twenty-one races that he ran.

But the performer who captured the public's fancy in the most basic way was Jack Dempsey. He started to capture it on the Fourth of July, 1919, when he destroyed Jess Willard and won the heavy-weight title—while Johnny came marching home. Tough, hellbent, savage—the right man at the right place at the right time.

To my father, raising three sons and a daughter in the Adirondacks in the years that followed, there was no taller hero and no greater fighter. It was a judgment that was drummed into our minds during story-telling sessions at his knee, and it was nourished by his old prizefight programs and memories of men named Firpo, Carpentier and Tunney and of awesome moments in world history like "the long count."

The judgment had long since become fantasy when an unspeakable event overtook my brother and me one October day in the late 1930s as we were trudging home from a kid football scrimmage on the playground of Hudson Falls, New York. It was almost dinner time, already dusk and wintry as we paused in front of the Public Library to watch a line of big, black limousines pull to the curb. That alone might have been an event. But nothing in our lives had prepared us for what followed: Out of the lead limousine in the caravan, directly before us, stepped the biggest and strongest and most improbable man we had ever seen. And, as he stooped to shake our hands, we chorused in total disbelief: "Jack Dempsey."

He was touring the upstate towns campaigning for Franklin D. Roosevelt, but we were stunned that our legend had come to life right there on Main Street. And that's what Jack Dempsey essentially was—a legend on Main Street. Years later, the legend is still flourishing.

Now, reflective and gentle, my fantasy has become my friend, and flanked by his vivacious wife Deanna and his stepdaughter and collaborator Barbara, far from the wild days and the wild applause, Jack Dempsey remembers what it was like—what America was like —in those roaring days when he was king of the hill.

—JOSEPH DURSO
The New York Times

DEMPSEY

1

The Move West

The Dempseys go back a long way. Just how far is hard to say, since very few of my ancestors could read or write and births and deaths were not generally recorded.

My father, Hyrum Dempsey, was a descendant of Irish immigrants from County Kildare. He lived in Logan County, West Virginia, widely known as "feud country" because of the pistol-packing, trouble-shooting Hatfields and McCoys. Hyrum was the nephew of "Devil" Anse Hatfield, whose motto, "Boys, never kick a cripple or go to bed with a fool," was passed on to his favorite nephew. Very little else was passed on.

The Hatfields and McCoys were just about the stubbornest feuding families in the history of Kentucky and West Virginia. Apparently they were so mistrustful of each other that they wore their boots and guns to bed—and probably slept with one eye open as well. Whenever a member of either family died, the next in line would assume the legacy, which was the slogan, "Shoot quick and straight!"

My paternal grandfather, Big Andrew Dempsey, was for a time sheriff of Logan County, as well as county surveyor. Somehow he managed to acquire several hundred acres of timberland while siring five strapping sons, of which my father was the oldest.

Logan County in those days was rugged country with a population of mainly Irish and Anglo-Saxon descendants. It was in rugged Logan County that tall, skinny Hyrum Dempsey met a petite, black-haired and very independent young lady who some- how prevented his getting to sleep at night. She had nerve, pride and a strong temper which, if provoked, knew no bounds. There was a special magic about this attractive, clear-eyed girl that made Hyrum think in terms of settling down. She was strong and quick of mind, and he wanted her. He knew deep down that she would turn out to be the type of woman who would be good for him. Unfortunately for Hyrum, she didn't want him. In time, how- ever, he managed to ingratiate himself with her father, who put in a good word.

Mary Celia Smoot, known simply as Celia to her family and friends, was Scotch Irish and, like Hyrum, a native of West Virginia. While she couldn't boast of the hardheaded Hatfields as relatives, she was the cousin of a U.S. senator, Reed Smoot from Utah. Celia had a strain of Cherokee Indian on her mother's side, which en- abled her to see and hear things the rest of us couldn't. At least that's what we thought when we were children; later we realized she was just smart.

The marriage of Mary Celia Smoot to Hyrum Dempsey took place on a Sunday afternoon, about 1868, in Logan County, after what seemed to Hyrum ten years of courting. Many showed up that day knowing they would get a good meal since Celia's father owned a small store.

It was, from the very beginning, not the best of marriages. The first years were hard and there was no money. Hyrum, the possessor of a roving spirit as well as a roving eye, was always scheming to get rich quick. He didn't like to stick with the same job for long because he figured the mind would get stale. Variety was a virus in my father's blood, and this caused a great deal of wran- gling between my parents.

My father drank when he had it and sometimes he managed to when he didn't. Money? Same thing. When he had it, it burned such a hole in his pocket that he threw it away. And he loved to play the fiddle. We all heard "Turkey in the Straw" so many times, it seemed to us like the national anthem.

When my father and mother settled down in West Virginia, he had a job teaching reading and writing at a local schoolhouse. He prided himself on having studied the formal usage, as he called it, of the 4 R's.

He disliked his job intensely.

"All a teacher needs to know is something you don't. If one is smart enough, he'll learn to ask lots of questions and notice things around him. Observation—that's all it is—observation."

By the end of his fourth year of teaching, he'd had it. He was thinking about escaping from the classroom when notices were tacked up all over town telling of the imminent arrival of a traveling Mormon "missionary preacher" who was coming all the way from Salt Lake City. By the time the preacher pulled into town, he had quite an audience waiting for him—a poor audience, but a receptive one; Hyrum and Celia included.

"Friends, there's a new life out West, a new opportunity to start afresh . . ."

Hyrum Dempsey tuned in to himself, having just heard what he wanted to hear. This was the green light he had been waiting for. Celia, on the other hand, saw and heard things differently. Leaning forward, she listened to each word that flowed out of the preacher's mouth and was impressed and touched by the fresh concepts of this new Mormon religion. The more she listened, the more she liked what she heard. She was convinced that this faith was tailor-made for her as well as for Hyrum. Both converted to the Mormon faith, each for completely different reasons.

Religion was one of the few things our family had in common. My mother embraced the faith throughout her life; at home she read and taught us stories from the Bible and made sure we said our prayers and counted our blessings—however few—at night. She was a God-fearing little woman who tried to show us that a good and worthy life is measured just by knowing the difference between right and wrong.

In my later years, I strayed somewhat from religion. If I were to describe myself, I would say I was a "Jack" Mormon—which wouldn't have made my mother very proud, but it was better than nothing, and it was certainly better than the personal code my father was practising.

Some have said that I prayed before fights. Nonsense. I was so intense and excited that to stop and pray, with people packed in the dressing room around me, was the farthest thing from my mind.

The only person close to me who could have used a good dose of religion was my father. From the beginning, he didn't live by any book. He believed in a practical rather than a spiritual approach to life. Even though he was told that just rewards were to be handed out in the next life, my father liked to play it safe day by day, reaping as much as he could in this life, never mind the next.

The words that the Mormon preacher had spoken that day stuck in my father's mind. He became like a man obsessed with one thought: to move! It was all he could talk about until he finally took hold of himself and decided to take action. He sold some acres of timberland that he had inherited from grandfather Andrew, along with what little else he possessed, and bought horses and a large wagon. Within a few days, after a number of tearful good-byes, my parents, with their two small children, were ready.

The covered wagon was stocked with provisions that included warm blankets, warm clothes, canteens of drinking water, and books for the long and lonely evenings. But it wasn't the material things that got them west; it was hope, courage and the pioneer spirit which helped them through the many hardships and God knows how many breakdowns. At times during the tedious journey the children were told to hang over one side of the wagon to help keep it from overturning. They were, I gathered later, very frightened, and seeing the number of dead animals on the road didn't help. Neither did those times when the water ran out, when they had to stop and dig shallow wells in the hope of finding some. When they found water, they stayed awhile; when they didn't, they pushed on.

The further west they pushed, crossing the plains and the Sierras, braving the terrible rains and dust storms, the more optimistic my father became, and the more sure he was that he had made the right decision.

The women, my mother among them, were the real pioneers,

the backbone of the west, the iron wills which mended the crumpled hopes and egos as well as the occasional bouts of frustration.

After pressing on for what seemed to be years and millions of miles through endless stretches of isolated backlands, Hyrum and Celia decided to settle in the small town of Manassa, Colorado. Manassa had been founded in the late 1870s by a struggling wagon train of seventy-two very tired Mormons. At the time, the Rio Grande Railroad was building a line from the north down through the San Luis Valley in Colorado. The Mormons thought this to be as good a spot as any, so they settled near the Conejos River, in the San Luis Valley.

Every member of this small community was a staunch supporter of the Good Neighbor Policy. Anyone who fell down on his luck would not be down for long, thanks to the helping hands that soon enabled him to stand on his own two feet once more. If there were something to be done for someone else, it was done without the asking.

These pioneers never experienced a real food shortage since there was lots of wild game around. Because of the availability of game, however, there did occur a shortage of ammunition.

To my parents, my older sister and my brother, Manassa seemed a new and promising place. By 1895, my parents were veritable old-timers, completely at home with a small farmhouse filled with children of every size and shape. In the center of town, the settlers had built a great white Mormon church in which I was later christened when I was eight years old. Up to that time, it was the biggest building I had ever seen; its steeple pointed towards the sky.

2

Manassa's My Home

On June 24, 1895, I, William Harrison Dempsey, became the ninth of what was to be a grand total of thirteen children. I was named after President William Harrison (naming children after presidents was then the fashion). I remember I had only one toy, a spinning top that my father had whittled out of wood. I didn't know any other toys existed, nor did I care; when you're very young you don't think in terms of how much or how many. I was happy with one thing, which was one more than nothing—and God knows how many owned nothing.

My father for some time insisted I was born on June 23, but my mother felt that she, having been present, should have the last word in the matter. And so it was. I weighed eleven pounds even. The midwife who attended my mother took twenty-five cents for her services, which in time proved to be a pretty good investment.

From the time I was small I realized what kind of people my parents were. My father was a dreamer and an egotist. He always felt he had to come first, no matter what—and then, if anyone wanted to follow. . . . I guess he just couldn't help it. As he must have figured it, whatever he did would somehow benefit his family. Sometimes it did and other times it didn't.

My mother, on the other hand, was a staunch realist. In my eyes she could do no wrong. She loved us all fiercely and was pre-

6

pared to stand by our sides at any cost, just so long as we didn't disgrace the family. She was unselfish and giving, and she really sacrificed for us in those early years.

Nevertheless, she too had rare moments when she allowed herself to get carried away. Once a painted gypsy dressed in vividly colored scarves parked her caravan not far from the center of town. My mother, who had never seen anyone quite like her, was naturally intrigued; without telling a soul she approached the gypsy to have her fortune told. The gypsy, seeing live bait, lit up. Finding that my mother had a silver dollar, she borrowed it to put under her tongue "to help the spell." Before the spell could be helped, the silver dollar disappeared. My mother, nobody's fool, demanded her coin back. The gypsy didn't move, so my furious little mother put her hands around the gypsy's throat and threatened to choke her either standing up or upside down, unless the money was returned. It was—fast!

Celia Dempsey was a tough, wiry little woman who knew exactly what she wanted; when she smiled, she could melt even the hardest heart. The haphazard, insecure life my father had thrust upon her wasn't to her liking at all. She had mouths to feed, bodies to clothe and honest citizens to raise. She always put her family first; she wanted us to make it. And she was responsible for instilling the "fight" in me, for her great hero was the famous old heavyweight boxing champion, John L. Sullivan.

"Just before you were born," she told me one day, "an old peddler came to the door and begged me to allow him to warm his feet and hands by the leadbelly stove he had seen glowing through the cracks in the shutters. Said he had traveled a great distance. Lord have mercy, I let him come in. After giving him some warm food and drink, I gave him a blanket near the stove, where he promptly fell asleep.

"Son, I know what it's like to get so tired your bones ache. I could see this man was on the verge of complete exhaustion. When he awakened, he was so grateful that he didn't know how to thank me enough, and he insisted I choose whatever I wanted from his sack of dusty wares. At first I told him I didn't want anything, but he was so eager for me to take something that I couldn't refuse. Since I had to while away the time, I decided to take a book. He thanked me profusely, God blessed me and then he left. Dusting off the cover I saw that the title was *Life of a 19th Century Gladiator* by John L. Sullivan himself. I read and reread this book so many times, son, that right there and then, I decided that if you turned out to be a boy, you could be just like him, because I felt you were going to be strong. I just knew it."

We were just about settled in Manassa, thinking of this little town as home, when my father lost his farming job. He decided to uproot the family and move on.

We headed for Creede and Uncompahgre, Colorado. We were among some of the highest mountains when things started going wrong near Leadville, one of the highest cities, if not the highest city, in the west.

One of the wagon horses who had pushed too hard up a hill quietly lay down on its side, heaved a great big sigh and died. Worse, and terribly frightening for us, my mother began feeling dizzy and then fainted a few times while experiencing shooting pains in her stomach.

"Don't worry," my father reassured us feebly. "Your ma will be all right. I've got a suspicion it's due to the high altitude."

His words were hollow ones. They meant absolutely nothing to us who were young, in strange unknown country and terrified. It had snowed, and for miles nothing was to be seen under the white blanket. It was icy cold, and our faces, especially our noses, were covered for protection against frostbite. My sisters cried and cried, clinging to each other. I tried to comfort them as best I could while my own insides trembled. My father realized he would have to get my mother out of the mountains at once.

He carefully counted and recounted all the money on hand and found that there was just enough to get my mother to my sister Florence, who was living in Denver.

It was decided that my mother would take the youngest ones, meaning me, my brother Bruce and my sister Elsie, while my father and the older children would stay behind and wait for our return.

We left them waving sad good-byes and managed to hitch a ride to a branch of the Denver and Rio Grande Railroad, where we mistakenly installed ourselves in one of the passenger cars.

After we had been on the train a while, I sensed someone standing over me. I looked up and stared smack into a brass button that was part of a navy blue uniform belonging to the train conductor, a big, burly, red-faced man with a thick neck and a scowl on his face. He demanded to see our tickets. My mother produced her single ticket and I froze. He overlooked Brucie, who was very small, and for some reason Elsie, who ignored him altogether by staring out of the window. He focused on me, his scowl worsening.

"I'll have to collect a half-fare for this boy, or you're all off my train. I've had enough of your kind."

My mother attempted in vain to win him over. She clutched his sleeve and tearfully told him of our meager circumstances and her illness; she showed him her almost empty homemade purse containing small change and frayed bits of paper. He was unmoved.

She tried again. "How can you think of putting us off the train in the middle of nowhere? Let us be and I promise, I'll make sure you get the fare somehow."

"Sorry, ma'am. Can't help you. Rules are rules, and I stick to 'em. You either pay the fare for the boy or he's put off at the next station. I'll be back!"

He glared at me one more time before moving off. My heart was beating much too loudly in my ears and I could feel the ice-cold trickle of perspiration making its way down my back.

As this scene was taking place there sat across the aisle a cowboy dressed in his entire regalia, including pearl-handled pistols at his side and beautiful boots with fancy spurs. He had been taking in the whole sorry situation. Now that the conductor was out of sight, the cowboy motioned to me.

"Tell your ma to stop worrying. If it comes to a showdown, I will pay your fare, sonny. But I don't think it'll come to that; I think he's bluffing. Don't you worry about a thing, pardner."

I was touched by these words of kindness. My eyes brimmed with tears which I would not allow to fall in front of this magnificent fellow. Humiliation felt like a pitchfork in my belly and it made me realize for the first time how poor we were. When we lived in a town where all the folks were struggling like us, I didn't pay any attention. We were all clean and scrubbed ("water don't cost nothin'; use it"), but here we were the ones who stuck out with our makeshift possessions and paper in our shoes.

I was ashamed. I vowed at that very moment—I was almost nine—that this wouldn't happen when I grew up. One day I would have enough money to pay for as many fares as I wanted. One day I would be grand, just like the cowboy.

My newfound friend turned out to be right; the conductor had been bluffing. We were mighty relieved when he came back through the compartment and passed us without saying one word, looking straight ahead.

Once in Denver, my mother felt better and pretty soon we were ready to rejoin my father and the others, who had managed in the meantime to get to Wolcott. When we informed him we were ready to travel, he sold the other horse and wired us the money.

We didn't have any trouble going back; this time we were all paid for. My father, who had had a fright even though he never let on, was extremely pleased to have my mother and us around again.

Stopping for a spell in Steamboat Springs, we hired ourselves out—we boys, that is—as farmers' helpers so that we could make more money and keep moving on. It was tough putting some money aside with so many mouths to feed, but we managed.

From Steamboat Springs we finally reached Uncompahgre, Colorado, where my father got himself a rancher's job. It was June, 1904, and I had just passed my ninth birthday. Despite our many moves, my mother always made sure we attended school wherever we were. Some of us did try our hardest to learn something, but it wasn't easy; the teacher was usually too busy keeping order to have much time for teaching.

It seemed to me that our mornings, before we headed for school, used to be as tiring as the days themselves. I hated getting up in the pre-dawn hours, realizing that before we could even think of getting breakfast the cows had to be milked, the wood chopped, horse manure cleared away and eggs collected. No chores, no food.

Not surprisingly, the kitchen was the most important room in the house. It was just about the only room that wasn't cramped and overcrowded, and it was warm and smelled good. Women cooked while the boys and men made themselves comfortable around the stove and told stories. Country ballads and gospels were sung and matters of Great Importance were discussed. Sometimes no one talked at all; occasionally thoughts would be interrupted by the sound of someone's chewed tobacco spit hitting the side of a spittoon.

In time we each acquired a horse, and one of our favorite pastimes was riding into the foothills to chase and rope the wild burros that roamed in small bands. It looked like a second-rate, badly staged rodeo.

We even tried skiing, but this was a very shortlived sport, for the barrel slabs that we used for skis were usually turned into toboggans, which were much more fun—especially when harnessed to the old family jackass. That ass certainly had his uses; my mother once tied one of my loose teeth to his tail and gave him a whack on the rump.

3

Our Gym Is a Chicken Coop

We were just about getting used to our surroundings and making friends when my father lost the ranching job. We had gotten pretty much attached to the farm and found it very difficult to accept the fact that once more we had to pick up and move. I think this was the first time I ever saw my mother in tears. I didn't realize that her tears were also being shed for her marriage, which was slowly turning sour.

Our next home was in Montrose. Gun country. Not dangerous, but each and every child was taught to hold a gun from the time he could walk. It was in Montrose that I picked up coyote trapping, laid traps for the bears up in the hills, and relied a great deal on my ten gauge shotgun. I remember its being old and incredibly rusty.

It was in Montrose that my tiny mother decided to take the financial welfare of her family into her own hands. She was tired of making ends meet halfway only to have to drop everything every time my father was out of work. She knew, deep down, that our way of life left much to be desired. She never allowed her worry over money to interfere with our upbringing. She preached the virtues of honesty with every passing day and incident.

"If you can't look at yourself straight in the eye with respect the morning after you done something, then it means I've done a bad job and you aren't fit."

There was even a sampler on the wall with words by Carlyle, which said:

**MAKE YOURSELF AN HONEST MAN
AND THEN YOU MAY BE SURE
THERE IS ONE RASCAL LESS IN THE WORLD**

Just a reminder, in case we forgot.

My mother's becoming a breadwinner happened this way: Around 1905, the Denver and Rio Grande Railroad was involved in building what was called the Gunnison Tunnel for the transportation of water. (Originally the railroads had come out west seeking ore, like everyone else who wanted to get rich.) Because of the tunnel's construction, workers and transients were to be seen everywhere. The construction of the tunnel dominated everyone's life, including my father's, who had managed to land himself a railroad job.

Looking around, my mother saw that there wasn't any decent eating place in the area of the construction site. Celia Dempsey, who knew how to cook, had a brainstorm; she decided to go into the restaurant business. The place was christened (with a jug of hard cider) the Rio Grande Eating House.

Celia Dempsey's Rio Grande Eating House consisted simply of chairs and tables clustered in small groups about a large room with a kitchen in the back. It was an instant success, crowded from the early morning hours right up to the time of the closing of the site, which marked the end of a long, hard day. The news of "good grub," including "the best beans in town," spread fast, and pretty soon we were all involved in one capacity or other. We did everything from shining customers' shoes (we had trouble finding eager clients—no one really cared what their shoes looked like) to mopping the floor, washing dishes and selling the local paper.

The construction period lasted quite some time, during which we came in contact with every type of person imaginable. I enjoyed sitting around with a few of the construction men, listening to their conversation. Between stories of this or that woman and gales of laughter, they liked to talk about current and past happenings. It was the telling of what had been that I loved hearing.

One story always seemed to lead into another, and there would be talk around a log fire until the early hours for those men who didn't have their families with them. Companionship was very important and the friendships that were formed were for men only. Women in those days had their place—and their place was not with the men.

Those nights I sat on lumpy crates or logs and listened were never too long for me. I watched cowhands play cards with construction workers, I watched the men smoke until the smoke got so thick that faces disappeared into thin night air. I was present when they gambled, drank whiskey and swore. It was very different from anything I had ever seen, and I knew that if I were ever caught . . . Somehow, though, I always had the feeling that my parents knew where I was but didn't say anything.

Everyone in Montrose worked hard. If you didn't, you were nothing but a lazy bum, a good-for-nothing. Though the people we came into contact with all seemed to be in the same boat, I was still conscious that there were the haves and the have-nots. Determined as I was to make it, I worked as hard as I could. So did other youngsters, for there weren't as yet any laws prohibiting child labor. Because we were so young, we were even made to put in longer hours.

When construction of the Gunnison Tunnel was finally completed, quite a number of people, including us, left town. The Rio Grande Eating House was sold and the money used to finance the move.

We stopped in Provo, Utah. It was approximately forty miles from Salt Lake City, which my mother hoped would be the final stop (whether anyone liked it or not).

Eventually we moved on to Lakeview. Here my father rented a 120-acre farm not too far from Utah Lake.

It was in Lakeview that I picked up my schooling once again, eventually managing to graduate eighth grade. My teacher, Ray Wentz, who used to commute to Lakeview on his horse and buggy every morning, was overjoyed to see his far-from-prized pupil finally get out. He was of the opinion that even though I probably absorbed very little, it might come in useful one day. He was right; it wasn't much of an education, but it did help me. I wanted to have a higher education, but it was obvious to me that I didn't have either the time or the money.

Lakeview was a town which held Saturday night dances and weekly meetings of the townfolk while attracting countless traveling medicine shows on the outskirts of town. These medicine shows were almost as exciting as seeing the circus coming to town and setting up its tents. We'd spot the hawker long before he reached town with the brightly painted van hitched up to a frisky horse. Not only was the van colorful, but it had a million signs hung on it. Stopping in a certain spot, the dapper medicine man would spring (they always sprang) down and start setting up his platform. This fast-talking man, dressed in his Sunday best (with top hat), would verbally attack the gathered crowd with some New and Exciting Offer. The more he talked, the more people couldn't help but listen, and, noting this, the more he talked without, as far as I could see, taking one gulp of air. He would motion to the group to "step a little closer," as he had in his possession (courtesy of some eminent chemists who preferred to remain anonymous) an Essential Product—usually a worthless tonic—which would revolutionize their lives. Guaranteed. My eyes were glued to his every move, my ears to his every lie, especially when he would produce living proof of his product's success—at which point a witness from behind the closed curtains would step forward and give an unsolicited testimony.

Some fell for his baloney, some didn't. Those who did insisted that it was goshdarned fine stuff rather than admit that they had been taken.

At this point I was still too young to have a really good time at the dances. All I ever did was go with some friends, stand on the side and whisper, snicker and point at the silly-looking girls who were staring our way. Ecch! As I say, I was very young.

After school I held a variety of jobs. One of my favorites was in a nearby barbershop where I shined shoes and kept the place clean. There were three or four barbers, but I liked one in particular because he let me put the hot towel on a few of his customers. I considered myself a tremendous asset in the barbershop, but the barber came to think otherwise. I experimented once with his favorite imported comb and broke it. Afraid he would get mad, I decided to conceal the evidence by sweeping it out the door—and right onto his feet as he was coming in.

Though I was never much of a reader, I found plenty of interesting things to read in the barbershop. Especially the *Police Gazette*. I devoured it, and whenever a new issue came in, the barber allowed me to take home an old copy. Anything that interested me would be cut out and tacked on the walls of the room where a few of us slept. (We couldn't put anything away in drawers because we didn't have any.)

These were my formative years, my longest years; they were the years while I waited impatiently to grow up. My older, bigger brother Bernie had become a prizefighter, taking on bouts whenever his money from mining jobs ran low. He alone knew of my ambition to become a fighter and decided to teach me a few professional tricks of the trade. He took me seriously, despite my being only fifteen, and he dedicated long hours to my training. Maybe he wanted to see for himself whether or not I was on the right road. I could have told him.

Bernie was a good fighter, but he had a glass chin, so he never quite made it. Nevertheless, in my eyes, he was the best. He seemed to know everything there was to know.

As far as Bernie the fighter went, he really wasn't making any money, so I figured that somehow, someday, I'd have to be better. At the time it seemed unlikely.

He helped me turn a chicken coop into a gymnasium. An old battered mattress was placed on the ground for tumbling and wrestling. We took a cloth bag and stuffed it with sand and sawdust to make a punching bag.

My younger brother Johnny also got involved with our fighting. Johnny and Bernie would alternate swinging a broom in front of me while I tried to hit it as it flew through the air. We took turns skipping rope to improve our wind. We would even sprint against one of our horses (naturally, giving ourselves a head start). This was supposed to improve our wind and our legs; at first, it only improved our appetites and our horse.

What with my normal boyhood scraps and the dedicated training at the coop, I actually felt that I might some day become a good fighter. But one problem remained: I was small and skinny and I didn't look like prospective champion stuff at all.

Nevertheless Bernie worked me hard. He didn't want me to have a glass chin. He taught me to chew pine gum, straight from the trees, to strengthen my jaw. Then, after a spell, he would test me to see if I had done enough chewing by throwing a left hook to my jaw. Invariably I would be knocked down. After dusting myself off, I would chew some more of the bitter-tasting stuff. I bathed my face in beef brine to toughen the skin. (Bernie called it pickling and said that if I ever got cut, I wouldn't bleed.) Once a day I would trek to and from the butcher shop, carrying back pails of the stinking stuff. At first the brine burned like hell, but then I got used to it. Eventually my face got as tough as a saddle.

"You don't want a fight stopped because of a cut, do you, Harry?"

"It'd better be worth it. Ugh!"

My family called me Harry. I didn't change my name officially to Jack Dempsey (officially in the ring, that is) until I substituted for Bernie in one of his fights. He used the fighting name "Jack," and when I substituted, I had to take over the name. The name originally belonged to the great Irish old-time middleweight known as Jack Dempsey the Nonpareil (the unequaled), who died in 1895, the year I was born.

It was hard work. The training was tedious. But it didn't bother me; I loved fighting. I was even getting pretty good with my fists and knocked Bernie down a few times.

After what had seemed a hundred years, my graduation from the eighth grade rolled around. I felt I had, at last, accomplished something. My mother and father were as proud as peacocks. My sister Elsie and I were the only members of the family to complete some kind of schooling.

"Son, you must, throughout your life, make every bit of your knowledge practical. If you do this, it will make you successful one day."

"Yes, Pa."

"Harry, are you going to quit studying now for good? Tell us, boy."

"Gosh, Ma, I've got a lot to do. Ain't got time for more studying. At least not right now. Don't worry, Ma, some day I'll make you proud of me. You too, Pa."

I was ready to leave home, ready to start earning a living on my own. It would be a whole new adventure. While my mother was sad to see me go, she knew I had to do whatever I felt was best. It was hard for her to see her boy turning into a man; she felt my boyhood years, no matter how brief, had passed too fast.

I can still hear her words.

"Remember, dear boy, if the truth should ever stand in your way, that will mean you're heading the wrong way. And don't you forget it."

"Ma, I—"

"Go, Son, go. And God bless you, Harry."

"God bless . . ."

4

Early Years in the Mines

From the time I left school I turned to mining whenever I wasn't fighting. Just like my brother. Bernie got me my very first serious mining job when I was sixteen years old. He had been mining on and off for a long time and was now shift boss at a copper mine in Bingham Canyon, Utah. I was a mucker, the lowest member of the mine crew. I worked after the others had finished for the day, loading the mined ore into small cars and getting it to the shaft to be hoisted to the surface. The job paid a lot of money— around three dollars a day.

My first day on the job the top boss ordered me down to the 3,000-foot level. Because of Bernie's skills, he assumed that I too was an experienced miner. I'd picked up a fund of general knowledge about mining, but there was a lot I didn't know. I kept my mouth shut and put on an air of confidence as I climbed into one of the small ore cars, head down so as not to hit the timbers and beams above me. At the 3,000-foot level, I found myself completely alone. If anyone else was supposed to be down there, they were now gone. After looking around, I started to do what I was supposed to do. I climbed out of the ore car and managed to push it along its narrow track to the end of the drift, the passageway through the rock wall. I was now in what seemed to me to be the bowels of the earth. I felt like someone in a Jules Verne book.

Extremely jumpy, I reminded myself to act like a man while I shoveled ore into the car real fast and then pushed it up the shaft toward the narrow passageway. At the mouth of this passageway, by a short spur track, was a white bell I had to push when the car was loaded. Three bells meant up; two bells, down; and one bell, stop. When the cage came down with an empty ore car I was to replace it with a loaded ore car and give the "up" signal.

Fine. I understood. But before I got to the end of this drift, my carefully loaded car jumped the track. At the same time I heard a hissing noise. If I had been jumpy before, it was nothing to what I experienced now. I felt the hairs on the back of my neck rise. I started running, but my feet, now blocks of wood, tangled, and I tripped and fell. My lamp went out and it was now pitch black. I was positive there was going to be an explosion—I had heard of so many of these tragedies that I prepared myself for the worst. I was convinced my end had come and that no one would ever find me. My life, unfortunately or fortunately, was still too short to flash before my eyes.

I waited, hardly daring to take a breath, to be blown to smithereens. My throat was so tight I couldn't swallow. My feet and hands were clammy. I couldn't think straight.

Huddled into a very tight ball with my eyes squeezed shut, I waited for *it* to happen. And waited. Nothing. The hissing was on and off now. Cautiously I started to move. I was still alive!

I tried to regain some of the senses I had lost in my fright and managed to get my lamp lighted again. Then I turned my head, looked around slowly and realized what had happened. When my ore car jumped the track it had bumped one of the compressed air pipes and knocked a joint loose. The hissing sound was only compressed air. I say "only" because this was nothing compared to being alone in the dark with the prospect of an explosion. I got the ore car back on the track and up the shaft. Whew!

Fighting soon followed me into the mining camp. My powerful fists were my prized assets—my only assets, come to think of it—and no one could take them away from me. A short time after I started working I came across a bully who thought tough, talked tough and looked tough. He weighed about 200 pounds and he kept picking on the smaller men. I knew that sooner or later he would get around to me.

One afternoon he walked by where I was working and threw a handful of dirt on me. I ignored him. He smirked. I looked up at him and grinned like an idiot. He grinned back and I continued shoveling. More dirt hit me, this time landing on my neck.

"Hey! Cut it out! I'm trying to work."

He laughed uproariously and threw another packed handful down on me.

"I said quit it!"

"What'll you do if I don't?"

"You'll see. Now if you know what's good for you, leave me alone or else . . ."

"Or else what? What, huh?"

I ducked more dirt he was chucking down and then my patience ran out. I started after him, going slowly until I reached the level ground where he waited, swinging his fists wildly. He was completely untrained. I had a distinct advantage despite the fact that he was bigger. We made such a loud commotion that the other miners stopped working and crowded around to see what it was all about. Some took bets, others yelled for us to stop. We started circling each other, neither landing a blow until I threw a right cross to his jaw that ended it.

The news of my quick victory spread like an epidemic. Everyone wanted to shake my hand, and I was no longer treated like Bernie's kid brother. The bully, on the other hand, was subject to so much name calling and derisive laughter that within a short time he gave up his job and moved on to camps where his talents might be more appreciated.

For the next five years I worked in the mines on and off between fights. Copper, silver and gold, I did 'em all. And it was tough and full of dangers; we didn't have the safety equipment they have now.

Bernie and I even went so far as to take a lease once on a mine located in Cripple Creek, Colorado. We solemnly promised the owner 25 percent if and when we struck ore. We worked like dogs, without helpers or machinery, doing everything ourselves. We sweated like pigs, we turned on each other, we collapsed in the sun, but we kept right on working that mine. The experience was one of my most unforgettable, for I really loved mining. Ore? We found none.

5

Fighting on the Move

As I covered ground, moving from place to place and from job to job, I came to the conclusion that I was master of my own fate. I was determined that if I didn't find a way to become successful, I would make one. As a young man, I saw no limits in what I could do; my options for success were countless.

My long-range goal was to become a Champion—and now I ate, slept and dreamed of it. I didn't tell too many people outside the fight game because I didn't want to be thwarted by jealousy or laughed at. I knew there were other fighters just like me, hungry and poor, but I really couldn't think of them—as I was sure they wouldn't of me. We were all out for ourselves, and if I didn't place myself first, who would? I no longer thought of them as competitors but as opponents to be defeated. It had boiled down to this: either work, and work hard, or starve.

By 1916 I had fought lots of guys, but all of them had been amateurs like me. I felt that the best thing for me to do would be to hit other towns, so I hopped a freight and rode the rods into Salt Lake City. There I decided that my best bet would be to walk into a gym, announce the grand arrival of Kid Blackie and add that I was willing to take on anyone. Unfortunately, "anyone" of any decent standing was not willing to have anything to do with me. A few who had nothing to lose agreed to take me on, and I arranged a few quick fights and made a few bucks. I was lucky to land a job as a porter in the Hotel Utah—for free room and board. I stayed there awhile, but pretty soon there were no decent opponents left in the gym. Many were on their way East, which was too big a step for me to take at this time.

I headed back to Colorado via the rods once more. It was harvest time; the trains were jam-packed with workers going where their skills would next be required. I didn't feel guilty about riding the rods; I was busted, and it didn't cost anybody anything to transport us. I say "us" because many others did it as well. Some guys even knew the trains' timetables backwards and forwards; it was from them that I found out that the mail trains went fast (up to seventy miles per hour) but the trains that rushed perishable goods to market were the best. Sometimes it got real cold under the train; you'd be hanging on with your eyes shut to avoid the hot blinding cinders and trying to keep warm at the same time. It wasn't easy, especially when exhaustion set in. When that happened I would tie my hands and feet (using anything from light chains to heavy cotton kerchiefs) to the train's lower rungs, making sure the knots were tied as strongly as I could make them.

From time to time train officials nabbed us and kicked us off, sometimes in the middle of no place.

On the banks of the railroad tracks, generally near a freshwater stream, were the "hobo jungles" or "hobo camps." Here hobos, tramps and those who had fallen on hard times would gather, all bundled up in their layers of old clothing and newspaper, warming themselves and whatever food they pooled, over a fire. As long as you threw a donation into the pot, you were welcome to eat. No donation, no feed.

The hobo worked when he could and traveled wherever the wind blew him. The tramp, on the other hand, traveled all over but didn't work. Nevertheless, they had respect for each other. Bums were a completely different story. They didn't travel and they didn't work. In fact, they didn't do a damn thing. Not surprisingly, they weren't welcomed in the hobo jungles.

The hobo enjoyed the wanderlust of his life. As a rule, he lived in the present; he was rebellious but quiet about it, a real loner and in peril of extinction. His home was the entire country from coast to coast. Some had their worldly possessions tied in a bundle to a stick; others were their own worldly possessions. From my encounters with hobos, I learned which towns were tough and which were not and that circus sites were the most generous with their jobs and their food. There was a strong bond of brotherhood among these hobos, and I felt it right away. No one interfered with anyone else—or anyone else's business—as interference and influence were part of the conformist world they were trying to avoid. The hobos who befriended me so many times in those early years were kind and generous men. To a young ignorant kid like me, that meant a lot.

Back in Colorado, I got fights by walking into saloons and announcing (with what I hoped was the grand eloquence of the great John L. Sullivan): "I can't sing and I can't dance, but I'll lick anyone in the house!"

Sometimes I wasn't taken seriously because of my high-pitched voice, which got even more ridiculous whenever I was nervous or unsure of myself. Whenever this happened I would clear my throat and say it all over again, taking great pains to make it sound like I had just finished eating gravel. On these occasions, all I could hear were hoots and howls. Nevertheless, I never lost my nerve. To show that I meant business, I would pass the hat, making the first contribution just to prove I had confidence in myself. It worked more often than not, and I did take on anyone who stepped forward, knocking him down and out as fast as I could. Then the hat would be passed again, and when it was all over, I'd beat it out of there as fast as my legs would go. The times I got licked were pretty rare; when it happened, I would only try harder.

Traveling around Colorado, I reached Montrose, one of my old home towns, where a former classmate of mine, now a blacksmith, Fred Woods, persuaded me to fight him in front of an audience during Fair Week in the local Moose Hall. Since this was a week that meant very much to the people of Montrose, I agreed and started training for the big match.

Fred designated me promoter and manager while he publicized the fight. Not wanting anyone to see me, I trained in a dilapidated wooden shed located in back of the blacksmith shop. Fred was, to anyone who had eyes in his head, the perfect fighting specimen: He was big, with huge arms and good legs. Because of this, I didn't feel like hearing any pre-fight speculation or comparisons by some of Fred's more ardent supporters.

While preparing for Woods, I practised new fighting techniques, from a low weaving crouch that made me harder to hit to variations of all the blows I already knew, including the powerful left Bernie had shown me.

Despite his muscle-bound body, Fred didn't really seem to have much of a chance—or so I hoped. In the end I won, but Fred gave me a good fight before he finally kissed the sawdust. When it was all over I had to pour a bucket of ice water over him to revive him. The total gate receipts for this fight between two unknowns was forty dollars, which covered expenses. Luckily for me, some remembered me from the time my family had lived in Montrose and kindly gave me hot meals and a place to sleep. After the fight, Fred and I pushed all the wooden chairs aside to make way for dancing and fiddling.

My next fight of any consequence was with Andy Malloy, who'd fought and beaten my brother. Andy was such a good sport that when I knocked him out he offered to teach me all he knew about ringmanship and suggested I take him on as my manager, to which I agreed.

And so Andy Malloy became the first of many managers I was to have throughout my career. Up to the time I teamed up with Jack Kearns, the managers I had were mostly my friends or well-meaning acquaintances who tried to help me get fights, arranging the small details so that I could dedicate myself to my training. I never signed a contract with any of them, not even Kearns. It just didn't seem necessary in those days; a handshake was stronger and more meaningful than any inked signature. The only ingredients necessary were respect and trust.

There is no doubt in my mind that a fighter needs a manager. Ideally, a manager gets up good likely bouts, arranges suitable dates and times and living accommodations, hires and sometimes fires sparring partners, "sells" his fighter's ability and skill to others by taking scouting trips and being a good press agent, and honestly handles all accounts as well.

This gives the fighter more time to keep himself in shape, running miles, punching bags, jumping rope, sleeping. Together the fighter and the manager are a team, pulling and pushing toward the same goal. If either takes advantage of the other, underestimates or oversteps the given role, then that's it; a loss of respect sets in and the whole relationship is shot to hell. If such a split does take place, it is usually the fighter who winds up with the short end of the stick.

I learned many things from my manager Andy Malloy. I learned to make my body a complete unit, the muscles of my feet, legs, waist, back and shoulders all contributing to the power of my arm. He taught me, in short, that my entire body was at stake in the ring, not just my fists. He was a good teacher.

Despite our good intentions, we soon came to the realization that business was bad. Maybe it was just our timing that was off. At any rate, we weren't getting anywhere as manager and fighter. Our purses were not even worth splitting, so we decided to go our own ways once more.

After Andy, I had a succession of business managers, all with very scant business sense. I wasn't happy with any of them and we always parted company soon after I realized that they were as green and unexperienced as I was.

Since I wasn't far enough into the game, it was becoming impossible to obtain satisfactory matches. It was discouraging but I never spoke of it; I kept my emotions to myself.

I fought just about anyone who was willing. I was so eager to obtain fights that I even fought out of my class, challenging rough miners from the mining camps around the area. I fought so many miners and went down into the shafts so often that I got a hankering for mining all over again. This couldn't have come at a better time.

So back I went, to doing the hard, dirty work no one else wanted. Lifting, hauling, moving a heavy load, wielding a pick, hour after hour, day after day, with no sun, no adequate ventilation. It was, as

always, the tops in terms of disciplining me both mentally and physically. And it kept my mind off my dismal fighting prospects. I still
lived, day and night, with the presence of my goal, knowing that its
attainment was not quite at my fingertips. I would wait and work,
as much as I'd have to and as much as I humanly could.

My reputation as a game fighter spread from mine to mine, but
now it had a different focus: I was no longer just a kid who challenged miners, but one of them—one who needed all the support
that could be given. And did I get it! One day the foreman of the
mine called me and told me that he felt I should get out and give it
another crack. He assured me I was a damn good miner and that I'd
always be welcome to join his mine crew. But he knew that my heart
was set on becoming a success and he didn't feel that I should waste
any time while I was still young and my enthusiasm was still intact.

I guess my "official" career started around this time. I began
keeping records of my victories and how long each took. I found
myself alert at all times, with my guard up, ready to protect myself
at a moment's notice if necessary.

Once, while traveling with my friend, Denver sports editor and
wrestling promoter Otto Floto, I had an opportunity to thank my
lucky stars that I was in good condition. Otto, one of the most colorful characters I ever met, had been hired by H. H. Tammen, co-
owner of *The Denver Post*, simply because Tammen felt (as he
often said) that Otto's name "was so beautiful." For years Otto liked
people to believe he owned a part of the Sells-Floto Circus, which
was in actuality owned by *The Denver Post*, which only used Otto's
beautiful name.

We had gone to a mining town in Colorado where Otto had
arranged for me to take on a few miners, one after another. It was a
terrible night; each miner was stronger than the last. By the time we
left, I was in pieces from fatigue and feeling more dead than alive.
The only consolation I had was several hundred bucks which Otto
and I had stashed in his well-worn briefcase.

It was dusk when we finally left town in Otto's car. Heading
toward Grand Junction, we were stopped by four mounted masked
gunmen who blocked the road. Menacingly, they dismounted and

walked toward us, their eyes glittering in the dark. They were eerie and strange in the dim moonlight.

The ringleader motioned us with his pistol.

"Awright, let's get outta dat machine, nice an' easy. Putchyer mitts over yer heads. Right. Atta boy. You too, kid. Now, don't try an' make a move or nothin' cause we've gotcha covered, understand?"

As if Otto and I didn't know! We were reduced to the status of paralyzed meatheads. There we stood, like hypnotized owls, blinking into the gaping barrel. It was too much, especially when I heard the hammer click. I guess Otto heard it too, for he immediately shut his eyes. Mine wouldn't dare close, even for an instant. The leader motioned us to hand over Otto's briefcase—which he got even before he finished his demand. One of the others opened it, took out the money, handed it to the ringleader without even bothering to count it and threw the briefcase back at us.

"Thanks, chumps. It's really swell of you."

Hah.

They laughed and then backed away. Jumping on their horses, they rode off. One of them, a real clown, shot his revolver into the air, sending us to the dirt.

When we finally managed to get up, we looked at each other in disbelief. After all my hard work, fighting all day and into the night, we had nothing left. *Nothing.* I felt like a fool. Sure, we had been outnumbered as well as taken by surprise, but still . . .

With heavy hearts, we managed somehow to get to the Grand Junction Hotel. I was still upset and angry with myself, and Otto wasn't doing a very good job consoling me. If I ever got a chance to get even! It was late when we pulled up.

Before heading for our room, Otto and I decided to get something to eat. We were hungry without having any real appetite, so we figured on a sandwich. We had no idea what we were going to use for payment, either for the sandwich or for the room, and we didn't care.

From the minute we sat down, my head kept twisting and turning as if I knew something were about to happen. I could hardly sit still; I stared at everyone who walked into the place. Otto told me to "sit still, for Chrissakes!"

All of a sudden, as if I had had a premonition, I recognized them by their clothes.

Leaning over to Otto, I whispered, "Otto! Aren't those the same bums who cleaned us out? No, no, not there—over *there!*"

Otto struggled to maintain his composure. He had a certain position to maintain (he was called a pal by crooks and bankers alike) and didn't feel like jeopardizing it by getting involved in a scuffle which could turn out to be messy. In addition, he had an artificial leg, and this didn't help his confidence.

He wouldn't even look. I was mesmerized with the shock of recognition, but they didn't even glance in my direction. They were too busy eating—on the dough they had just taken from us!

I was really steaming mad, and a raging anger took hold of me. Before I had a chance to think, I found myself leaping through the air, landing right on top of them.

Taken completely by surprise, they didn't have a chance to reach for their guns as I punched, with fists and feet, until all the fight was out of them, making sure of getting my money and their guns before grabbing them one by one by the seats of their pants and tossing them out the door.

Otto, who had sat like a stone through the entire spectacle, now patted my soaked back, telling me that I might have been killed if I hadn't taken them by surprise. He was absolutely right. At the time I had been so blinded by fury that I hadn't considered what could have happened to me. I slid to the ground exhausted. Between the miners and this, I wasn't fit to stand up. Otto pushed a chair toward me and helped me hoist myself onto it, telling me that he was real proud, yessir, real proud, my reflexes had never been so good as they had been when I was spurred on by necessity. No one needed to tell me that; it was blood money that I fought for, and now that we had it back, I felt a damn sight better.

Did we pack the food away that night! We resembled two refugees from the land of famine. And we didn't even have to pay for it—compliments of the management!

6

Kid Blackie No More

There were days when fighting only got me a buck or two if I was lucky. I guess whoever made up the phrase "mind over matter" really knew what he was talking about. It was only the thought of future monetary returns that kept me in the sport; it didn't feed my belly or keep me warm at night, but it kept me going.

Small fight and athletic clubs were scattered around. These clubs staged special boxing shows during the week, giving a chance to anyone willing to try. Like me.

Salt Lake City was among the better fight towns. There a local promoter named Hardy Downing ran a boxing club which held amateur and semi-professional boxing on Monday nights. One day I approached Downing and told him that I wanted to be part of his bill the following Monday. He agreed reluctantly.

Monday night finally rolled around. I had been training all week, somewhat more than the others, since no one took me very seriously because of my size. I, Kid Blackie, was slated against Kid Hancock. When I stepped into the ring, thin and unshaven, I was loudly greeted by razzing, hoots and hissing. I got rid of the Kid twelve seconds later and went to Hardy Downing to collect the five bucks owed me. I was handed two dollars and fifty cents.

"Say, what's the big idea? What happened to the five bucks?"

"Sorry, kid. That's all you get. You put Kid Hancock away too fast, you didn't give my crowd out there a good fight for their dough, and that's not the policy around here."

"Wait a second. All I did was sock your boy in the belly, then on the chin. It's not my fault he can't take it."

"Well, maybe you've got a point there, kid. Tell you what I'm gonna do. I'll give you a shot at his brother and that way you'll get the other half of the dough. Whaddya say, kid?"

What could I say? I agreed and took on Kid Hancock's brother, who had the same fighting ability as his brother. This time, when the fans saw me in the ring, they went wild. Kid Hancock's brother was a joke.

Later Downing paid me in full and suggested I stick around.

At Downing's place I engaged in a series of three fights with a cigar maker/salesman/fighter named Jack Downey. He had a shiny, bald head and looked mean. Surprisingly, he turned out to be one of the best boxers I'd met up to this point, and a nice guy as well.

As we fought, Downey smiled with confidence. He blocked nearly all my blows, exhausting me. By the fourth round I was beat and Downey rightly got the decision. Our next bout ended in a draw; in the third and last bout, I managed to knock him out. Incredibly, he smiled when he kissed the canvas.

A couple of scouts from Price, Utah, approached me. They matched me up, for a quarter of the gate receipts, with a black fighter named George Christian who figured me real easy pickings. He was wrong by a first round knockout, which made it even harder for me to find new opponents. I had already put away anyone of any decent standing in Salt Lake.

I went to Reno, Nevada, where I signed to fight Anamas Campbell. Anamas was hesitant to fight me; he didn't want anyone to put him in a bad light. Not taking any chances, Anamas asked me to spar with him before the fight in order to size me up. I didn't see anything wrong with this, so I went a few rounds with him just to prove that he really had nothing to be afraid of. He was satisfied. But not for very long; I knocked him out easily.

I didn't get a real chance to prove my stuff until my brother Bernie contacted me from Cripple Creek, Colorado, where he was working the Golden Cycle Mine. He had signed to fight a tough guy named George Copelin and then changed his mind after the whole thing had been arranged. He told me that I had to take his place. He never explained why. He didn't have to. As I figured it, he was starting to feel past his prime and didn't want to risk failure in front of co-workers who had come to see him fight. I asked if my substituting was the right thing to do and he assured me that everything would work out fine.

George Copelin, Bernie told me, was not only a good fighter but had earned a reputation as one of the best ore shovelers around. This was almost enough to make me change my mind.

"Harry, remember this: You gotta beat the hell out of him before he beats the hell out of you. You just gotta win!"

For this fight, a fifty-dollar guarantee was offered beforehand, which Bernie used to cover our expenses. He was banking on the money he would get from the bets.

Cripple Creek's altitude affected me so much that I felt weak and lethargic. All I wanted to do was sleep. But Bernie made me work hard—he was my manager, sparring partner and trainer rolled into one. He even insisted I take his fighting name, Jack Dempsey, instead of Kid Blackie.

When the crowd saw me at fight time, wearing Bernie's white trunks and climbing into the ring instead of him, they jeered at me and demanded their money back.

The promoter, furious, rushed up to me and threatened to kill me with his bare hands. Bernie hadn't bothered to tell him of this last-minute change.

"Who the hell are you and where's Jack Dempsey?"

"I'm Jack Dempsey, sir."

The promoter was hysterical. But it was too late: The bell clanged.

I fought with everything I had. The high altitude bothered me worse than before. I felt that the fight was taking place in a dream. The more I staggered, the more George staggered as well. I even remember thinking, "If George goes down one more time, I'll go down with him!"

Two things kept me going: One was the amount of successful fighting I'd already done—if I could keep in there long enough, I'd somehow manage to win in the end through skills. The other was that I felt compelled to show my best whenever I stepped into the ring. The roars from the fans, their enthusiasm, the glory and the money— I had to prove myself worthy of these things. And Bernie. I just couldn't let him down.

I launched a final attack in a blur of exhaustion. When the referee stopped the fight, held up my hand and proclaimed Jack Dempsey winner by a technical knockout, it took me a few seconds to realize I was Kid Blackie no more. My legs were so wobbly that I almost crawled back to my corner. Bernie was jumping up and down like a rabbit, making me dizzy. I glanced toward George. He looked like I felt.

Bernie and I went to collect the additional money due us from bets placed. When we got to the promoter's office, he informed us that he didn't have any money and that even if he did, we wouldn't get it because of our last-minute substitution. We argued that he had gotten a pretty good fight for his money; he asked us to please remove ourselves from his office as he had nothing more to say.

Since Bernie had spent 90 percent of the advance money, we were back to broke.

It was an empty victory for me. I was winning but I wasn't getting any recognition; what's more, I was often being cheated out of my pay. Promoters were dismissing me after the fights. I couldn't understand them. Did they want a good fight or not? What the hell was I supposed to do, lose so they could put together a rematch? Forget it!

All this badly dented my confidence. I seemed to be the only one who was proud of my ability, and that hurt.

It was not an easy time for me. I had to work things out, to see if boxing was really worth the aggravation. Only one thing was clear: I didn't want to do anything else. I couldn't.

Something inside me told me to give myself one more chance. I didn't know that I would have three heartbreaking and disappointing years ahead of me.

7

Enter Maxine

I proceeded westward from Salt Lake, finding one unimportant fight after another. Some I kept track of and some were just too crummy to mention, but I won them all and my confidence started rising again. In Goldfield, Nevada, I was approached by an old-time fighter, Jack Something, to take on Johnny Sudenberg, whose scheduled opponent had gotten sick. For one hundred dollars. I didn't hesitate.

In Goldfield I trained at the Northern Bar, which had been owned some years before by gambler Tex Rickard. Jake Goodfriend, the promoter, kept his eye on me the whole time I trained. He had his doubts about me, so I engaged in a pre-fight bout with Slick Merrill in a gambling house in nearby Tonopah. Once I had put Slick away—fast—Goodfriend left me in peace. While training, I kept knocking my sparring partners out. I wanted to look good, and I was out for myself.

Much to my discomfort, I found the altitude in Goldfield just as weakening as that of Cripple Creek. My lungs felt as though they were on fire. I looked at Johnny Sudenberg and saw that he wasn't faring too much better. My arms and legs were like putty; every time I sat in my corner, I almost dropped off. And this time brother Bernie wasn't around to scream me awake.

The fight was scheduled to be a ten rounder, and I was relieved when it was over even though Sudenberg got the decision.

When I woke up the following morning, I felt as if I had been in a stampede. I couldn't move at first. I was stiff and my head just wouldn't stay upright. I doused myself with ice water and managed to pull myself together before going to see my so-called manager, Jack. Not finding him, I asked some of the boys hanging around the pool hall if they had seen him. Sure, they had seen him, all right; he'd even told them to say good-bye to me and tell me he was sorry. Everyone kept passing the buck until one guy finally spoke up. It seemed that Jack had taken my earnings and had celebrated, blowing every last penny in a heated all-night gambling game. Since he knew I'd be mad, he left town. Mad? I was burning with rage. If Jack had walked across my path that very second, I would have beaten the daylights out of him. He'd made a damn fool out of me. Again I had subjected myself to poundings and had nothing to show for it. Again. I was getting sick and tired of the same tune.

I sat tight and waited for something to turn up, and, sure enough, it did. A Tonopah promoter who'd seen me in action with Johnny Sudenberg wanted me for a return match—if I was willing. Was I! I was willing to fight for nothing since that's what I was making anyway. I was offered one hundred and fifty dollars for this fight.

Sudenberg met me at the Mizpah Hotel in Tonopah and we both trained vigorously, right up to the fight. Throughout the bout we stood toe to toe, slugging at each other, landing good blows and knocking each other down with the final result being a fair draw. The fans got their money's worth and I got paid. That was more like it.

In Tonopah, Johnny and I had become pals, so we decided to stick together awhile. Since we both needed work, we went to Reno and put on a few exhibitions. We weren't good and we weren't bad. The local paper wrote about us once or twice and we both got copies to mail home to our folks.

This was the first time I got publicity; it was small-town publicity, but it went a long way with me, especially when I'd walk down the street and be greeted by name by those who'd read about me or had seen Sudenberg and me fight.

Sometimes we'd go into the local saloons and challenge the house. When that didn't work, we'd challenge each other. Those saloons were friendly places, as long as we stayed away from guys who were on a bender and those involved in poker games.

The men, while drinking, sang, and Johnny and I joined in whenever we could. I still remember the words from a song we were all fond of singing—in our flat, off-key voices. Judging from the words, I'd say it was composed before its time.

> If I was a millionaire and had a lot of coin,
> I would plant a row of coke plantations, and grow Heroyn,
> I would have Camel cigarettes growin' on my trees,
> I'd build a castle of morphine and live there at my ease.
> I would have forty thousand hop layouts, each one inlaid
> with pearls.
> I'd invite each old time fighter to bring along his girl.
> And everyone who had a habit,
> I'd have them leaping like a rabbit,
> Down at the fighters' jubilee!
>
> Down at the fighters' jubilee!
> Down on the Isle of H. M. and C.
>
> H. stands for heroyn, M. stands for morph,
> C. for cokoloro—to blow your head off.
> Autos and airships and big sirloin steaks,
> Each old time fighter would own his own lake.
>
> We'll build castles in the air,
> And all feel like millionaires,
> Down at the fighters' jubilee!

We had laughs singing that song in unison. In later years, however, just thinking about it filled me with a tremendous sadness, since the tragedy of hard drugs eventually destroyed my younger brother Johnny.

In Reno people were starting to talk about me. Not that they said very much, but at least it was a start. It was here in Reno that one opponent walked up to me with a proposition to throw the fight. I heard him out with disgust. Then I told him off with the strongest language I could muster. He was off in a flash. But later he had to look at my face in the ring and he knew he was beaten before he started.

In those lean days, everyone was looking for an opponent with a Big Reputation who wasn't much good. I was good, but I didn't have the reputation.

My next fight was with the Boston Bearcat in Ogden, Utah. The Bearcat was pretty much an unknown in the midwest, but it was rumored that he had stayed on his feet with the great Sam Langford. That made most young fighters unwilling to meet him. Not me.

The Bearcat was his own best press agent. He would stand outside a saloon bragging to one and all that he was the Greatest Black Fighter who had ever lived. There wasn't any man who could whip him. He let the curious feel his arm and stomach muscles as they came staggering out of the bars.

I realized how big he was when I stepped into the ring and saw him stripped to the waist. He was enormous. I got into my fighting crouch and delivered about half a dozen blows. He went down. The round wasn't nearly over! The referee had begun the count when the Boston Bearcat raised his hand and interrupted him by saying, "The Bearcat is through." I couldn't believe it.

The fight with the Bearcat really spurred me on. Now I fought more and more and trained harder than ever, running six or seven miles every morning before sunrise to strengthen my legs and my stamina. I adopted different methods to suit my size and talents. If a man fought down low, then I'd have to get down low too. If he was a puncher, I couldn't box him; I had to fight him.

Above all, I really got to know myself, to know my ability to take a blow and to know the extent of my endurance under different conditions. Missing a target only weakened my strength; it was better to duck, feint and weave. I practised ducking my head from side to side when charging in, making me harder to hit.

When I was in the ring, if it was going well, very little went on in my head. I didn't have time to think because I had to concentrate on what I was doing. If I got hurt and pain seared through my body, I'd hope that the fight would soon end.

I was always aware of the lust for blood of a portion of the fight crowd. There was that unconscious wish to see something dramatic happen. Often those who seemed the most timid would be the ones who screamed their lungs out at ringside, hoping their voices would mingle with the others. But the fight crowd was an essential part of the fight game. Without the people, there would have been no color, no stimulation and of course no gate.

My next bout was with Joe Bond. Joe had recently returned from a tour of Australia with his manager, Jack Kearns. He and Kearns had just split up and now Joe was on his own. Nevertheless, it was rumored that Jack Kearns, even from a distance, was keeping his eye on Bond as well as his opponents.

At this point I needed another manager, so I asked Hardy Downing if he knew of anyone. He suggested Jack Price, his brother-in-law. I knew Price slightly and liked him. He was a heavyset, good-natured guy who was willing to try anything. His ambition was to become a famous dancer in New York, so when I approached him with the offer of becoming my manager and told him that I was thinking of going East, he jumped.

Going East meant only New York. Even the name was exciting. It was where everything was happening, where so many wanted to go but never quite made it. New York. Where the big money and opportunity were. The city of lights. The door to fame and fortune. At least, that's what I thought.

The prospect of going to New York made me fairly leap out of my skin. Only later did I realize that New York never wants you—it's you that wants New York. These were words that Damon Runyon repeated to me many years later. He was absolutely right.

One day Price and I walked into Maxim's, a saloon/cabaret on Salt Lake's Commercial Street, to discuss the trip. Commercial Street was, in those days, a controversial strip in the center of a more or less red light district, a seedy side of town where anything and everything went on. Mormons shuddered at the thought of Commercial Street, but there was nothing they could do about it. It was flashy and it was cheap, but it was inevitable.

Price and I sat down to work out the details of our trip. When-

ever anyone glanced in our direction, Price assumed they were looking at him and he would puff out his chest and look important. He
begged me to "pay attention," but my eye kept wandering to the
piano player who was giving me the come-on. I was flattered that a
talented woman could be interested in someone like me. I excused
myself and walked over to the piano.

"What's your name, stranger?"

"Harry, ma'am. I mean Jack." I could feel my face turning
colors.

I was still shy. While I knew about girls, I didn't know about
women. And this woman was making me jittery. She wasn't pretty
by a long shot, but she was all female and she knew it. Her name
was Maxine Cates and she hailed from Walla Walla. She told me that
she was now in Salt Lake after having done a stint in San Francisco.
Not knowing her way around Salt Lake, she would be most grateful
if I could show her around after she finished work. I looked at
Price, who was trying to get my attention by wagging his head and
waving his arms. No, I really didn't have time—this time—but next
time, when I came back to visit my family . . .

Maxine. I couldn't take my eyes off her. She made sure of that.
When she spoke to me she would lean toward me so that her breasts
would strain against her dress. And every time she did, I would
pull back as if she had electrified me. She was amused by my
awkwardness.

She played the piano really well. Her fingers were like feathers
on the keyboard, and I was impressed. I had never met anyone quite
like her. Sometime later I realized I would never meet anyone like
her again.

Maxine asked me to make sure I looked her up again, and I
agreed. Then I said good-bye to her, somewhat stiffly, and returned
to Price, who was annoyed at me for having stayed with the dame so
long. He looked at Maxine one more time and dismissed her. I
thought he was being unfair but I didn't say a word.

Within a short time we were off to New York. While traveling
we used our cardboard suitcases as pillows.

8

New York–That Wonderful Town

We finally pulled into New York with less than thirty dollars between us. New York in 1916 was experiencing one of its hottest summers, and it seemed even hotter to us, since this was the first time we had ever been in the middle of a big city in this much heat.

We must have looked a sight. Price was wearing his ten-gallon hat and what looked like, after our long journey cross-country, a ten-cent suit. I looked worse; I was the color of an old saddle from the sun and I was in need of a shave and a bath. I wore shabby clothes and carried a cardboard suitcase as well as an empty stomach.

There we were, wondering what to do next, each waiting for the other to make some move, when a fancy car pulled up near us. I raised myself to my full height and puffed out my chest, thinking I'd been recognized. Instead, a uniformed driver hopped out and helped two ladies descend. I stared. I had never seen such beautiful creatures before in my life. They were dressed in white with big white matching hats and they carried ruffled umbrellas and freshly cut flowers in their arms. They looked like a painting I had once seen in a book. Price lifted his hat and bowed. They didn't even glance in our direction; in fact they made sure they kept their distance from us, two dirty bums from God knows where.

We were at the corner of Forty-second Street and Broadway. There were lots of people around and a few looked our way with vague curiosity. Price told me to ask a policeman where the Great White Way was.

"Why don't you go?"

"Because I have to watch our stuff."

I walked over to one and asked.

"Are you kidding, sonny?" He looked at me from head to foot. He walked over to where Price was standing.

"Where are you from, boys?"

"Well, sir, my friend and I are from Colorado and we just arrived and seeing how everyone's always talkin' about this Great White Way, we were wondering . . ."

"Whoa, young fellow. Catch your breath and don't be in such a hurry. You want the Great White Way? Well, son, you're standing on it."

His face crinkled and then he burst into good-natured laughter. He was still chuckling as he swung his nightstick in the air and walked away.

All I saw were lights, thousands, maybe millions, making up a twinkling strip, as if a bolt of lightning had crumpled into jagged pieces and was now stilled. These lights made up a grand, no a great, white way. Boy, did I have a lot to learn.

Depositing our suitcases in the baggage claim area of the Grand Central depot, we decided to attend to more important matters. That first day I visited almost all the New York sports editors to let them know I had finally arrived, in case they were interested. They really weren't. In fact they couldn't have cared less. Then it struck me that the city must have been full of young hopefuls like me.

The only writers who did show any interest in me were Jim Price of the *New York Press* and Damon Runyon, who hailed from Manhattan, Kansas. He had seen me with the *Denver Post* journalist Gene Fowler somewhere out west. Jim Price assigned a young Nat Fleischer, later to become a top expert on boxing, to interview me for the Sunday edition of the *New York Press.*

In my pockets were wilted, well-fingered clippings that told of my twenty-six knockouts. They didn't, of course, tell of the times I fought for nothing, of my disappointments and of the times I buried my head in my pillow at night and beat it with my fists out of exasperation. Clippings never do mention these things. No one even bothered to read them through except Damon Runyon. To the others I was an unknown, with no reputation to speak of, and I was, as far as they were concerned, just wasting their time.

I remember boasting of my knockout of the famous Boston Bearcat who, according to his manager, had built up quite a following in the east. The editors' reactions were all basically the same.

"Who?"

"Never heard of him."

"Listen, kid, no one here ever heard of the pug or of you either. Why don't you just head back home?"

It didn't take long for them to show me the door. Once, standing alone in a hallway of the *New York American,* I was approached by Runyon, who told me not to give up: It was never easy making an impact on New York. All I had to do was to face the city slickers head on and bounce back every time I was knocked down. The important thing to remember, he told me, was to keep my mouth shut and never let on to *anyone* what I really felt deep down inside, since no one really cared or had time to listen.

I understood what he said, but I really didn't know if I'd ever be able to follow his advice. I told him that I didn't know how to deal with people in anything less than an honest and forthright manner. Runyon told me that it was about time I learned.

His words meant a lot to me. Around this time, Runyon was just one journalist among many. He didn't become the superb raconteur of Broadway until years later, when, according to Broadway wags, Runyon turned to writing Broadway fables to pay for an upcoming appendix operation.

About the time of my arrival, there was a fistic man in New York, Jimmy Johnston, in whose office all the sports journalists used to gather to chew the fat. One day, while sitting in Johnston's office, Billy Roche, an old-time referee who'd been out west, mentioned my name as a fight hopeful. Johnston paid no attention and discussed others. Roche tried again, and again Johnston didn't pay any attention, so Roche dropped it. Runyon, who was present, saw that I might be getting the bum's rush and decided he would help me out by writing a small piece on me in his column. He realized that Johnston had his hands full with the eastern crop of new fighters and therefore really couldn't be bothered by some kid from out west.

Jack Price and I made more rounds. We went to all the newspaper offices we could think of, getting the same reactions in different words. I was told to go home and forget the fight game so many times that it sounded like a scratched record, and I felt like placing my hands over my ears.

Our money was down to virtually nothing when Price and I began to get on each other's nerves. Neither one of us had made any progress. We were holed up in a dingy room which had only a bed, a sink and a light bulb. It must have been the crummiest hotel and the smallest room in New York's hotel history. We even had to scrounge a three-legged chair from a neighbor who lived in bed.

At last, through Tom McArdle, whom we had met on one of our rounds, Price was able to land me a fight with Andre Anderson, a big blond fellow from Chicago, at the Fairmont Athletic Club. Billy Gibson, who was later to team up with Gene Tunney, ran it.

Andre had just about the same reputation as I had, but he was so big that no one wanted to fight him. (It seemed that I was often fighting the guys no one else wanted.) But I wasn't choosy. It was the only way I knew to get some money to live on.

I went to the gym after Price and McArdle had arranged everything. I weighed 173 pounds and looked lighter. Anderson weighed about 215 and looked heavier. Except for the Boston Bearcat, he was then the biggest fighter I had ever met. Billy Gibson approached me, looked me over and started yelling for Price.

"Price! Where is that son-of-a-bitch? Price! What the hell is the matter with you? I oughtta put you in jail for allowing this kid to fight Anderson. Why, he'll get murdered!"

Price and Gibson yelled at each other for a while, but in the end Price convinced him to allow the bout. If anything happened, it was my hide and I knew what I was doing.

In the ring Anderson's blows crashed down on me, knocking me off my feet several times. I didn't know how long I'd be able to take it. At ringside they were debating whether or not to stop it. By the fifth round, Anderson miraculously began to tire. As he weakened, I felt stronger. Seeing him show some strain encouraged me to try harder. At the end of ten rounds, *he* was trying to get away from *me*.

There weren't any official decisions in these exhibitions. Decisions were made by the sports writers present. Damon Runyon was one of those who named me the winner of the Anderson fight. He said something to the effect that I looked very promising, that with the right training and management I could get to the top.

In New York I trained at Grupp's 116th Street Gym. There I gained valuable experience as well as insight, since many of the well-known heavyweights and promoters often came in and gave out free pointers and advice.

I was now officially known as Jack Dempsey. Only my family and childhood friends still called me Harry. Nat Fleischer in later years referred to me as Manassa Jack, but it was Damon Runyon who gave me the nickname Manassa Mauler. It was to stick to me for the rest of my life. I was very proud of it.

I found it hard to get accustomed to this big, impersonal city, but I had no real complaints. At times I still felt like telling some guys off, especially those who gave me the brush-off. But I didn't. Outside the ring I tried to be nothing less than a gentleman. I wanted to respect people and to have them respect me, which was harder. I was, however, still just another fighter—one of many—with no concrete identity.

Then came bad news and trouble. Jack Price received a wire from Salt Lake City informing him that his mother was sick, possibly dying, and asking him to come home as soon as possible. He had no choice. In a way I felt he was glad to be going home, despite the circumstances; he had been homesick for a long time. We said good-bye and parted, and we both knew we wouldn't see each other for a long time.

I was now completely alone and as lonely as one can be only in a big city. I had no money so I couldn't go anywhere, and I didn't have friends I could call. Some time later I learned that the telegram had been sent by someone who wanted Price out of the way.

A few days after Price left, I was approached by John the Barber. John the Barber, who had gotten his name from a Broadway barbershop, was a shifty character whose real name was John Reisler. He was known around town as a slick operator and gambler. Many said he would have sold his mother's blood for money if the price was right.

"Hey, Dempsey, I'm in charge of you now. Your pal Price sold me your contract, see? He knew you wouldn't mind. Incidentally, he also borrowed fifty dollars against your next fight."

I couldn't believe my ears. Price's selling me out was crazy after all we'd been through together.

"What is this? I never had a contract with Jack Price!"

"Sorry, kid. A deal's a deal. Here's some dough. Go out and buy yourself some decent clothes. You look like a goddamn bum!"

I protested, but he told me I would fight for him whether I liked it or not. I really didn't have a choice.

First he wanted me to take on Sam Langford. No way. Then he suggested Gunboat Smith. I told him I thought he was daffy; Gunboat Smith was a real pro. As much as I was willing to fight anyone and everyone, these guys were really out of my league. I refused again, telling him to let me get some more opponents under my belt first. This made him mad.

"Listen, you punk. I'm giving you one more chance. You fight John Lester Johnson next week. He's good and that's what you want, right? Now don't give me any of your lip. If you don't fight him you fight no one, see?"

I feared getting blackballed. It could ruin me.

The bout was held uptown at the Harlem Sporting Club. Before the fight John the Barber told me I would be getting 25 percent of the total gate receipts. Now he was talking!

Big, burly Johnson had the reputation of being rough and dangerous. That was an understatement. My bout with him almost finished my career. He socked me like a bulldozer and grunted every time he made contact. This was one of the few fights that I remembered for a long time because of my agony. One blow, which landed in the second round, really made me double over from pain and see stars. Three rounds passed before I was able to straighten myself up. I sensed Johnson had cracked a few of my ribs. I couldn't move well but I stayed in there and did my best. It felt like my worst. I managed to land some solid blows despite the excruciating pain.

The sports writers were divided. Some picked Johnson, some picked me and still others called it a draw. At least I had made a decent showing.

Nevertheless, I was through for a while, both physically and mentally. I had been overmatched and hurt and I was being treated like scum by the Barber. I knew I had to stop fighting for a while.

John the Barber paid me one hundred bucks for the fight.

"Here's your end."

"What about the gate receipts?"

"What about them? Listen, you get what I pay you and let this be understood once and for all. Am I making myself clear?"

I told him that I wouldn't be able to fight for some time. I was tired and running some kind of on-and-off fever as well as being in pain from the cracked ribs. I needed time to heal.

He was unmoved. He had no feelings, at least not toward me. But he knew that I was in no shape to fight.

"Okay. You go and rest up," he said. "I'm tired of seeing you and your long goddamn face hanging around here. If you weren't a halfway decent fighter . . . You know, I didn't mind you at the beginning, but now you're starting to give me a real pain. Well, what are you waiting for? Go and get your rest, but don't forget to come back. Remember, kid, we've got a contract."

I couldn't wait to leave. I bought myself a coat with some of the money I had managed to save. It was orange-checkered with big, shiny buttons and I considered it the most beautiful thing I had ever owned in my life.

It was now July, 1916. My boyhood pal Gene Fowler was getting married, so I stopped off in Colorado to see him. There was a difference of five years in our ages, but we knew each other from the time he was in high school and I was selling newspapers on the street. He and I used to spend Sundays together, catching wild horses.

Now Gene was in love. He had met Agnes Hubbard one day while he and his friend, Jack Kanner, a boxing promoter, were strolling through the complaints section of the Health Department, where she worked.

When Gene and Agnes tied the knot, we were all very happy for him; he seemed to be finding what everyone else was looking for. Gene persuaded a Free Methodist minister, former mule skinner and ex-wrestler Reverend James Thomas, to perform the ceremony. Kanner was best man and a professional gambler known as Cincinnati acted as chauffeur. Some time after the ceremony, Gene showed the Reverend his appreciation by publishing a photo of him in the newspaper in fighting pose.

Because Gene didn't have an overcoat, I lent him my new one. Gene told me afterwards that Agnes was pleased at the elegant way he looked, even though the orange coat had a mile-long visibility. She asked him where he had gotten it and he told her that it belonged to me, Jack Dempsey, a pal of his who would soon become Champion of the World.

In the fifties we lived near each other in California. He was a superb writer and I was a fighter. I loved him like a brother; he was very close to me, and we understood each other perfectly.

I remember an occasion when someone who didn't know either one of us very well came strolling into my house looking for me. Seeing only two messy, splattered house painters, he decided to make himself at home. Plopping into an armchair, he helped himself to a drink, paying no attention to the painters, who kept making a big production of slapping their paintbrushes on the walls. After sitting and drinking awhile, he decided to find out where I was and when I was expected, and he walked over to the two painters to ask. It took him a full five seconds to realize that the two painters were none other than Gene and I.

Back in Salt Lake, after Gene's wedding, I stopped off at Commercial Street and looked up Maxine, the piano player. She was happy to see me and insisted I stick around so that we could get to know each other better. I guess I was pretty starved for attention, and affection as well, because one thing led to another and pretty soon Maxine was discussing marriage while I was idiotically agreeing.

For the longest time, I couldn't figure out why she wanted to marry me. I had very little or nothing to offer her. But she was insistent, I couldn't see any reason why not and before I knew it we were man and wife. She was fifteen years older than I and quite an experienced woman, even though she denied it. She was sweet and friendly when we married, but it didn't last long. Her moods were constantly changing and her friendliness turned to hostility once the honeymoon (in a tacky hotel room) was over.

She didn't seem to mind when I told her that because I was a fighter we would have to be separated, sometimes for months at a time. Since there didn't seem to be anything for me to do in Salt Lake, I planned to leave for New York just as soon as I got back into shape. I lumberjacked and worked some mines, and when I felt better I stopped by to see my mother to say good-bye once more. All we ever seemed to be saying were hellos and good-byes. My family hadn't taken the news of my marriage well at all. The mere mention of Maxine produced fireworks, so I decided to be on my way, hoping the matter would blow over.

I gave some money to Maxine and used the rest of what I had to help me get back to New York. I still hadn't given up on New York.

The first person I saw in town was none other than John the Barber, who had been waiting. But this time it was different; I had regained my strength and had patched together my pride. I knew exactly who I was, what I wanted to be and for whom I was well matched (as well as who I couldn't take on, no matter what the price). I knew that John the Barber knew these things too but didn't give a damn.

"Well, here I am. I guess I'm ready to fight again."

He worked fast and immediately arranged a match.

"You may have to take a licking, kid," he said. "But there'll be real money in it for you if you do it the way I say."

"I don't want that kind of money. I want a good honest fight. Who's my opponent?"

"Gunboat Smith."

I protested again. I didn't want to meet him and I couldn't understand why John the Barber was trying to push him on me. Gunboat Smith was really a topnotcher and no match for me. At least, not yet. I wasn't in his category, and I still winced on remembering what John Lester Johnson had done to me. It wasn't easy to forget pain.

"I won't fight him. I can't fight him. What're you trying to do to me?"

"You won't fight him, you say? Listen, you punk, it's either him or no one, just like I told you before."

In the end he gave in to me for what was to be the last time. I thought I had made my point with him; a few days later I realized I was wrong.

"I've arranged another match for you. Frank Moran. This should get you into the big time."

Frank Moran. He was even tougher than Gunboat Smith. Just the sound of his name made me squirm. Why, Frank Moran fought in Madison Square Garden—some even thought of him as the next champion! What was I, a patsy? Just another victim for Moran to tuck under his belt? Was Moran afraid of endangering his top standing by agreeing to fight me? A thousand questions flashed through my mind at once. Reisler wanted to run me to the ground, and I didn't want any part of it.

I refused again and this time he got furious. I had never come up against such a vicious person before. He threatened me with everything he could think of, but I was firm. I knew I was right. I wasn't going to take orders from anyone who was willing to sacrifice my whole career just for the sake of one gate. Reisler was poison and I knew it.

Taking a stand against him was not pleasant, but it turned out to be one of my wisest decisions despite its costing me plenty in terms of money and opportunity.

"Either fight this guy or get the hell out of town," he yelled. "If you don't fight, I'll make it impossible for you to fight in this town—or for that matter any goddamn place else!"

He humiliated me and called me every name in the book. He

said he was through with me, that I was nothing more than a lousy ingrate and that I'd better be on the first train out of town.

I sensed that if I stayed in New York he could, and would, make it impossible for me to fight. On the other hand, by leaving I'd be breaking clean. I had to do it. I couldn't stand the sight of him any longer. He was trying to scare me with his threats but I wasn't afraid. Outside New York, no one would be even slightly familiar with his name. Or so I hoped. There was nothing to do now but to go home.

I left Reisler still shouting at me as I slammed his door for good. In my opinion, Reisler was a man completely twisted with hatred and rage. I knew that if he ever had the opportunity to make my life miserable, or maybe even just difficult, he would do it. And he did. I hated his guts.

I was so upset on leaving his office that I had to take a walk to clear my mind. It seemed that everyone I came into contact with was either no good or vindictive. I couldn't understand why. Maybe I was too trusting. Maybe I was a fool. I felt like I had reached the end of a track leading nowhere. I just couldn't face the prospect of being a failure—not with so many pulling for me back home, not after my hard work and sweat.

I couldn't wait to leave. I had put all my hopes and dreams into New York, and now I was being driven out. But I vowed I'd be back, even though I didn't know when or how.

I was alone. I didn't seem to have one friend that I could count on, nor did there seem to be anyone who cared enough to advise me. I packed my very few belongings together and headed away from New York City. It wasn't exactly the grand exit I had expected.

9

I Should Have Warmed Up

I took a train from New York to Philadelphia.

In the City of Brotherly Love I found it impossible to see any-one of any consequence. Sports editors and promoters were cool and distant. Doors slammed in my face. No one wanted any part of me, even though I offered to take anyone on, just for exposure. No dice. John the Barber had made his rounds just as he had promised.

I rode the rods and stopped in Kansas City, where I had heard that Frank Moran was training to fight big Carl Morris. I went to Moran's training camp to ask if they needed sparring partners. The men in charge took one look at me and smirked, so I went to Carl Morris's. Being smaller than Morris, I managed to convince them that I'd be good, fast practice for Carl. After all, sparring partners were not that easy to come by in those days, especially since Carl Morris was six foot four and weighed around 235. Those who fought him thought of Carl Morris as a potential killer. I didn't care; I wasn't in any position to.

Carl Morris was everything everyone said: He was fast and he was good. He was also obnoxious. He had saved up some dough and he liked to show off.

My daily pay was seventy-five cents, which went toward my room and board—well, whatever board I could afford with the money left over. Once, while I was eating a doughnut in a lunch-room, Morris walked in and sat down next to me. He called the waitress over and ordered a steak with all the trimmings and then turned his attention to me, commenting that I sure must have been hungry judging by the way I wolfed the doughnut. I looked at him and told him that I still was—just as his full, steaming, hot plate was set down in front of him. Hoping he would offer to buy his sparring partner something, I stared at his meal. He ignored me, de-vouring the food as if he hadn't eaten in months.

Then he turned to me and said, "Listen kid, why don't you get someone to buy you something to fill your belly and quit staring at my grub. I'm sure you can manage to hustle someone."

Angry and humiliated as I felt, I rose and said so long. I hoped he would choke.

I had been at his training camp three or four days when the fight was called off. It was rumored that both Morris and Moran figured they couldn't afford to be beaten at this stage, both being heavyweight contenders for Jess Willard's heavyweight crown. So I was out of work again. Everyone cleared camp and said their good-byes. Tempers were short and everything that wasn't nailed down got lost in the moving process, including my one and only suitcase, which contained my New York suit and a pair of much-needed tights and shoes. One of Morris's handlers told me not to worry, that things got misplaced all the time. He told me to a leave a forwarding address and forget about it—the suitcase would be sent to me.

A week or so after I arrived in Pueblo, Colorado, I got a notice saying that a C.O.D. package had arrived. Not only did I have to work to eat, but now I had to have the money to collect the pack-age as well. After a week or so I found that I still had the shorts, and later I borrowed some dough from a guy in the local pool hall.

There was talk around this time of the Great War in Europe that was now approaching year three. Everyone had figured it would last only a few months, but now men were beginning to look fearfully toward their families and themselves. The United States wasn't involved as yet, but local hospitals and the Red Cross had already started collecting blood just in case. I offered mine, only to be refused and told to keep it since I looked like I could use it my-self.

From Pueblo I went to Salt Lake to see Maxine and fight some local boys. Our marriage, from the start, had been on shaky ground, and I didn't want it to crumble if I could help it. My money was constantly running out and my absences weren't doing the situation much good. Being an independent spirit, she kept busy with her work while I carried on with mine. It was the way she wanted it, so it was okay with me.

I didn't realize how Maxine was changing toward me. I was still blind, whether out of lust or love. She constantly reminded me that it was a husband's duty to provide his wife with money. After all, she had to live, didn't she? Money. The one thing that ruled her. The one thing I wasn't giving her enough of. When I had it, she got it, but she wasn't interested in how or what. She was only interested in more. She needed lots of things and if I couldn't provide them, well . . .

But I loved her—in my own way. Maxine was my woman and I realized I'd have to do as much as I could to keep her happy.

My folks still wanted no part of Maxine. My father called her a slut when I was out of earshot and my mother figured that anyone who worked in the Tenderloin district of town couldn't be any good. But it was my life, and if Maxine was what made me happy, then she must also be, according to the Good Lord, what I deserved. Nevertheless, I didn't dare bring her home for a long time.

A few weeks after I came back, I found I couldn't stand the continual battling, the unending ridicule and the harping. I told her that I was going back into serious training and that I couldn't concentrate very well in Salt Lake. I asked her to accompany me, but she refused, saying she couldn't leave the saloon at this time. I pleaded with her, thinking that a separation at this point would lead to many more, but she refused to listen. Maxine only did what Maxine wanted, so she told me not to come back until I knew the meaning of marriage and its responsibilities.

In Pueblo I got a wire from a promoter I had once met, Fred Windsor. He'd heard I was looking for work and could arrange a bout for me with Fireman Jim Flynn. I wired him back to go ahead with the arrangements. Why not? Flynn was good and I was eager. Perfect match, right? Not quite.

The fight was held in Murray, Utah, where several hundred fans rooted themselves hoarse for Flynn. Fred Windsor remained on the west coast, having arranged the fight through an intermediary. My brother Bernie was once again in my corner, and that made me feel better.

From the minute the bell clanged, I knew I was in trouble. I had made the mistake of not warming up properly. What a dumb oversight on my part—it was probably going to cost me the fight! I should have shadowboxed in the back room! I should have done this and I should have done that! I kept berating myself when—*bam!*—down I went. I barely managed to get up when—*crack!*—down again. I got floored a few times, and the worst part of it was that I knew it was my own fault! I was just about getting my second wind when Bernie threw the towel in.

"What's the matter with you, gone daffy or something? What'd you have to go and stop the fight for? What'd you do to me, Bernie?"

"What was I supposed to do? Stand around and watch you get your block knocked off?"

"Sure, it's my hide. You should have let me go on!"

I screamed at him, I think, for the first time in my life.

"Listen, kid, you're my own brother and I'm probably the only one around who really gives a damn about you! Lemme tell you something, Harry. Even the best of champions get knocked down once. Throwing the towel in don't mean nothing!"

"So, why didn't you stop me in Cripple Creek?"

"That was different. You didn't need it then. Now you take a good hold on yourself—and remember, kid, it's your brother Bernie talking."

"Get outta my way, Bernie!"

"Now don't get sore, kid. It's for your own good!"

Sore? I was steaming. I felt sick—and later I was to feel even worse when some people insinuated that I blew the fight for dough. Dough meant a lot, but it sure wouldn't make me blow a fight.

After the Flynn fight I showered, dressed and walked into a saloon where I knew a lot of sports people hung out. Bernie accompanied me though we weren't talking. When I sat down a number of men at the bar turned around, pointed at me and snickered. That was too much; I got up and left Bernie sitting there.

From Murray I returned to Salt Lake, where I took a room and waited for Maxine, who had let me know before the fight that she had changed her mind and was going to meet me. Every time I heard footsteps in the hall I called out her name, only to be greeted by silence. The minutes and the hours passed. I was so tired from the fight that I could hardly keep my eyes open. I put my winnings behind the bedpost and dropped off to sleep.

Maxine sauntered in at three o'clock in the morning, reeking of whiskey and cigar smoke. I asked her where she had been and she said that it didn't matter, she was with me now. I was too tired to argue, so I accepted the fact that she was there and showed her my money. She took the bills without saying a word. When I woke up in the morning she was gone. Bernie came around to see how I was and I told him to leave me alone. I guess I was taking Maxine out on him. Poor Bernie.

A few days later Fred Windsor wired me again from Oakland and said that he wasn't displeased with my showing against Flynn. He asked me to join him as soon as possible.

Before leaving for the coast, I made sure I found Maxine. Seems I was always doing that—and then getting a nice, swift kick in the butt.

I asked her to come with me and this time, much to my surprise, she agreed. In San Francisco things actually seemed to be ironing themselves out—that is, until she flew out of control for no obvious reason. She became hysterical, throwing things around the place, screaming at the top of her lungs. She threatened to throw herself out the window while I yelled at her to shut up and tried to find out what had set her off. A frightened neighbor called the police. The minute they walked in, Maxine told them that I had belted her and she could hardly move. I couldn't believe Maxine would lie like that; I just stared at her.

The police, having better things to do, told us to settle the family quarrel but to please keep it down.

For the next few days Maxine was subdued and acted as if nothing had happened, making me think that one of us had a screw loose. Everything seemed normal once more—until I had to leave her for a couple of days to engage in a bout. She said good-bye and told me to hurry back. I did. When I returned, she was gone without a trace. According to neighbors, she had left to visit her brother and then to go to Yakima, Washington, to see her mother. I should have known then that Maxine and I were through, but I didn't. Maxine Cates Dempsey never returned.

I hired out as a lumberjack in Seattle and worked out in the local gyms, waiting for Fred to get in touch with me. In time he arranged for me to meet Al Norton, a very distinguished guy of Spanish origins, whom the ladies loved.

The fight was scheduled to take place in Oakland, and I couldn't wait. Al looked like anything but a fighter while I looked like nothing but a fighter—with my upturned, pug nose and a face which was thin but cried out for a shave. I'm afraid, though, that I never sounded like a fighter. I did everything I could to lower my voice, from grunting and growling when I was alone to talking with my head down. It didn't do much good; every time someone spoke to me, up it went.

The fight was a four rounder, the main event. Seats had sold out for two bits each (there was no such thing as a scale of prices).

Al climbed through the ropes and into the ring. He was the local champ and the cheers were deafening. When it came my turn, it sounded like a snake convention; I never heard so many hisses and boos in my life as I did that night.

I followed Al around the ring, trading punches. By the end of the second round I saw three Al Nortons standing in front of me. I kept looking for openings even though I could hardly stand. Four rounds. Four long rounds.

In the end, the fight was a draw. Even Al's fans agreed with the decision, which must have been a first.

Fred Windsor was pleased and said he would try to sign me up for a return match. In the meantime I took on fat Willie Meehan and a number of unknowns who never managed to make the record books. Willie was a clown fighter. He looked like pure blubber—but I was warned to watch out. No matter what he looked like, it was dangerous to underestimate him. He was damn good, but I felt I wasn't too bad myself. After all, Fred had gotten me several fights and he must have had confidence in me.

Willie and I got together in the ring and gave it all we had, but the fight turned out to be such a bore that the spectators started leaving before it was over. Willie Meehan didn't seem to be able to knock me out, and I couldn't knock him out simply because I couldn't reach him.

Because people had been talking about the Meehan fight, Fred decided it was high time for me to get some publicity. One afternoon he marched me into the sports department of the *San Francisco Bulletin*. I remember how self-conscious I felt, dressed in old khaki pants, a worn sweater and black shoes. I carried my trunks in one hand and my ring shoes in the other. When Fred announced me, no one showed even the mildest curiosity. They were used to Fred, but that didn't keep him from talking nonstop about me, my prowess in the ring, my bouts past and future and other assorted subjects that came to mind.

Rooted to the spot, I heard someone behind me laughing and I turned to see who it was. I saw a pale man wearing a short-sleeved shirt and a bow tie and sitting on the corner of his desk. He told me his name was Edgar Gleeson—but call him "Scoop." I glared at this "Scoop." He motioned me to come closer and told me that he wasn't laughing at me but at my noisy, windbag manager. I couldn't help grinning. In Scoop's opinion, Fred Windsor was his very own banner headline, one who lived up to the nickname "Windy." This was my first encounter with the grand art of ballyhoo.

When Fred had deflated himself in the sports department, he took me by the arm and ushered me into the art department, where I changed into my ring outfit and posed for pictures in my fighting stance. Scoop came with us so as not to miss one minute of Fred's performance.

Scoop asked me to stay behind for a story. I was impressed by his gentleness, his incredible memory and his encyclopedic knowledge about everything and everyone. Including me. He said that he wouldn't be at all surprised if I were to become the heavyweight champion of the world. No one had ever said that to my face before. He couldn't have known that I lived and breathed it with each passing day. Ol' Scoop. A kind but shrewd fox who was to be in my corner, win or lose, in the coming years.

The second Norton fight took place, and this time I won. Nevertheless, the Flynn fiasco had lowered my attractiveness at the gate. Some fighters were convinced that there was very little to be gained by beating me. Others dismissed me altogether. I couldn't be built up as being dangerous; I didn't look it and I didn't have any pulling power. So Fred sadly came to the conclusion that he couldn't do anything more for me. He told me he was sorry, but sometimes those who think they're cut out for fighting really aren't.

10

A Letter from Jack Kearns

Nineteen hundred seventeen. Time was pressing forward. God knows I wasn't.

After my split with Fred Windsor, I decided to do something constructive, so I got a job at the Tacoma Shipyards in Washington. They needed men badly; the European War was expanding and Preparedness was uppermost in men's minds. Patriotic in my own way, I figured that working in the shipyard would be a useful thing to do.

I had a week to kill before the job started, and I didn't know anyone in Washington. I was lonely and ashamed that I was. I decided that the best thing for me was to be around people. I needed company, I needed to hear conversation that wasn't about me, about fight gates or about fighting in general.

I walked into a saloon a stone's throw from the Oakland ferry. I didn't drink, but what the hell—it was as good a place as any. The saloon was packed with shipyard workers, sailors, card sharps and toughs. It was a rough place, but the customers weren't overcharged or rolled—there was plenty of time for that outside. It was a popular watering hole which stank of whiskey and sweat.

I sat down and looked around. I knew I was out of place, but I didn't really feel lost; there was too much going on. A cheesy dame approached me and wanted me to buy her a drink. Boy, did she have the wrong guy! I told her to get lost, I wasn't in the mood.

Meanwhile, some trouble was brewing at the far end of the bar. Two guys were having a row, and they were getting louder and more abusive. Everyone, including me, turned to see what was going on. The two were holding half-empty bottles and facing each other like a pair of snarling dogs, nose to nose. The guy nearest me was a big, beefy lunk who was surrounded by his pals. The other was a smaller man, very dapper, wearing a vested suit, a diamond stickpin in his necktie, and a flashy ring on his little finger. They didn't look as if they could speak the same language. Both were stinking drunk and could hardly stand up. The smaller guy's face was hard; it was obvious he wasn't anyone to tangle with.

The name Darcy kept cropping up. I assumed it was the smaller guy's name. Men started rising from their seats and moving away from the bar.

I don't recall who threw the first punch, but in a flash what had been an argument between two men turned into a free-for-all. No one really knew for what they were fighting or for whom. And I was there, right smack in the middle. I saw the big guy and his friends gang up on the smaller guy. In my eyes, only cowards pick on someone half their size, so I jumped in to help the little guy. I landed a haymaker on the big guy's chin and was pleased to see him dazed. Fists were swinging; I felt myself clobbered from behind; I turned and laid some guys out. You could hear thuds, resounding smacks and grunts accompanied by the sound of tables and chairs overturning, mirrors shattering and bottles splintering. The saloon was reduced to a disaster area with the bartender in a flap, hollering that he had called the cops and that there were damages to be paid. That's when I walked out.

I turned the corner, my legs barely holding me up. I was so hot I just leaned against the wall and slid down until my butt rested on solid ground. The cool wall felt good against my throbbing head and soaked back. I looked around. I was surrounded by masses of accumulated garbage. The thought crossed my mind that maybe this was where I belonged.

Men were streaming out of the saloon and gathering in clumps within earshot. They all seemed to have something to say. From what I could hear, the crowd agreed that it had been a good brawl and that it was Jack Kearns's fault. I turned his name over in my mind—Jack Kearns—if memory served me right, he was Joe Bond's former manager from Oakland, a good manager that those in the fight game either hated or liked, with no in-between.

As the conversation shifted to another topic, I got up, brushed myself off and left the area, wondering if I had been in my last fight. If another pro fight came my way, I'd have to think about it.

The shipyard job finally started and I worked long, hard hours, satisfied that I was helping the country as well as myself. I figured that if I stayed put, I could learn something about myself and where I was headed. I settled in and the months passed.

When I was least expecting trouble, I got a distress wire from my mother in Salt Lake. My younger brother Bruce had been stabbed in a street fight while selling newspapers. Please come home. Quickly. I felt as if I had swallowed a chunk of lead. Bruce stabbed. The baby of the family, only fifteen years old. He was a good kid who never harmed anyone and always tried to help the other guy. He took after my mother more than anyone else in the family. He had a bleeding heart, but he was far from being a sissy and he could handle himself in a scrap as well as anyone. Bruce, who so many times had enthusiastically welcomed me home and waited, wide-eyed, to hear where I had been and whom I had met, who considered me his hero. His favorite big brother. Please, God, I thought, don't take him away.

I hopped a slow freight—couldn't even get a direct one. I made it home only to be told that it was too late, Brucie was gone.

I couldn't bear to look at my mother's face, puffy from grief. My father sat in a corner and stared straight ahead. The shock had been great for him, too. I begged him not to do anything rash to avenge Bruce's death, but he didn't even hear me.

My mother tearfully insisted that everything that happened was God's will. If this was God's will, I thought, then it didn't make any sense at all. The pain and the sense of injustice over Bruce's death stayed with me a long time. I found it hard to accept death, especially when it came to someone young like my brother.

No one ever found out the motive behind Bruce's senseless killing, and in time my young brother became just another statistic in the files.

Now I really didn't know which way to turn. I couldn't stay home and I couldn't go to Maxine. She had proved she didn't give a damn about me, and I had no idea where she was anyway. Nothing and no one could penetrate the heaviness I carried around with me. I had even lost my shipyard job; I had been so upset that I had neglected to ask them to hold it for me.

Then a letter arrived from Jack Kearns in Oakland. I ripped open the envelope, nearly tearing the letter into shreds. I read it over three times before I could make sense of it. I had been right about Kearns; he had been the manager of an old opponent of mine, Joe Bond, and had split with him just before our fight. It appeared from the letter that Kearns had kept his practised eye on Bond and, subsequently, on every one of his opponents, including me.

He didn't mention any of my fights, and I hoped he hadn't heard about the Fireman Jim Flynn fiasco. He wrote that "it took a tough man to take on tough opponents and win." He said he had seen me fight and liked what he saw. He was interested in taking me on and, if things worked out, becoming my manager! That is, if I was interested. Was he kidding?

I wrote him back immediately, telling him that I was interested and quite available. Then I waited for his reply. I couldn't imagine where he had seen me fight, but it didn't matter to me. He wanted me and that was good enough for me.

That week just didn't seem to move. I haunted the postmaster in town. I think he wished for the return letter almost as much as I did, if that meant getting me out from under his feet.

The letter finally arrived. Kearns sent me a railroad ticket from Salt Lake to Frisco and a fin to eat with. I couldn't believe it: Here was a guy I had never met, sending me five bucks and a ticket. This Kearns, as far as I was concerned, had class.

I said good-bye to my folks and was on my way. Before leaving town I stopped to see Maxine (someone had given me an address) one more time, but she wasn't home. Or maybe she just wasn't home for me. Maybe, if I had had money, she might have cared to see me.

I had supported her to the best of my ability, and if it wasn't enough, there wasn't much more I could do. Time was running short; I left her a note saying that if things got bad she would be welcome in my family's house.

I rushed to the station and climbed into a compartment on a passenger train. (Riding in a compartment instead of under one!) I couldn't get there fast enough. Kearns was to meet me at the depot and I hoped he'd recognize me; I had no idea what he looked like.

In San Francisco I was on the platform even before the train had stopped, but I was enveloped in a cloud of steam. I moved away, turning my head from side to side, looking for him, when I heard a raspy voice behind me calling my name. I whirled around.

It was Jack Kearns, wearing a vested suit, a diamond stickpin in his necktie and a flashing ring on his little finger. It was the same guy who'd been in the brawl in the Oakland saloon, the guy I'd helped.

So Jack Kearns the fight manager wanted to hook up with Jack Dempsey—young, semi-retired, hopeful. I hoped it would work out. I had nothing to lose and, as he told me, neither did he. Things hadn't been going well for him. His wrestling days were over and he had decided to dedicate himself to boxing again when a fighter of his, Marty Farrell, got thrown out of a ring for stalling. Because of this, he had had to scout around and find himself a new prospect. He wanted to make a name for himself and he wanted dough. After scouting the field, he had decided to take a gamble on me, figuring I was as good as most—or better. As it turned out, we came into each other's lives at precisely the right moment.

I was aware that he was disappointed when he saw me up close. Because of Brucie and my trouble with Maxine, I had let myself go; I was thin and exhausted. I was also hungry, which was nothing new.

Seeing me in this state, Kearns figured I could use some rest before taking anyone on, so he took me to his mother's house in Oakland. Mrs. McKiernan (Kearns's real name) was an exceptionally nice woman. She was warm and understanding and she treated me like a son. Better than a son. She baked bread for me, canned fruit for me, fussed over me. I guess she thought I needed it pretty badly. I was so grateful that I trailed her around like a shadow. Kearns wouldn't allow me to train until I got back into shape.

Mrs. McKiernan's outlook on life was the most optimistic I had come across in a long time. She didn't want for anything, thanks to her son. In a way, she reminded me of my own mother's always looking out for me. She even yelled at Kearns to make sure I got an even break.

From the time we met, Jack Kearns and I got along pretty well. While we weren't like brothers, we trusted each other enough to form the basis of a more or less stable relationship.

We spent a good deal of the time talking and getting to know each other. He told me all about himself and his past. He was twelve years older than I was and he had a sister he never talked about.

Kearns was born in Michigan and raised in Washington. At fourteen he ran away to the Klondike in Alaska (along with others, such as Jack London). In the Klondike, Kearns told me, he had proved to be a jack of all trades, a gold weigher in a saloon, wrestler, fighter, unsuccessful peddler of cemetery plots and door-to-door Bible salesman—not to mention gambler.

Jack Kearns was not the type of guy to sit still and watch the world go by. He tackled just about anything, whether it was acceptable or not. He was a crafty alligator, a real slicker, as expert at making a fortune as at losing one. He was a man who connived for success, and any method was good enough just so long as it worked.

Jack Kearns would stop at nothing, and nothing would stop Jack Kearns.

11

Off and Running at Last

I talked more to Kearns in those few days than I had to
anyone in quite a while. He seemed to understand me; he listened to
everything I had to say without underrating my goals or my dreams.
I told him of my fear of disappointing my family, of my poor showing in the Flynn fight. I told him about Maxine, how I had made a
mistake, how I didn't even know her whereabouts half the time,
though I sent her as much as I was able.

While my personal affairs were really none of Jack Kearns's
business, I felt the need to spill what was inside me. At this point in
my life, Jack Kearns was just about the only guy who had the time
and patience for me, and I was grateful.

He told me, in that raspy voice of his, not to worry about a thing.
He, too, had made a hell of a lot of mistakes, some of them unmen-
tionable. His only downfall was dames. Booze? He drank a lot but
handled it well, most of the time.

Under his and his mother's supervision I came around, slowly
but surely. I was skinny—165 pounds soaking wet—and didn't look
like much of a bargain. Kearns was about to take quite a gamble.
But he told me he knew good championship stuff when he saw it.

Kearns rigged up a makeshift gym in the back of the house.
Here I worked out from morning to early evening, determined
to prove that he hadn't made a mistake by approaching me. He

even got his old fighter Marty Farrell to come over and spar with me. Marty was good and he was fast. The faster he threw his punches, the less awkward I felt. He helped me perfect my left hook but didn't, as many have said, tie my right behind my back. He showed me how to punch out of a weave as well as how to increase my speed.

Kearns liked what he saw. He brought friends and acquaintances to watch me. I felt embarrassed in front of these spectators—it was different from being in a ring—but Kearns said he was banking on word of mouth to spread my reputation.

One day I noticed a familiar-looking fellow watching me intently. It was Teddy Hayes, whom I had met with Al Auerbach in Salt Lake. He seemed surprised to see me, too. After all, it was a long way from Salt Lake City to Jack Kearns's house. Kearns had approached Teddy to train me at some date in the near future. At first Teddy Hayes was a bit skeptical, but he was soon snowed by Kearns's exuberance and sales pitch. I guess no one could refuse the man.

People kept coming and going while Mrs. McKiernan remained glued to her stove, trying to stretch her meals for the newcomers. Some didn't faze me one way or another, but others were incredible. One, a promoter friend of Kearns named Simpson, pointed to me, turned to Kearns and snickered:

"That's the kid who won the decision over Joe Bond in Nevada? That's the one you was telling me about? You must be kidding! Why, he ain't worth two cents!"

"Well, I think he is. All he needs is a little time."

"All he needs is a little time? Christ, he needs a hell of a lot more than that! What're you doin', Kearns, playing nursemaid to this kid? Why don't you feed him? Wouldn't do him any harm. Maybe with a little weight he'd look like something—not much, but something."

I almost shoved my fist in his face, but Kearns held me back.

"Listen, Simpson," he said, "what would you say if I put the kid against someone like 'Slapper' Willie Meehan?"

"I'd say you was a damn fool."

Within the week Kearns had signed me to fight Willie Meehan again.

"Don't worry, kid. Meehan's a clown. You just get in there and pull up your socks. We'll have the last laugh when we're rollin' in the dough!"

Rollin' in the dough! Those four words sounded pretty good to me.

The Meehan bout was held in Emeryville, just outside Oakland. Three thousand people showed up—to root for Willie. His fans loved him. It was, under California law, a four rounder. I lost the fight, but Kearns was far from disappointed. He called it a good showing; Willie was deceiving but he was tough.

Now Kearns felt that I was ready to go all out, so he arranged another bout with Al Norton, which I won. Rematch. I won again. Kearns was satisfied and pitted me against Meehan once more. This time I won. The months went by quickly. Al Norton again, two draws in bouts with Meehan, KO'd Charley Miller and beat Bob McAllister in Oakland, as well as several others off the record.

Kearns felt I was now ready to take on hard-hitting Gunboat Smith in a four rounder in the Mission Baseball Park in San Francisco. Gunboat had once beaten the champion Jess Willard, and Kearns figured this fight would prove a lot of things. I knew it was my big chance. I also feared that if I blew it Kearns and I would probably be through.

I wasn't afraid of taking on the Gunboat anymore, but I made Kearns promise, just as a precaution, not to throw in the towel, no matter what. He agreed.

While waiting for the Gunboat match, we made almost daily visits to the city sports rooms, right up to the day of the fight. Kearns was obviously setting the stage for further appearances. One of his first converts was Warren Brown, who later became a sports editor in New York and Chicago. Warren was sharp; he and Kearns understood each other from the start.

Jack Kearns was determined that I would fight Jess Willard. One afternoon he put a come-on to Willard in the *San Francisco*

Examiner. But getting it in print wasn't enough for Kearns. He rushed out into the street and grabbed a newsboy by the scruff of his neck.

"Say, kid, what's your name?"

"Willie."

"Willie, you look like an ambitious young fellow. How'd you like to make yourself a buck or two?"

"Sure thing. What do I have to do?"

"Get me a couple hundred *Examiners* and make sure every goddamn sports editor in this city has a copy on his desk."

Willie moved fast. By sunset Jack Kearns had also managed to send a copy to every sports editor he knew around the country.

The fight with the Gunboat wasn't an easy one. He was a hard puncher, and I remember being socked hard with a long right to the chin. I was out and yet, unconscious, I managed to stay on my feet and keep moving. I saw stars and I felt I had lost, even though I hazily heard Kearns and my second, Spider Kelley, screaming their lungs out, spurring me on.

"Keep goin', kid! Soften him up and put him away!"

"You're better'n he is! Go to it, kid!"

The fight mercifully drew to a finish. I was beat and I was disgusted with myself. In the dressing room I apologized to Kearns. At first he and Spider didn't hear me; they were standing in the doorway trying to keep people out of the dressing room. Everyone was ranting and raving. Maybe they wanted to get me for such a poor showing. I tried again.

"I guess I'm no match for Gunboat. I'm real sorry I let you down. I guess I'm not what you thought I was."

I stopped in mid-sentence and looked up. Kearns and Spider were staring at me as if I was out of my head.

"What're you guys starin' at?"

"Kid, you won! The Gunboat hit you with a right and I thought it'd kill you, but you nearly killed him!"

Spider chimed in, "You're in, kid. You're in! What the hell are you apologizing for? Save that for the Gunboat, kid. You're going to be the next champion!"

I passed out.

I'd heard people talking about "champion stuff" before and hadn't paid any attention. Maybe now it would be different; Kearns knew what he was doing as well as what I should be doing. He never even asked me to sign a contract—we trusted each other and that made us a good, solid team. That's all that mattered; I was now on the right road and he was there to guide me.

It was right after the Gunboat Smith fight that Kearns got the nickname "Doc." Whenever he approached me about some arrangement, I had gotten into the habit of saying, "Whatever you decide is okay with me. You're the doctor!" The nickname stuck, and through the years I was never able to think of him as anything else but Doc.

In October, 1918, I took on Gunboat Smith again. I wasn't afraid of anyone now, and I knew there was no stopping me. My confidence had been restored. I won again.

Then came Carl Morris. The same Carl Morris with whom I had sparred. And the same Carl Morris who had humiliated me. I told Kearns about me and Morris.

"Don't let it bother you, kid. Morris is just a big lug with no brains. Remember one thing, kid: A quitter never wins and a winner never quits. Now you're a winner, so get in there and make mincemeat out of him!"

Six feet four inches, 235 pounds of mincemeat, against my 180. A couple of days before the fight, Doc and I bumped into Morris in a hotel lobby.

"Well, well, well. If it isn't my little sparring partner. And who's this dude, your manager, sport?"

He made my blood boil. As he figured it, if I had been his sparring partner for a few bits a day, how good could I possibly be now?

Doc told him to keep his trap shut and be prepared to pack his gear after the fight. Morris laughed, but Doc laughed louder.

That night the betting was in Morris's favor. The Dreamland Pavilion in Frisco was packed. Among the masses sat Wyatt Earp, Rube Goldberg and Al Jolson. All of which convinced Doc that we were slowly but surely gaining a following. I tried explaining that Earp and Goldberg were probably covering the bout for their papers, but he wouldn't listen. "All the newspapermen will sit up and take notice by the time I'm through. The name Jack Dempsey will be up in lights!"

Carl Morris still had the reputation of being a wild beast in the ring. He not only wasn't, but he had the annoying habit of hanging his weight on me. I couldn't lose this bout, and I didn't.

We were off and running and planning to head east. Doc had some ideas for publicity that impressed even me. "Watch me, kid, and do as I say. I can see it now, big cars, gorgeous dames . . ."

The ballyhoo was about to begin.

12

The Ballyhoo Begins

Doc could probably have made it east entirely on his own steam. I was uneasy. I couldn't forget the last time. I was in a different position now, and I had Doc by my side, but just the same I was uneasy.

We stopped in Denver, where Doc and I went to see H. H. Tammen, co-owner of *The Denver Post*. Doc barged into Tammen's office and bellowed that Tammen was one of the privileged few who was being given the opportunity to meet the future heavyweight champ. Tammen wasn't too impressed by my appearance and was even less interested when I opened my mouth and a high-pitched "how do you do" came out. Doc tried to talk to Tammen but was gently pushed out the door, Tammen insisting he had to attend an important meeting.

This didn't stop Doc. It wasn't every day, he said, that we could just stroll into the office of someone like Tammen. On the street, Doc stopped dead in his tracks. In front of us, walking alone, was none other than Jess Willard. Not being one to miss an opportunity, Doc leaped across the street, cornered poor Willard and tried to arrange a match between us right there and then. Willard looked at me without interest and then looked toward Doc with obvious distaste. I could tell he couldn't stand him. I couldn't believe Doc's nerve—he not only didn't possess ethics or scruples, he had no fear.

Willard tried to back away from Doc but found it impossible; he was too big and Kearns was too cagey. The more Doc talked, the more nervous Willard got. Jess finally told Doc that he wouldn't under any circumstances even think of defending his title while the war was on. Doc accused him of placing boxing in a state of suspended animation and of being afraid of losing his title. Willard denied this, so Doc calmed down and made Jess promise—for what it was worth—that I would get first crack once he was ready to fight again. Jess agreed. I think he would have agreed to anything at this point, just to get away from Kearns. Doc relaxed and Willard managed to get away fast.

Doc turned to me and said, "Learn something, kid. It's only the beginning. Most folks are willing to believe anything you tell 'em, no matter what. It's all in how it's presented. You gotta sell them good, kid, make 'em buy anything and let them think they got the best end of the deal. Did you see the way Willard was cornered? Well, I know he wasn't interested, but I forced him to stay and listen. Now he thinks he's pacified me with that nothing of a promise, thinks he's made a fool of Jack Kearns. No, siree. Just you keep your eye on him from now on and you'll see who winds up with the short end of the stick."

After Willard had vanished, Doc turned around and headed right back to the *Denver Post*. There we bumped into Otto Floto, just the person Doc wanted to see.

"Listen, Floto. Keep this under your hat. We just met Jess Willard and he's agreed to fight my boy for the title, with the proceeds going to charity."

Otto listened intently and then said that this was too big to keep quiet; how would Kearns like it if the *Post* were to put out an extra regarding this new development?

Kearns thought for a split second and then agreed, "only because it's you, Otto."

The *Post* came out with the story and Kearns was satisfied. He was also curious as to what Willard's next move would be.

Before heading for Chicago, I stopped in Salt Lake to see my folks, promising Doc that I would catch up with him in Chicago.

My father had come down with a crippling rheumatism and in his pain he was snapping at everyone, especially my mother. My sister had lost her husband and was having a problem taking care of herself and the kids. Joe wasn't well, and Johnny had had to undergo several operations. It was heartbreaking, especially since they all depended on whatever I could contribute.

I asked around for news of Maxine. No one had seen her for quite a spell. Following slim leads, I traced her from city to city and finally tracked her down in a dance hall in Illinois. She wouldn't see me. Through a friend she informed me that she had resumed her career and didn't want to have anything more to do with me.

I rejoined Doc outside Chicago and we took a train into the city. This time I carried a leather valise and wore patent leather shoes, a three-piece suit and a linen handkerchief. Everything had been bought on credit.

When we arrived the snow was knee-deep and the temperature near zero. We checked into one of the best rooms in the Morrison Hotel.

"Don't ever check into a crummy joint, kid. People'll think that's all you're used to. Remember, in a dump they'll always ask for their dough in advance, while a classy place waits till the end of the week or month. And as we know, kid, anything can happen in that time."

A week? A month? With Kearns all hell could break loose in ten minutes! From the time we arrived in the windy city, we played the roles of Big Time Fight Contender and His Manager. We generously tipped everyone in sight—and before we knew it, we could have used a tip ourselves. I came down with a rotten cold, but it didn't stop Doc. He made the rounds of the newspaper offices, from sports rooms to city rooms, inviting every editor to come and meet me at the Morrison. They came and they saw. Doc apologized for me, saying I had sprained my ankle. And there I sat with watery eyes and swollen, runny nose.

When our dough ran out Doc turned to Jim Mullen, a promoter, who helped us out by lending us money to buy warm coats.

He also introduced us to a young woman whose mother, Mrs. Sheehy, ran a rooming house where all the sports editors and writers stayed. Perfect. We left the Morrison and moved into Mother Sheehy's. (I never knew how Doc paid the bill.)

Doc had the habit of hanging around and conducting business in hotel lobbies. No matter where he was, he made sure that a pre-paid page boy called his name every twenty minutes or so. If he was with exceptional company, he would even go so far as to refuse the trumped-up calls, dropping the caller's "name" in his refusal. Surprisingly, it always worked.

One day, strolling through one of his lobbies, Doc heard his name called. He turned around and found himself confronted with a fuming Jess Willard. Seemed he was mad over the article in *The Denver Post*.

"That was a cheap trick you pulled, Kearns. When *I* decide to fight again, it'll be with someone who's earned it."

He made it clear that he didn't want me or anyone else Kearns had in mind. The scene was so embarrassing that I backed away. Jess was insulting not only me but Kearns as well. Willard really incensed Doc before walking away. The whole lobby was staring, and Doc was pretty annoyed at having been humiliated in public.

He sat down and wrote Willard a letter, stating in effect that Willard's not wanting to fight me was a disgrace, since the proceeds were to go to charities that were helping boys overseas. Before he sealed the letter he showed it to me. I tried to convince him not to send it, but his mind was made up.

"That's the only way to put that fat, arrogant Willard in his place!"

Some time later word reached us that he had reacted bitterly, saying that he never, but never, wanted to see me or the lousy Jack Kearns again.

In Chicago Doc arranged for me to appear on stage shadow-boxing and jumping rope. In our off-hours, Doc made sure we patronized the "right places." We had invested in a few more suits, on credit again. They were expensive and flashy, just like Jack Kearns. I tried to imitate him in dress and habits (and continued to do so until dapper Tex Rickard took me aside some time later and suggested I polish myself up).

One day Doc decided it was time to get me some publicity, so he called a press conference. When the sports writers arrived, he introduced me as the next champion. Then he startled everyone, including me, by offering to bet $10,000 of his own money that I could beat any two fighters of the press's choice in one night!

I stood by him and couldn't believe my ears. Ten thousand dollars of his own money? *What money?*

I shook my head. Now, I thought, he's really done it. We had hardly had enough to pay for the streetcar! We couldn't even afford the press conference.

I took Doc aside and whispered, "We ain't even got two bits, Doc!"

He laughed and said, "Don't you know that's the name of the game, kid? Look, it's great publicity for us, and what's more, no person's got that kind of dough to lay out."

"Oh, I see." I really didn't. That was one hell of a lot of money to risk on a bluff! I was afraid someone would take him up on his bet, but Doc proved right. No one had that kind of dough.

Many writers must have recognized Doc's bluff; nevertheless, it worked. It gave us priceless publicity. All of a sudden, we were making news. Doc started inventing tales about my strength, my heritage, my fierce temper (I had none) and whatever else he could think of. The publicity mounted.

I kept myself busy by training in Kid Howard's gym. There many of the sports editors whom Doc had approached came to see me work out. They weren't too taken with me; I never looked good working out. But Doc kept up the Ballyhoo until he had arranged a match with Homer Smith in Racine, Wisconsin. I knew everyone was waiting for us to take a fall, either through Doc's inflated words or my actions.

Like me, Homer was pretty new in the top contender category. He'd earned his slot by getting a draw against Bill Brennan. Homer and I both knew that we had everything to gain and a lot to lose.

Homer's showing did nothing for his career. He was flat on the canvas in one minute, fifty-nine seconds. But he was a good sport, especially after the fight. According to some, he was a bit dazed for a couple of hours but wouldn't admit it. He even smoked a cigar and took a couple of slugs of whiskey—his first cigar and his first slug. He ended up not only dazed but sick.

Doc now referred to me as Jack the Giant Killer, the Man-Eater and similar names his fertile mind invented. This time people listened.

We seemed on the threshold of some kind of success and some piece of the spotlight. Sports writers were now writing about me. They had no choice; we couldn't be avoided. Several of them, who found Doc obnoxious, hoped that I would be defeated just so he'd fade away.

In the meantime, Doc learned that Charlie Murray, a Buffalo promoter, was arranging a fight between Carl Morris and Fireman Jim Flynn. Kearns wired Murray and offered to have me take either one of them on before the fight, for a substantial guarantee. Morris didn't want it, but he felt that he had lost face with me in the San Francisco bout. Since his standing and reputation were at stake, he needed time to think it over.

Flynn, on the other hand, liked the idea of making some additional money before his fight with Morris. Nothing to it. He figured if he had knocked me out once, it would be twice as easy now. He told Murray he had nothing to lose. We met and I demolished him in the first round.

Doc immediately telephoned Murray and offered to substitute me for Flynn in the upcoming Morris fight. He told Murray how big and tough I was and how easily I scored knockouts. By the time Doc was through talking, Murray was almost sold. He figured Doc had a giant on his hands and he was definitely interested. He sent us money to get to Buffalo so he could see me.

We took the train and, when we were almost there, we got caught in a raging blizzard. After a long delay, we finally pulled into Buffalo. We checked into the Hotel Iroquois, exhausted from the long trip. It was pretty late and Doc figured that, because of the hour and the storm, Murray would wait till morning.

I went into the other room, peeled down to my drawers and

socks and sprawled out on the bed. Doc unpacked his bottle and prepared himself a drink. He had just about settled into an armchair when there was a heavy knock on the door.

It was Murray; his curiosity just couldn't wait.

"Awright, where is he?"

Doc called to me to come out. He introduced me to Murray and I put my hand out. Murray didn't make a move, just stared at me in disbelief.

"Okay, Kearns. A joke's a joke. I know this kid's some middleweight you keep around. Now, where's Dempsey?"

Doc assured him that I was Dempsey. Murray refused to believe him.

"What's the big idea? You told me he was six foot two, weighing at least 230. This little guy doesn't even come near 190. I can't put him in the same ring with Morris. The public wouldn't stand for it!"

Doc argued that I was good and that I had been in a four rounder with Morris a year before, and won.

"So what!" Murray shouted. "He's too goddamn little. Morris is tougher than he was a year ago. This time he'll kill your kid!"

My stomach muscles crunched. I looked at Doc. He was as upset as I was, but he wasn't going to lose this one for anything. He paced back and forth, his hands clasped behind his back.

"Listen, Murray. Don't let his size fool you. He's good and he's fast. Why don't you give him a chance? What's it to you if Morris's willing?"

And so it went, back and forth, endlessly. Whenever they stopped arguing, I'd put in a word or two for myself. I needed this chance pretty badly, but Murray was really being pig-headed. After a while, I was so exasperated that I wanted to call the fight off—but it wasn't mine to call off.

I thought Murray would never come around. I tried one last time.

"Mr. Murray, you've gotta let me go ahead with this fight. Tell you what, if I don't lick Morris, you can give my end of the purse to the poor kids in Buffalo. Listen, we need that dough. Please, let me take him on. It means everything to me."

Murray chewed on that for a moment and then reluctantly agreed. Doc and I smiled at each other. Doc assured him he wouldn't regret the decision.

It was an ugly fight. Morris, who had really wanted Flynn, was faced with me instead. Throughout the fight I was under the impression that he disliked me so much he couldn't look me in the eye.

Carl Morris had a terrific swing he called his "Mary Ann." And Murray was right, it was a tougher Morris. I threw as many body punches as I could. Finally, I could see he was in trouble. I aimed for the jaw, but Morris was tough and wouldn't go down.

The more I pounded him, the lower he landed his blows, until the sixth round, when referee Dick Nugent, who had warned Morris several times, disqualified him for fouling and awarded the fight to me.

I felt fine. Doc felt better.

13

Finally, a Following

We were finally beginning to make money, though we kept very little of it. Either we owed someone for something or I sent my share home.

Soon after the Morris fight Doc felt the time was right for me to meet Bill Brennan. Instead of issuing a direct challenge to Brennan through his manager, Leo P. Flynn, Doc asked various sports writers for their suggestions for my next opponent. They tossed around a few names. Every time Brennan's cropped up, Doc would enthusiastically support the choice. The writers, spurred on, would boost a Dempsey–Brennan fight.

The pressure mounted until Leo P. Flynn, no longer able to ignore the indirect challenge, approached us. Brennan was willing; fighting me, in his opinion, wouldn't be too much of a risk, so Flynn and Doc signed the necessary papers. In his haste to sign, Doc found that he was short, so he borrowed the hundred-dollar guarantee from May Brown, Mother Sheehy's daughter. May was nice about it; she was behind me all the way, handmaking my boxing trunks right up to 1926.

I had originally met Bill Brennan in 1916 while working in Billy Gibson's gym in New York. At that time I was a sparring partner for just about anyone, and I had gone a few rounds with Brennan.

He stopped in my dressing room just before the fight. He was

Finally, a Following **8 1**

pretty confident, and he let me know that he had Jess Willard just about tied up. All he needed was a match with Fred Fulton and he'd be set for a crack at the championship.

"Sure, Bill, I understand. I'd like to meet Willard myself. Listen, we're pals, so may the best man win!"

Leo walked in and told Bill to get ready. The Milwaukee Arena was filling up and he had a couple of two-way bets riding on this fight. He sized me up and down and then broke into a chuckle.

"Everyone's underestimating you, kid, but I've got a feeling you pack dynamite in those hands."

I was surprised to hear this from my opponent's manager.

The fight lasted six rounds. I tried for a first round knockout, but it didn't work. I did manage to floor him a few times before the second round was over. By the sixth round, he was groggy. I hit him as hard as I could. He spun around and I heard something snap as he fell. The fight was over, but I was horrified. The snap had been so loud that I was convinced he had broken his leg. I rushed to his dressing room and found that he had in fact broken his ankle.

Leo P. Flynn was asked by several sports writers after the fight what he thought of me. He said, "Can Dempsey hit? Say, he hit my man so hard he broke his ankle. Did you ever hear of anything like that?" He went on to say that if Doc wanted to get out of the fight game, he'd be more than glad to take me on.

Now I had a reputation. I had knocked out some of the best, and the field was becoming narrower. Only a handful now stood between me and Jess Willard.

The press watched me closely. They no longer dismissed us as noisy newcomers. We had wedged ourselves in, and it was obvious that we weren't going to give up.

I licked the other contenders one by one. I worked damn hard in the ring, and Doc worked his tail off outside it. Our goal was to force people to recognize me as the leading contender. Doc didn't waste a moment, but sometimes we had to control our impatience; if certain contenders were unavailable, we had to wait until they were.

Doc spread as many stories as he could, varying them according to his mood. Often writers actually argued among themselves over who got the correct version.

When I read about myself in the papers I had the eerie feeling I was reading about someone else, someone who was fighting, staging exhibitions and selling liberty bonds. I did everything and anything Doc told me to do.

The more publicity I got, the more Doc stepped up his verbal campaign. By now I had developed, according to him, the "killer instinct": "Just look at that scowl."

Everything was going smoothly until one fight manager threw in a monkey wrench. He wanted me out of the way in order to give his fighter, who had served some time in the armed forces, a chance. He told Doc that I was monopolizing the ranks and that I should be overseas like his boy had been. Doc told him to mind his own goddamn business and not go around shooting his mouth off when he didn't have the facts. He wasn't about to explain Maxine, my folks or the draft papers I had filled out. He wasn't going to point out how much I was raising for the Red Cross or how many bonds I had sold. No, Doc wasn't going to tell him any of it.

A west coast editor also lashed out at me. He had approached us with an offer to stage an exhibition for a local charity, and we had refused because of a previous engagement. Miffed, he too attacked us. I guess I was the perfect target.

When things started to cool down, there came more bad news. John the Barber stepped out of the shadows and told Kearns that I was under contract to him. He wanted me or a piece of the action. Doc told him to get lost, so Reisler instigated a lawsuit, the first of many, against us.

Doc asked the Barber to produce the alleged contract. He couldn't. Then he told Doc that he had advanced me some money.

"How much?"

"Five thousand dollars."

"Why, you reptile. We haven't got that kind of dough!"

"Well, it's either five grand or Dempsey. Take your pick."

Doc asked me if the Barber had really advanced me that kind of dough. I told him no. Nevertheless, John the Barber could make our lives miserable. Doc was desperate. He called Bill Farnsworth, the journalist, to whom he spilled the whole story. Farnsworth was sympathetic. They put their heads together to think of someone who would have that kind of dough. Then it hit Farnsworth that Colonel Jake Ruppert, part owner of the New York Yankees, was just the man. All Doc had to do was convince Ruppert we were worth bailing out. Doc agreed to try.

One midnight, Doc, accompanied by Farnsworth, knocked on Ruppert's door and asked to see him. They explained our problem. Ruppert looked Doc over and asked Farnsworth to vouch for Doc, which he did. A half hour later Kearns and Farnsworth walked out with the money. Doc paid John the Barber off and told him never to show his ugly face again.

In St. Paul, Minnesota, I met Billy Miske. He didn't look impressive, so his toughness in the ring came as a big surprise. Throughout the fight, Miske kept landing more blows than I did, and he seemed to be really piling up points.

"Pull up your socks and smack him down," Doc yelled. "Get rid of him!"

Easier said than done. Both Miske and I were tired, and even though I was able to drive a few in, he covered up well. In the end I got a draw. The fight with Billy Miske taught me not to underestimate anyone or anything.

The Miske bout was followed by a succession of first round knockouts. In July Doc arranged through promoter Jack Curley a match with Fred Fulton, the Minnesota Plasterer. Curley was a good-natured guy who, like Jack Kearns, had tried his hand at just about everything, including, in later years, managing Rudolph Valentino when Rudy quit pictures in a moment of anger to go on a coast-to-coast dancing tour.

Various reform groups who were attacking alcohol and tobacco now criticized us, saying it was morally wrong to pay for a fight while the country was at war. The Spanish influenza was reaching epidemic proportions, and some claimed it would get even worse if masses of people sat together at a prizefight. Doc paid no attention and made another publicized donation to the Red Cross.

Suddenly, certain factions did an about-face, saying that sports were badly needed, at home and abroad, for entertainment and morale —especially when portions of purses were given to the Red Cross.

About this time I filed for divorce from Maxine. We hadn't been in touch for quite a while, and Maxine had obviously wanted out for a long time. While she preferred her independence, her own way of life, she didn't mind my money. I charged desertion and the divorce became final in a matter of months. She never contested my action; she simply didn't care.

Because Fred Fulton was a good fighter, Doc took no chances. He took me to Long Branch, New Jersey, where I was trained by the professor himself, Jimmy De Forest. In Long Branch we stayed at Mother Hughes's Boarding House.

De Forest was the expert in his field. He was the best, and Doc knew it. I was nearing the top, and Doc didn't want any amateurs around me.

De Forest was a shrewd little guy who was never seen without an unlit cigar in the corner of his mouth. It didn't seem to interfere with what he had to say, which was plenty. Doc said he talked too much and poked his nose everywhere, but he knew his stuff. I liked him and respected him. He gave me fine points on hitting and blocking, footwork and anything else he thought would help me, criticism as well. Jimmy De Forest was to be my trainer right up to the Willard fight. Then Doc, over my protests, let him go.

My sparring partners while training were Jamaica Kid and Jim Johnson, both veterans of the ring, fast and tough. Doc saw to it that I had the best possible preparation for the fight. We both realized that winning this fight was vital.

Because the advance ticket sale was slow, our $12,500 guarantee from promoter Curley had to be reduced. Even so, it still amounted to more than that of all my early fights put together.

The fight was scheduled to take place in the old Federal League Ball Park in Harrison, New Jersey. The high-priced seats were empty, so the lower-priced ticket holders knocked each other down in a rush to get to them.

Fred Fulton was a tall guy with a good reach and a glass chin.

Once in the ring, I worked fast, wearing him down till he dropped his guard, whereupon I went straight for the jaw. He was counted out in approximately eighteen seconds of the first round, a bad break for ticket holders who came in late.

One friend, who had bought a high-priced ticket, told me after the fight that the minute he saw Fulton go down he had rushed outside and managed to sell his ticket, for twice what he had originally paid, to an anxious fan who was standing toward the end of the line.

We got nine thousand dollars for eighteen seconds' work. After the fight I was mobbed by enthusiastic fans—for the first time in my life. They tore at everything, just wanting to take a little piece of me home. They even trailed me to the Treat Hotel, where I was staying. Fans. Up to now I never thought of myself as having any. Fans. They were to stay with me for the rest of my life.

I was real proud of myself. After the Morris fight, I had helped my mother make a down payment on a house in Salt Lake. I remember sending her some money wrapped in newspaper clippings about her son. Now, after the Fulton fight, the house was completely hers.

Because Jess Willard had counted on fighting Fred Fulton next, I was now the logical contender. All we had to do was to find someone who would be willing to promote a Willard–Dempsey fight. New York was where everything was happening, but as circumstances would have it, boxing was not regarded too favorably there. My expenses were mounting and my "entourage" was growing, so Doc decided to bide his time and make some money elsewhere. (Strange about an entourage—every time a clean sweep was made, new deadwood replaced the old.)

We made our way to San Francisco, where Willie Meehan was to be my next opponent in a benefit for Navy Relief. Since I had seen him last, Willie had trimmed down and was now a seaman. How things had changed for both of us in just one year!

We slugged away at each other in the Civic Auditorium in Frisco. So intense was our fighting that at the end of the fourth round neither one of us heard the bell. Willie got the decision, accompanied by a roof-raising cheer from his fellow sailors.

The decision didn't hurt me. It was a benefit, and I was too far along to be concerned.

Doc feared my getting stale from training too long, so I stopped and did very little for about two months, until Doc could line up a suitable opponent. I was just beginning to enjoy my idleness when Doc announced that we were off to Philadelphia, where he was to negotiate a bout with Battling Levinsky.

After Battling Levinsky, only ten men seemed to be standing between me and Jess Willard.

14

Of Tex Rickard and Jess Willard

The war was just about over. Doc and I felt that we had, in our own way, boosted the war effort by raising just under a half million dollars for the Red Cross in addition to selling bonds. We were cooperative and tried to help anyone who contacted us.

In Philadelphia Doc was approached by a representative of the U.S. Government, accompanied by Cody Drennen of the Sun Shipyard. They asked Doc if I would agree to pose in the shipyard for recruitment purposes. It'd be good publicity, both for the shipyard and for me. Doc, completely immersed in the Levinsky contract, didn't give it much thought but figured it would be all right. Everything was arranged for the following day.

In the shipyard I was given a pair of stripped overalls and told to slip them on over my street clothes. Snap. Then I was handed a riveter's machine. Snap. "One more, Jack." Snap. Snap. And that was that.

The next morning I unfolded the newspaper—and there I was, dressed in those crisp overalls, with my shiny patent leather suede-topped shoes sticking out like sore thumbs. I couldn't believe it. What was this picture doing in the newspaper? I picked up another paper. It was in that one, too. I shut my eyes and a million questions flooded my mind. Had Doc known it would hit the press? Had I been mistaken in thinking the photo was for the Sun Shipyard and not for publication? Damn Doc and his lust for publicity!

Doc and I had registered for the draft and been deferred because of my needy family and Doc's mother. At one point I had even attempted to enlist in the Navy. So why, I asked myself, should this photo bother me? My conscience was clear. I worked hard and I sent money to Maxine and to my family in Salt Lake.

I told Doc I was disturbed.

"Listen, kid. What're you worried about? You're makin' a big deal out of nothing!"

Still, the entire matter made me uneasy.

When the war had first started, it had been considered strictly a war for Europeans. The United States maintained an isolationist attitude; we weren't going to get involved in a foreign war and we weren't going to send our boys over. But the tide gradually turned. Those who had been pacifists were seeing their closest relatives off to Europe. I wanted to go, too. After all, wasn't I a fighter? In my mind, it didn't matter where I fought; I was strong and I never shirked my duty in life. I wasn't afraid, especially if it meant representing my own country.

I tried pushing the entire shoe episode aside. I had to concentrate on my career without interference or anxiety—at least that's what Doc kept telling me. The more lightly he took the matter, the more the pressure built up inside me. We were starting to quarrel, so I decided that I'd keep my trap shut and my thoughts to myself. It hurt me to read the criticism the press dished out, but nothing could be done about it.

Still smarting, I met Battling Levinsky for the prearranged bout, and I won. It was around this time that Doc and I were approached by his friend, trainer Teddy Hayes. Hayes was an officer attached to the Great Lakes Naval Training Station, which boasted 15,000 men, including some outstanding all-around sportsmen. Teddy told Doc that he needed a heavyweight to represent the United States Navy at a boxing meet in London in December. Admiral Moffett had given Teddy the papers necessary to enlist me as a First Class Seaman. Teddy, with the papers in his pocket, was now at the Vendic Hotel telling Kearns that I was needed for the tournament. But Doc wouldn't have any part of it. I was more than willing, but

Doc told Teddy that we still had to fulfill some engagements for the Red Cross, the dates of which conflicted with those of the tournament in London. Wounded soldiers, widows and children needed our help more than the Navy's tournament did.

"We can't get out of this, Teddy. What's more, it'll put Jack in good standing with the public. How about if we join you some time later?"

Teddy figured it'd be all right; he'd just have to speak to someone who would be able to arrange my release from the San Francisco draft board where I was registered.

Teddy left for New York, the papers still in his pocket. He recruited Jack Heinon to take my place.

That very week the Armistice was declared, but the U.S. Naval Station's tournament took place as scheduled. I was convinced one and a half years later that I would have been better off going with Hayes instead of listening to Doc.

Doc kept me pretty busy in the following months, fighting several unknowns in exhibition bouts as well as having me meet some top contenders, including Carl Morris in New Orleans. He was still riding high; his loss to me some time before, based on a foul, really wasn't taken seriously. I still couldn't stand the sight of him, and he knew it. (Not the trusting sort, Carl collected his share of the purse from the promoter before stepping into the ring and stuffed the dough in his shoes.) I knocked him to the mat in fourteen seconds of the first round. I knew the bum wouldn't get up.

Doc had started putting ads in the paper for sparring partners. One guy, Marty Burke, joined up with us just before the Morris bout. He went some rounds with me for a couple of days. He was an amateur champ, and at the end of the three or four days I gave him twenty bucks. He croaked, "Jack, you're making a professional out of me."

By this time nothing that would help promote me was overlooked. We went to all kinds of events, all civic group gatherings. If something was on, we were there. Doc was the perfect scene stealer. If someone was having his picture taken, Doc'd make sure the lens was somehow directed towards me instead of the original subject. He started catering to and patronizing the big shots, the big names, the rulers of the game. At first they weren't too friendly, but they listened to him—they had no choice. Doc had sharp eyes; he knew all the tricks and kept them brushed off and ready to be used.

On December 30, 1918, I knocked out Gunboat Smith in what turned out to be a two round bout. I was now so impatient that I was managing quick knockouts, moving closer and closer to the target.

We stopped making appearances in small towns and started making them in the big cities where the publicity would have more clout. We checked into top hotels, ate in expensive restaurants and took cabs. A hotel management, adamant about the bill, once cornered us for payment. Doc solved the problem neatly. He inquired when our "pal" in the next room was checking out. Informed of the date, Kearns checked out beforehand, leaving the bill to our neighbor as a token of our friendship.

He made sure we were with the right people at the right places. Tailors started making our suits faster than ever, sewing like lightning. All on credit, accompanied only by a handshake. Even our car bills and expenses were mounting. It was no longer just Doc and me now that we had the "entourage," which meant that I had to support more persons than ever before.

In 1919 Doc decided we needed a gimmick to attract attention, so we went on the vaudeville circuit. We joined Barney Gerard's American Burlesques, and Doc devised an entire stage routine. We were usually the third act on the bill, pacing nervously in the wings. Most acts, in those days, carried their own sets, curtains, drops and wardrobes, so we had to wait while they cleared the stage.

Then Doc would step to center stage, dapper and perfumed, and bellow the benefits of boxing, explaining why every good American boy should box. Then he'd announce grandly that he had the next heavyweight champion of the world backstage. I'd come out, introduce myself, skip rope, punch some light bags and do some shadowboxing. After a ten-minute workout with Marty

Burke, who had joined us, Doc would step forward and offer $1,000 to anyone who could stay three rounds with me, patting his pocket as if the full thousand was there, rather than a crumpled monogrammed handkerchief.

While the crowd debated the offer, a young man would present himself, shaking with anticipation for the thousand: our shill, Max "The Goose" Kaplan. With one punch, he would lay down flat. We had practised our act so many times that his timing was ace-perfect. Doc had told Max to make sure he beat everyone else in getting to me. He did. And the audience ate it up. Max was really good; he could fall over like a store dummy.

We traveled from state to state, playing every place from the legitimate theater to the dive, always attracting a full house. Even the press started taking notice. Whether they were interested in us or whether they were waiting for a story headlined LOCAL TOUGH LICKS CONTENDER, I don't know. At least they were keeping tabs on us. Doc was convinced they were all holding their breath, hoping we'd lose our steam.

Doc was making such a fuss that the champion, Jess Willard, told one journalist that if we ever met, it would only be because I still hadn't been knocked out by some second-rater. Apparently he still felt that my eighteen-second knockout of Fred Fulton had been a fluke. That was the extent of Willard's comment before he dismissed me altogether. He thought I was a jerk and he considered Doc a gangster as well as a pain.

Things ran pretty smoothly while we were playing vaudeville. Once, in Pennsylvania, Max didn't get to the stage on time. He tripped and fell, and by the time he had managed to scramble to his feet, it was too late: Some loudmouth named Curly had come up. Doc was fuming. He tried to get rid of Curly by telling him that I wanted to see him show his stuff, so why didn't he go a few rounds with this other young fellow, Max, who was climbing onto the stage. Curly reluctantly agreed and floored Max in a split second before tearing after me. He went up and down like a yo-yo and then it was all over. Doc paid him fifty bucks and thanked him.

But it wasn't over as far as Curly was concerned. The next

night he was sitting smack in the first row, surrounded by his tough pals and supporters. He shouted to Doc even before Doc had had a chance to ignore him. He'd been training all night, he said, and was ready for action. Doc looked at me and, seeing he couldn't deter the guy, shrugged his shoulders. He nodded to Curly, who leaped on stage. He was big, but there was no reason for me to be concerned. He must have been desperate for the thousand bucks. I let him stay one round and then I ended his dream of glory with a left hook to the stomach. As he fell he grabbed the curtain, causing the ring to collapse and dragging down the scenery on top of him, leaving in his wake a bunch of gaping chorus girls, electricians and maintenance men. The audience howled with laughter as Curly and the curtain were hauled away.

Then came other fights, other towns, other cities. I remember Doc pacing the floor and wringing his hands, his face betraying nothing, Doc writing down the names of useful contacts and breaking his pencils from anxiety. I wasn't used to his being agitated. It unnerved me, but he kept telling me it had nothing to do with my fighting. Some sports editors, he said, had started putting some kind of heat on him because of an incident in his past. He didn't want to talk about it.

The turning point came in Pennsylvania. We had been paid for a show and had spent the dough the night before on some broads. We were sitting backstage the following day, discussing how our contacts were starting to wear thin, when the theater manager burst in on us and demanded his rent in advance.

"Rent in advance? Out of the question."

"Out of the question? Well, in that case, wise guys, out of my theater—and stay out!"

We tried telling him that this was not the usual policy, but the man told us it was *his* policy. Out meant Out. Kearns decided the time had come to go to New York "to see who or what I can hustle up."

He was gone forty-eight hours. When he came back he seemed a changed man. He told me he'd hooked up with Tex Rickard, the guy who'd built the stadium for the Jack Johnson–Jim Jeffries fight, the one in which Johnson had pushed Jeffries through the ropes. And then the words poured out:

"When I arrived in New York I met a pal and we went to the Biltmore. There I spotted Wild Bill Lyons. You remember, he had been a sergeant-at-arms in the Colorado State Senate. He joined us, along with John McGraw (I knew him in my Klondike days), and pretty soon we got to talking and drinking when that Rickard came along. You know, kid, when McGraw introduced us, that crafty, shiftless gambler pretended he'd never set eyes on me before. Gave me that crap, 'Say, haven't I seen you somewhere?' Damn right he had, so I set him straight by telling him that I had been the gold weigher in his Northern Bar Saloon. He sure didn't like me remindin' him, kid. But he played it straight and then said that maybe he *did* recognize me, but I had changed. We then got to talking about this and that, and I told him all about you, how I was your manager and all."

Doc seemed to take great satisfaction in telling the story.

"So?"

"So listen! Ya know, kid, he'd heard your name around New York. See? Publicity, kid. Publicity. Anyhow, I told Rickard we was interested in meeting Willard, but he didn't bite. Said he had the shorts and that he wasn't interested in promoting fights. I think someone told him you weren't too big, 'cause he said something about his not wanting to be responsible for your gettin' killed. Said the 'public wouldn't allow it.'

"That Rickard. When I told him I thought we could make Big Money his eyes lit up. Sure, I got him all figured out by now. He knows and I know fat Jess's no good anymore, he's been out of action too damn long. One thing led to another, and before he knew it, he was sending the champ a telegram. I guess I convinced him when I told him I'd take care of raising the $100,000—the amount we figured that fat so-and-so would accept as a guarantee. Ha! By the time I got through with him he was convinced I knew what I was talking about. Yessir, you leave it to Doc, kid. Why, I even told him you'd be willing to meet Jess Willard for nothing!"

For nothing! Was he serious? From then on Doc's motor was

running. He couldn't stop talking, he didn't stop drinking and he wouldn't stop thinking—waiting for Willard to answer. He assured me nothing could go wrong. That Willard wasn't a real threat to anyone and especially not to me. But he worried all the same; he almost wore a hole in the carpet and was probably working on one in his belly, too. He didn't seem to need sleep at all. Night after night he would invite pals in and they would talk and talk.

Willard's answer arrived in a matter of days. Tex Rickard's call reached us while we were on stage at the Arch Street Theatre in Philadelphia. Doc walked off stage and left me to fend for myself. When he came back he was grinning from ear to ear.

We were to meet Rickard in New York the following afternoon. Meanwhile, Rickard would meet Jess Willard in Chicago. While I had seen Rickard briefly some time back, I really hadn't had a chance to observe him, and I found him different from the picture Doc had given me. He was a cool customer, but he was likeable and he called the shots as he saw them. While Doc referred to him behind his back as a "crafty son-of-a-bitch" or a "chiseling gambler," Tex didn't mince words either; he called Doc everything from a "sneaky no-good" to a "cheap conniver." It was obviously not a mutual admiration society. Here was one con trying to out-con the other.

Tex Rickard was in fact a gambler; when he won, he won big, and when he lost, he lost big. In his early days he discovered he had a natural instinct for promoting—anything and everything. Once he had put a purse filled to the brim with twenty-dollar gold pieces in the window of his Northern Bar Saloon to sell tickets to a Joe Gans fight. Seeing gold displayed turned out to be quite a come-on. Within three days the fight was completely sold out.

Rickard, a solitary man since being orphaned at ten, grew up on a Texas ranch. He had been a cowhand, a wrangler and later a Texas sheriff. He had been in the Klondike gold rush and had struck it rich in the famous Bonanza strike. With the money he set up a saloon and gambling hall, only to lose it all eventually on a bad wager. He lumberjacked for a spell and then returned to the action. Some time and money later he opened another saloon and became even wealthier before losing it all again on worthless gold claims. His Northern Bar Saloon was just about his last venture in the west. From the time I met him, I treasured his friendship and loyalty.

Tex told me how he'd met Doc at the Biltmore and how Doc had stiffed him for a twenty, pleading he had no small bills. Tex was no fool; he knew Doc had tried to pull a fast one. He couldn't forget he'd known Doc from way back, when Doc, in the Klondike, had vaselined and gold-dusted his hair for effect. He remembered Jack Kearns all right. He hadn't trusted Kearns then, didn't trust Kearns now and would never trust him. But they managed to get along pretty well in public—for the sake of the buck. I defended Doc; he'd been good to me.

Many who really knew Tex Rickard loved him, as Grannie Rice, Bill Corum and I loved the man. If he was disliked, it was usually because he wasn't understood. He wasn't a man who gave openly, he didn't spread his friendship around easily or indiscriminately. He was discreet. He was his own man—a lone, sensitive man—who didn't want to be obligated to anyone. Doc used to say that while he respected the guy, that didn't mean he had to like him.

Tex, like Doc, was always available to the press. He would interrupt the most crucial conference for a newsman. I remember walking into his office and finding him behind his desk, slowly chewing tobacco, while the press boys, with their feet up, made themselves completely at home. In addition to liking the press, he also liked to set them straight every so often. He fairly jumped with glee when the press prophesied some disaster and he, Tex Rickard, proved them wrong.

Rickard thought I was crazy for wanting to fight Willard, but he couldn't help smiling when I told him I was six feet and still growing. I was so anxious that I think I would have said just about anything.

15

Signing for the Big Fight

I guess my fight with Carl Morris was the one responsible for
my getting a crack at Jess Willard. When Jack Curley, Morris's manager, sent Tex Rickard's press man, Ike Dorgan, to New Orleans to
collect his 25 percent, he was in for a big surprise. Seems the promoter in New Orleans told Dorgan that Morris had personally collected the money before the bout and that he had no inkling of
Morris's whereabouts.

As it happened, promoter Tortorich told Dorgan that he was
planning to offer Jess Willard $75,000 to fight me, since he had
liked my style in the Morris fight. Dorgan, who didn't particularly
care for Tortorich or any of his cronies, listened carefully to what
Tortorich had to say and became convinced that the promoter would stand firm on the $75,000 offer. After an hour or so,
Dorgan said his good-byes and took a fast train to New York,
where he scrambled to Tex Rickard's office and told Tex to offer
Jess Willard not less than $100,000 so that Tortorich wouldn't have
a chance.

Tex digested Dorgan's information and said he would think
it over. So, when Doc and Tex met in the Biltmore, Tex was already
in the know though he pretended he wasn't. He faked astonishment at Doc's proposals for a Willard match. He was actually confident of getting Willard to come around, but he couldn't bring himself to allow Doc the slightest bit of satisfaction.

Tex and Doc never saw eye to eye except when it came to money. Even then they fought over the amounts, since Tex was conservative and Doc just the opposite. Tex told Doc that, assuming all systems were "go" with Jess Willard, I could not expect to get a guarantee of more than $20,000 or $25,000. Doc thought that $25,000 was ridiculously low.

"Well, Kearns, how much do you want?"

"How much do I want? Listen, Rickard, this isn't just an ordinary fight. I'm pitting the kid here against Jess Willard, and that ought to be worth at least fifty grand!"

"Too much," Tex replied. "If the purse is too big, then it's no good; I can't make the gamble. Besides, you and I know you could afford to fight for nothing. If Jack here can beat him, it'll be worth half a million to you fellows inside a year. If he can't, then it isn't worth any $50,000—or for that matter even $10,000!"

As I figured it, Tex was right. Willard was the champion and I was just a contender; why should I be entitled to the equivalent of one-half of the champion's purse? For once I was afraid Doc would blow it. Nevertheless, I kept my mouth shut, especially when I saw that Doc wasn't about to let Tex off the hook.

"Listen, Rickard. Let's be reasonable."

"Forget it. I'm leaving."

Then Doc had an idea.

"Tell you what I'm going to do. The kid here has grit, a clean, straight mind and a good punch. He knows what to do and he'll give you a good fight. Why don't we put this to the boys of the press?"

Tex thought about it, decided it was fair and agreed. Doc was more than pleased, since he had made a point of getting to know all the sports editors. Not only would they give us a fair shake, but we'd get publicity—the name of Doc's game—as well.

Tex turned to me and gave me a somewhat skeptical look. He and I were both aware that I didn't look the type to fit the bill, but I quickly assured him that I would do my best, and that was a promise. What else could I say that I hadn't said already?

Doc asked Bob Edgren, one of the best-liked sports writers around, to call a press conference for the following afternoon.

Among the newspapermen who showed up were Bill Farnsworth, sports editor of the *Evening Journal;* Jim Dawson of the *New York Times;* Eddie Frayne of the *New York American;* Gene Fowler; Grannie Rice; Rube Goldberg; Hype Igoe; and Damon Runyon. Just seeing Fowler and Runyon there made me feel a damn sight more confident. They had been through plenty with me.

As the writers were assembling, Doc appeared to have the upper hand. Every time Tex started to say something about me, Doc would jump into the conversation and within forty-five seconds dominate it completely. Tex didn't like that, but he didn't want to lock horns with Doc at this point.

Tex called the meeting to order by rapping a chair with his malacca cane. Taking the cigar out of his mouth, he announced:

"Gentlemen. Jess Willard has decided to defend his title against Jack Dempsey. As yet, we haven't picked the site for the fight, but it has been agreed that Mr. Willard will receive $100,000."

He then went on to describe the gamble he was personally taking by staging a championship fight. He added that it would be worth it to Doc and me to meet Jess Willard for nothing if I thought I could lick him.

Doc glared at him and silently mouthed something.

"Nevertheless, gentlemen, I feel that $10,000 or maybe even $15,000 should be considered, since Jack will have training, lodging and living expenses and—"

Doc interrupted him and emphatically declared that he, Jack Kearns, had been the one to get Rickard to approach Jess Willard in the first place. Without his push, Rickard would never have had a fight.

"You're just trying to worm out of paying us, Rickard. Jack's string of knockouts makes him a pretty good draw, so don't sell him short."

He pointed out that Jess Willard had, after all, been out of action for the past three years while touring with the circus and Buffalo Bill's Wild West Show. In addition, if he wasn't mistaken, "Jess's heart has never really been in the fight game. I hear he signed 70 percent or 80 percent of himself away, so he's sour.

"The only real boxing exposure Mr. Willard gets these days,"

Kearns continued, "is when he's in some exhibition, sparring with his close pal, Walter Monaghan."

If giant Jess Willard beat me—an impossibility as far as Doc was concerned—then and only then would my value fall to zero.

"It should be plainer than the noses on your faces that this boy deserves at least half as much as Willard."

There they all were, discussing my merits and my liabilities, while I stood to the side, silent and hopeful. Every so often one of the boys would turn to stare at me, probably sizing me up. It was uncomfortable, to say the least.

I felt I was being verbally tossed back and forth like a yo-yo. Rickard was annoyed, Doc was annoyed and the press was amused. They sensed that this Kearns–Rickard duo was going to be around quite a while, that they were colorful, cunning and ambitious, and what's more, they had me—which might or might not be a good thing.

Rickard offered us $25,000. Firm. Doc countered with $30,000. Then it was given to the press to decide. Within ten minutes it was settled: $27,500, more money than I had ever been offered in my entire life.

I glanced at Runyon. He gave me a broad wink behind his thick glasses. That meant it was good, and I was pleased, knowing he was pulling for me.

The only person who wasn't happy with the situation was Tex Rickard. He had promised Willard $100,000 and another $27,500 to me, he had to find a fight site and he had to promote the fight. And he didn't have the money.

Doc told him not to worry until he made a few contacts. A certain prosperous big shot named Addison Q. Thatcher, an eminent member of the Toledo Athletic Club, felt that Toledo, Ohio, would be a good place to hold the bout, and he was willing to put up the necessary cash. Unlike New York, Ohio wasn't affected by any adverse boxing legislation; there the local authorities could okay fights. The final clearance, however, would have to come from Governor James Cox. So Doc called Rickard and told him they were on their way to Ohio.

There they managed to get into an Elks convention, where

Governor Cox was the featured speaker. Tex and Doc, posing as brother Elks, managed to get the governor aside and to put the proposed fight to him. Before the governor could answer, Doc mentioned that he had quite a number of eligible voting relatives living just outside Toledo. The governor listened to Doc and Tex attentively and thought the idea a fine one. Ohio and Toledo would prosper, and it would be good publicity. Before long the entire matter was settled. Doc got the $100,000 in cash from Frank Flournoy, a friend of Thatcher who in 1919 became Rickard's partner, sharing the billing on storefront headquarters in Toledo.

The idea of promoting a fight never failed to appeal to a broad spectrum of people. Frank Flournoy became one of the most enthusiastic backers I had ever come across.

In New York Rickard called a press conference and announced that Toledo, Ohio, had been chosen as the site for the proposed championship bout—whereupon we were all promptly attacked by none other than the Ohio Ministerial Association. Tex was adamant; he wasn't going to let hell, high water or members of the Ohio whatever-it-was stop him now!

He contacted Major A. J. D. Biddle, whose great passions included the U.S. Marching Marines and boxing, and asked for his help in pacifying the Association. Biddle told Tex not to worry. He'd calm down the Ministerial Association through the Biddle Bible Class, which handed land tracts every so often to members of the Association. Biddle requested a small favor in return. He asked to assist in naming the officials and to be allowed to have his Marines put on a show before the Dempsey–Willard fight. Tex couldn't refuse him, and so Biddle, along with others, picked Ollie Pecord as referee and W. Warren Barbour, later to become a U.S. senator, as timekeeper.

Because it was illegal to sign fight articles in New York in 1919, we boarded the ferryboat for New Jersey, where the contract was finally signed, with a borrowed pen, in a dismal railroad waiting room. It was February 11. Despite everyone's tight nerves, there was no dickering. One of the contract's stipulations was that I start training a minimum of six weeks before July 4, 1919, the date of the fight.

From February into early spring, I fulfilled as many vaude-ville bookings as Doc could arrange, as well as staging several exhibitions. I had to be more careful now than ever; because of the advance publicity, all eyes were on me.

Between engagements I boxed once with Eddie Eagan, who later became the amateur heavyweight champ, at a benefit for the Red Cross. My old pal Otto Floto of the *Denver Post* acted as referee. I wanted to knock Eddie out from the moment we started, but Otto growled that I'd better take my time, since it was a benefit! After the bout, Eddie stopped by my dressing room to discuss certain fighting techniques with me. He seemed impressed when I showed him how I held my jaw in, down close, protecting it with my shoulder. Eddie wanted desperately to become a professional, but I told him to stick to law. Maybe his outlook would be the same when he got out; maybe it wouldn't.

Many people still made a big squawk about prizefighting. Some attacked it, others were merely convinced that those who were in it were nothing but glorified bums. Since nothing ever went smoothly, we soon encountered a potential setback: The Ohio State Legislature adopted a resolution calling on the governor to prevent the fight. Thankfully, the resolution was never formally passed.

We were in Toledo by the middle of May.

16

Training in Toledo

Toledo, Ohio, in the heart of the midwest, bordering the western shore of Lake Erie and the Michigan line to the north, was in those days a haven for prominent gamblers and hustlers who were on the lam. Once in a while local authorities would crack down and crap games would suspend until new locations were found. As the hotel rooms varied, so did the games.

Tex Rickard managed to construct his arena with the best new lumber he could find—which was a mistake. The hotter the temperature became, the stickier the seats got as the sap oozed out. He was so proud of his beautiful arena that he would take walks around it, praising it like a newborn baby. He even had it inspected by the building inspector.

The Overland Club, where I trained, was located on the shore of Maumee Bay in Toledo. From the moment we arrived, the air was tense with excitement. Newspapermen were all around and Doc took full advantage of their presence.

"We've got to move fast, talk fast and hope that the odds'll change."

People seemed to be coming from all over, and private homes in the area rented rooms and offered home cooking. The favorite pastimes were speculation, prediction and contradiction; journalists excelled at all three. Otto Floto and Scoop Gleeson came out for me before any of the others.

Damon Runyon, who was very busy in the weeks before the fight, proved to be an invaluable friend. He had become one of my favorite persons. I always felt that if I ever fell down, I could safely land on either Damon or Gene Fowler. Damon would sit and talk with me for hours, listening to my ideas, my plans and my outrageous Kearns-like philosophies. He was the most patient man I knew. He went through ups and downs like everyone else but kept his problems to himself, not wanting to inflict himself on others.

"You know, Jack, people don't really give a hoot about what you're saying. Most of them are just sitting there waiting for you to pause so that they can interrupt and retread the conversation back to their favorite subjects—themselves."

He told me that a man of few words is, as a rule, more respected than one whose words foam in his mouth. Damon used to laugh at some people because of this; seems that every time he clammed up (which was often), others would start babbling furiously, as if they felt the necessity of talking for two. Because of his friendship with me, and because he was privy to little-known information, Runyon was frequently resented by the other newspapermen—some of them the same ones who had slammed their doors in my face several years before.

I was training in Toledo long before Willard arrived. My trainer, Jimmy De Forest, an incredible dynamo, dedicated himself to me morning, noon and night. He and Doc, as always, disagreed on all but one thing: Neither of them wanted me to overtrain and go stale, so they had me alternate one week of training with one week of rest. The rest weeks always seemed to be too long, but the locals who came to see me kept me occupied. Kids would take turns sitting on my lap or at my feet while I told them tales of wild bears and moose. I could play baseball on the beach with friends or I could run the 100-yard dash. In short, I could do anything I wanted to do that week except train.

In addition to training, I would lay off food one day a month to give my body a rest. It seemed strange to be doing such a thing out of choice, when only a few years ago I didn't eat out of necessity.

Moods in training camps can always be felt from the very beginning. In mine, monkey business and shenanigans were kept to a minimum and morale was high. Sure, we had the usual hangers-on, kibbitzers and experts—everyone did—but mine were unique. Some of them were to hang on tightly for the next fifty years.

Doc lashed out at Willard every opportunity he got. It was easy since he wasn't around to defend himself.

"Beat Willard? Why, I'd like to take a crack at that big stiff! A cinch, nothing to it! After this is over, I'm going to try and sign Jack with Georges Carpentier, who I hear is fighting again. If he won't come here, why, then, we'll go to France. Or Britain!"

He knew just what to say and, what's more, he thoroughly enjoyed reading what he said afterwards.

"The challenger is ready to go into the ring and he is in condition to box all night against any man in the world!"

Box all night? For a moment he really threw me, but then I remembered he'd say anything.

Doc continued jabbing verbally at Willard until Jess finally decided to speak up, countering with, "Kearns is just talking off the top of his head. This will be one of the easiest bouts I ever had! What good fighter gets knocked out in the first round? I hope he comes rushing at me. I'll fix him good!"

Many didn't care too much for Jess, thinking in terms of what ring history supports—that the best heavyweights are never extra big, only big enough. Some even felt that a big man was frequently not mean enough or fast enough. And the underdog always appeals to the crowd. For some reason the most cheers are usually reserved for the smaller man, even though the bigger one may be the true underdog.

I was fully aware that this was my big chance. The spotlight was on me, even though I still stood in Willard's shadow.

By the time Willard arrived in Toledo on a Saturday, I was firmly established with the locals. Everyone was waiting at the edge of town for Willard, but many of them were talking about me. When he pulled into town he found his training grounds hadn't been completed and that he lacked such necessities as downy quilts to lay under the canvas in the ring, rubdown lotions and tapes. So he went shopping, accompanied by a journalist who couldn't believe the variety of stuff he bought.

Now that Willard had arrived, publicity was split right down the middle with tales and countertales. Rumors ran rampant. One said that Jess had gotten so fat that he could hardly move. Another said that I had had a fight with Doc and was packing my bags and leaving camp. One absurdity followed another.

My sparring partners were Jamaica Kid and Bill Tate, a Senegambian whose wife was the camp's cook. (She wrapped cooked meat in toweling to drain off the fat and grabbed my hand to make sure I didn't touch any roughage.) My two sparring partners were probably the finest I ever had.

Doc made sure everything ran smoothly. He was as capable then as he would have been if he had had at least ten champions under his belt already. Surprisingly enough, Willard showed up without a manager. He was apparently trying to save money, but being his own mouthpiece certainly didn't help. He just didn't seem to fire the public spirit and imagination.

Jess was altogether different from me. He'd gone through all the hullabaloo before, and he wasn't touched by it. Reportedly, he was a suspicious man who hated crowds. He was more retiring, more reticent and of course much older and more weathered. When he wasn't training, he preferred to stay quietly in a fine rented house on one of the best streets in Toledo. It had a large lawn with flowers and shrubs and—unlike my own quarters, which lacked the barest necessities—it had everything. But that was Jess. I guess I was a victim of an American syndrome: If anything's too easy, then it can't be any good. It's got to be rough, even inconvenient, to be of any value.

Doc and Tex were my biggest boosters. I absorbed it all and basked in whatever attention came my way. They agreed that I had all the makings, that I was going to be the next champ and that they had made the right decision. They patted each other on the back and treated each other with the utmost courtesy—that is, until after the fight, when I was relieved to see them once more aiming for each other's jugular.

Day after day I trained, up at six, then seven to ten miles of jogging followed by a hot and cold shower and a rubdown until breakfast, which consisted of meat and vegetables. After breakfast, a quick nap and then off again, sprinting a few miles. I just couldn't believe the crowds that jammed the roads to see me!

My typical afternoon consisted of exercising and sparring, which could be watched by anyone willing to shell out two bits. Afterwards, more sprinting until dinner. At night everyone settled down to chewing the fat or playing gin rummy. Experts argued with experts, and many a nose was punched. No drugs, no drinks and no women were allowed on camp grounds. Those were the rules.

That June was the hottest and most uncomfortable I can remember. Sweat flowed like water from a broken tap. Even the lakeward breeze didn't seem to affect the temperature, which hovered around 104°.

Gossip cut a deep furrow from my training camp to Willard's. Willard's "secret service" even accused Doc of having visited Willard's Casino training grounds incognito and having had the nerve not only to spy, but to mingle with the crowd, paying the four bits admission fee. Normally I wouldn't have put this past Doc, but we both knew that with so many members of the press around, he'd never take the risk of being recognized—or for that matter of bumping into Willard, who still detested Doc with a passion.

Willard, who scoffed at the very idea of Jack Kearns in his training camp, nevertheless said, according to friendly sources, that if I really wanted to send someone, I should send my sparring partner, Bill Tate, who would gladly be given a line. Big talk on Jess's part. Everyone knew Willard didn't want any black sparring partners, no matter how good they were or what kind of reputation they had. Since his win over Jack Johnson in Havana, Willard had been so ridiculed and abused by Johnson's fervent fans that he was alleged to have developed an intense aversion and dislike for the entire race. This came out when Harry Wills, a good black heavyweight, applied to join Willard's camp and was flatly refused. Subsequently Ray Archer, Willard's on-and-off manager, made for New York to get some other sparring partners and was severely criticized along with Willard. Archer lashed back and said something to this effect:

"I can't hire everyone who asks to be taken on; you can't

tell what some of them might do. I'd stake my life on the boys I've got with me."

He was obviously referring to Willard's close pal, chief advisor and sparring partner, Walter Monaghan, who was on a forty-day Army furlough, and Jack Lavin, a fat Cleveland heavyweight who looked like he couldn't fight (but could).

Not only did Willard lack adequate sparring partners, but he acted as his own trainer as well, figuring he knew his own condition better than anyone else. Why should he pay good money for some outsider's system?

One afternoon, sparring in the ring, Willard accidentally knocked his pal Walter out cold, causing a great deal of commotion. In a fight camp, then as now, everything is blown up and, no matter how insignificant, becomes newsworthy—especially when there are only two contenders for a big event and the press is tired of rehashing all the well-worn statistics. So the next day, Walter Monaghan's statement made the news.

"My, how Jess can hit when he is in earnest. We were only fooling around this afternoon, but you saw how that right came over, didn't you? I saw it coming, and accustomed as I am to boxing with him, I could not get away from it. You can imagine how the big fellow will hit when he gets into the ring July 4. Say, if he hits Dempsey on the jaw with the old right, they will probably pick up Jack Kearns's hope in the $10 seats somewhere."

This infuriated Doc.

"Fooling around? Why, that Willard doesn't have the brains to fool around. That entire camp is beginning to give me a real pain. If Monaghan has any more comments, he should come directly to me. Why, Jack'll put Willard away in the first round!"

This in turn annoyed Willard, so he invited me to watch him train anytime I wanted. Naturally, his offer was turned down. Doc didn't want to risk my becoming anxious, especially since he'd placed a bet on me (this news he kept from me until I was ready to step into the ring). It seems that Doc had approached John "Get Rich Quick" Ryan, a gambler around town. Doc asked Ryan what the odds on a first round knockout were, for a good friend. Ryan gave him 10 to 1. That sounded pretty good to Doc, as well as to Damon Runyon, who was along.

Ryan asked Doc, "How much does your friend want to bet?"

"Ten grand."

The bet was on. Doc and Runyon then hustled around for the dough. It took them all night. Now, if I put Willard away in the first, we would stand to make $100,000 in addition to our guarantee.

Inwardly, Doc didn't think Willard had ever been judged accurately as a fighter. Around the time of the Jack Johnson–Jess Willard fight in Havana, a law was passed prohibiting interstate shipment of fight films. It was only a good many years later that the film of the fight was seen and analyzed, revealing an even contest between Johnson and Willard for twenty rounds before Jack Johnson was apparently knocked out. Doc had somehow seen the fight film and was convinced that Jess Willard was far from being a natural fighter. To Doc, he lacked the animal instinct, the inner fury and the all-important lust for battle.

Jess Willard might not have been a natural fighter, but he sure was confident—confident enough to worry about killing me.

The heat in Toledo was mounting, affecting moods and tempers. It seemed to get hotter and muggier from hour to hour. In the training camp, we found we appreciated as many laughs as we could get, so Max Kaplan appointed himself camp comedian and told old jokes. On a few occasions, Max, Jimmy De Forest and I entertained the camp, strutting through the grounds with a huge banner proclaiming ourselves to be "The Great and Grand Maumee Bay Band." We would sing, dance and take turns blowing on the kazoo. Kids would trail us as if we were pied pipers. Anything for a laugh. That is, until Max sang his medley of old Yiddish songs. Then everyone cried and cursed Max for making them blubber. We were like one great big family—for the first and last time.

Doc, like everyone else, had his good days and his bad days. He seemed to have difficulty in finding suitable outlets for relaxation. He drank a lot and spat words out like bullets until I'd get worried and speak to him. Then he'd go dry. Just like that. Cold. With no hangover, nothing. The man was truly unique. The only times he would get really sore at me were when I'd take the wheel of the Stutz (borrowed on credit) and go for a drive with Doc sitting beside me. As he saw it, I was now a large investment, and investments shouldn't drive.

Doc could usually be found with the newspapermen and photographers who swarmed around both camps. The majority were from New York and Chicago; a few were from the midwest and the west coast.

One of the unforgettables was the former lightweight, Oscar Matthew "Battling" Nelson, who had been assigned by the *Chicago Daily News* to cover the fight. Instead of staying with the other reporters, Battling Nelson set himself up in a pup tent by the arena, which was a fair distance away from the training activities. It was his big assignment and he didn't want to chance missing the fight. Once, at two o'clock in the morning, someone suggested paying Bat a visit. When they got to the tent he was sleeping soundly. Within seconds the pup tent's pegs had been pulled, leaving poor Bat all tangled up in the tent. By the time he emerged, there was no one in sight.

The days wore on. I trained, I rested and I thought. I was seldom inactive—inactivity led to laziness, and laziness led to a dead end. No, thanks.

Once, while I was sparring with Jamaica Kid, a gash opened over my right eye. Doc panicked, thinking of the bet, the guarantee —and the fight. I assured him it'd be okay by fight time.

Someone suggested my wearing a headgear. Doc couldn't see the "practicality of the damned thing," but I could, and I insisted on wearing it. The headgear protected my brows and kept my ears from getting knocked in. As soon as Willard's men saw this, they suggested that maybe he should consider wearing one also. He scoffed at the idea. It was newfangled junk. If he didn't think of something first, it wasn't worth a plugged nickel. He told a few people that, strange or otherwise, my training methods would end for good on July 4.

"And after that I'm going to New York to negotiate picture deals, and after that to my land which is a sand strip next to where they've just discovered oil. I'll be very busy where the big money is. No stage appearances for me!"

I guess Jess Willard was overly sensitive about his size, especially after having appeared in Buffalo Bill's Wild West Show. There, he had always been Big Fellow, Big Jess. In a way I felt for the guy.

By the time my brow gash had healed, I had been on a five-day layoff and was impatient to be moving again. I had everyone on their toes, particularly Jamaica Kid.

My twenty-fourth birthday rolled around and Doc went all out to celebrate. Everyone packed away as much booze as was humanly possible (Prohibition was just around the corner). Everyone was talking about it, how they had started hoarding some time back, and screw the authorities. Doc laughed.

"Me worried? Nah. Pay enough and you'll get enough. If any of you get stuck, come and see the Doc. He'll fix you up good."

That was Doc, confident as always. The press liked Doc despite his having to be in command at all times. He was the master of one-upmanship. When he was with writers, he could write; with actors, he became the biggest ham; with the press, well, he'd show them what was meant by good copy. . . .

June, 1919. That month dragged. The days passed quickly enough but the nights were long. I couldn't sleep and I would wander around camp in the early morning hours. Sometimes I could hear Doc and the others in the distance, talking and laughing. It annoyed me. I was irritable and anxious, but dared not show it. With everything on the line, I felt the responsibility weigh in my gut.

The one person who mattered who didn't think I had a chance against Jess Willard was my own father. His Harry was a go-getter, but he was no champion. He supported Willard right up to the finish. Then he changed his mind.

A pre-fight party, with wall-to-wall people, was held in the rundown farmhouse that was part of camp. I put in a brief appearance and then hit the sack to the faraway strains of curses, arguments and songs. It was like a noisy Fourth (which was in fact only hours away). While Doc gave his party, Jess Willard met with Tex

Rickard to discuss plans for the future. According to some of the boys present, Willard downed an entire bottle of gin. Even Tex was surprised; after all, the fight was the following morning. Rickard apparently asked him if the booze wasn't pretty potent medicine. Jess reportedly replied that it wouldn't do him any harm since meeting me in the ring would only be exercise.

That night I, William Harrison Dempsey, known as Jack, young aspirant to a world heavyweight crown, slept with my eyes open.

17

"I Did It! I'm the Champ!"

Morning finally dawned, a dawn I was to remember for the rest of my life. Doc came over to see how I was doing. I was aware of his presence but I couldn't digest his words. I seemed unable to shift my concentration away from the coming events of the day.

He told me that Willard was still sleeping, since he didn't want to strain himself unnecessarily before the bout. Why should Jess worry? Fighting me was going to be a snap.

I worked harder that morning than ever before, punching bags, throwing and catching the medicine ball to strengthen my stomach muscles, pulling weights and doing some last minute sparring before the weigh-in.

"Don't show no emotion, no anxiety, no nothing, kid. The press is just waiting for you to crack—it'd be good copy. Be careful!"

Doc had a point. I made sure that I didn't even look into Willard's face for fear my eyes would give me away. Staring at my own feet was safer. I couldn't take a chance on being psyched out.

I weighed in at 187 pounds and Jess Willard at 245. Almost sixty pounds and five inches separated us. Jess was like a mountain; he was even bigger close up, in those blue trunks of his. I ignored him and he sneered. We weren't to meet until 4 P.M.

Willard was the 5 to 4 favorite and was pretty damn cocksure. He even had the nerve to approach Doc for legal immunity in case he killed me. For Doc this was the last straw. He wouldn't tolerate

1895. A gathering of the more infamous side of my family — the Hatfields — when they were fighting the McCoys.

1916. One of my earliest fights in Hardy Kay Downing's gym in Salt Lake City.

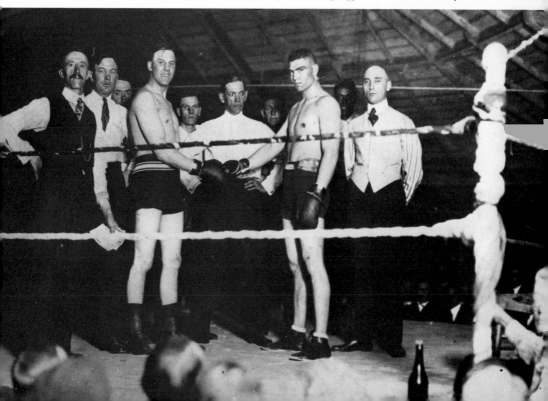

1918. Gene Tunney and I meet, not realizing what was yet to come for both of us.
(*Courtesy Dave Margolis*)

Pausing in my Liberty Bond Drive to pose with some members of the United States Marine Corps. (*Courtesy Dave Margolis*)

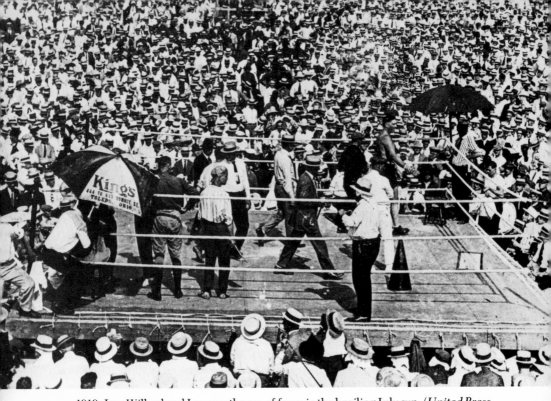

1919. Jess Willard and I survey the sea of faces in the broiling July sun. (*United Press International*)

Standing in the center of the ring with champion Jess Willard. It was the most intense moment of my life.

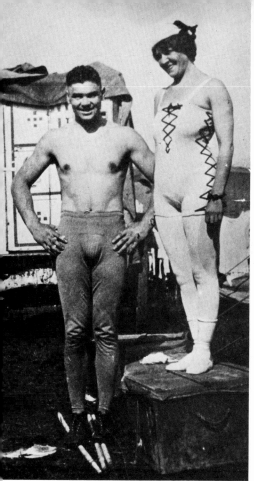

1919. Relaxing with a friend while appearing with the Sells-Floto Circus.

father and mother. (*United Press International*)

Here I am, at my slacker trial, flanked by my mother, father and attorneys.

Posing on the Santa Fe with leading lady Josie Sedgwick and starlet Ruth Langston on the way to our Mojave Desert location to wrap up *Daredevil Jack*.

Jack "Doc" Kearns with me in one of our earliest pictures together. (*Commercial Studios*)

Bernie and I, among several others, in a scene from the movie *The Health Farm Wallop*. "That man is after your title." (*Culver Pictures*)

Getting into my Chrysler Imperial sports sedan in Hollywood.

My first house in Los Angeles, on Western Avenue.

any more of Willard's snide remarks. He'd been waiting for this moment as long as he could remember, and he told Willard off good.

By noontime the temperature in Toledo hovered around the 106° mark, causing the pitch and resin to flow more freely out of the new wooden seats in the arena. Tex had enjoyed telling one and all that not only had the construction taken two months and 520 men, but if the boards were placed end to end, they would reach from New York to Chicago. Needless to say, the cushion and umbrella sellers were the only ones who had no complaints that day. Those who hadn't purchased a cushion faced the alternatives of ruining the seat of their pants or standing for the duration of the fight. Drink vendors declared a liquid catastrophe—they were sold out in an hour. The ice cream vendors didn't have a scoop in sight, and sandwich stands were stuck with gooey, unsold stock.

Bat Nelson got up early that morning. Because it was a special occasion, and July 4 as well, he decided to take a bath whether he needed it or not. One of the more enterprising concessionaires, obviously anticipating a great rush, had moved several barrels of lemonade into a hogshed located near the arena. As luck would have it, Bat came across the hogshed and mistook the tubs of lemonade for water. He jumped in, cake of soap and all, and had his bath. Because no one and nothing went unnoticed in camp, word spread like a brush fire. No one knew exactly which barrel had been contaminated, so the lemonade went completely untouched by those who knew. Tough luck for those who didn't.

The arena's seats weren't selling quite up to Tex's expectations. He'd priced the reserved ringside seats at $60—an exorbitant sum in a year when many made only $10 a week. The general admission seats were $10 and the cheapest seats $2. Not many people were ready to fork out sixty bucks for this bout, so the scalpers and the sharks took turns standing by the gates, approaching anyone from men in uniform to women. Many griped about the special women's section, an innovation. (The women's representative and leading mouthpiece was the theater's great Ethel Barrymore.)

Outside the arena, near the scalpers, stood a somewhat stocky, spruced-up guy with a curled moustache and carrying a fancy cane: Bat Masterson, the former lawman, an avid fan of Jess Willard and Otto Floto's archenemy. He had appointed himself Official Collector of all spectators' guns and knives. His assistant was a balding Wyatt Earp, who had been referee for the Bob Fitzsimmons–Tom Sharkey fight. Between the two of them, they got things done. At first all equipment was placed neatly in piles, but by fight time the guns and knives were in a disorderly heap. Some of the rowdier boys refused to relinquish their six shooters without a scuffle.

Bat Masterson was a master of all trades as well as a gentleman. He'd been everything from buffalo hunter and scout for General Nelson Miles during the Apache uprising in '86 to card dealer, wrestling promoter with Otto Floto in Denver and lawman. Now he was a sports writer and boxing authority for the *Morning Telegraph*. He was a sharp observer of the world around him, right up to the day he died about two years later, with the following quote in his typewriter:

"There are many in this old world of ours who hold that we all get the same amount of ice. The rich get it in the summertime and the poor get it in winter."

At three o'clock in the afternoon I was told that there were about forty to fifty thousand paid admissions. Whatever the number, Rickard's 90,000-seat arena was far from filled, despite the fact that all roads led to Toledo! Bay View Park was clogged with cars, bicycles and people. Rickard, not wanting to take too big a loss, managed to sell the arena to the American Wrecking Company for $25,000 and felt better, even though it had cost over $100,000.

Suddenly it was time. Willard's camp sent Walter Monaghan and Ike O'Neil over to supervise the taping of my hands. Two of my men were in Willard's dressing room as well, while Doc ran around feverishly. Jimmy De Forest taped my hands and then slapped me on the back to wish me luck. It was a big moment for him, too.

Before I left the dressing room, Doc walked in and told me of the bet he'd placed on me with its 10 to 1 odds. Among my well-wishers were Grantland Rice, Ring Lardner—the deadpan wit who'd gotten a release from the *Chicago Tribune*—Jimmy Johnston from New York, Ned Brown, Rube Goldberg, Hype Igoe, Bugs Baer, Harry B. Smith, Bob Edgren, Boxing Commissioner William Muldoon, Tom Mix, Governor James M. Cox, Beany Walker, Nat Fleischer and, last but not least, Damon Runyon. De Forest had his hands full keeping people out.

Three forty-eight in the afternoon. I was straining to go, having been cooped up in the dressing room for an hour and a half, having had to wait for the end of an eight-round semi-final bout and Biddle's beloved Marines' exhibition of bayonet work and marching.

Time. Out of the dressing room and quickly through the aisle to the ring. Waves of heat rose from the ground. Ringside was surrounded by a sea of straw boaters and white short-sleeved shirts. I had never seen so many people gathered for a fight before. Not for one of *my* fights. The crowd stood up and cheered as I sprinted down the aisle accompanied by Doc, Jimmy De Forest and Bill Tate.

A large umbrella was set up in each of our corners. Willard's was paper-bag brown while mine was plastered with advertising from the local merchants. (Doc had made sure to tap anyone who had a buck.) In the ring, a second supporting canvas had been laid down and fastened.

When Willard stepped into the ring the crowd roared its salute. I stared at this crowd, at first seeing absolutely nothing. I danced and pulled at the ropes automatically, but I was only conscious of one man: Willard. There he was, a standing giant with what seemed to be an expression of boredom and stupidity on his face. His look of annoyance in turn annoyed me. He made noises whenever he turned his back to me. His hair was plastered with some kind of goo which flashed in the hot sun. Of course, I didn't look that great either; I hadn't shaved in three or four days, and I was burnt the color of dark cork. I hoped I looked mean and tough enough.

Rapid gum-chewing Ollie Pecord was the referee. It was his first championship fight and he was agitated. Funny, it was my first, and I wasn't agitated—I was downright scared.

Tex Rickard was judge on one side and Major Drexel Biddle judge on the other. In my corner were Doc, Bill Tate, Jock Malone, Jimmy De Forest and my brother Bernie. Ray Archer, Walter Monaghan and Jack Hemple were the main persons in Willard's.

Doc was fairly twitching from nerves, which had caused his feet to swell in his shoes. Bernie was no better, having suddenly developed an uncontrollable itch. Bill Tate, my sparring partner, sweated oceans, and even Runyon, who could be spotted from my corner, was said to be unable to sit still for more than a count of five.

Scoop Gleeson, my old supporter and new pal from the *San Francisco Bulletin,* sat on the Willard side with H. W. Walker and Otto Floto. From the time I'd met Scoop in San Francisco with Fred Windsor, he'd become quite the expert on me. In addition to being a good newspaperman, he was also an effective publicist. A couple of years before he had handled press relations for a colorful and dynamic dentist whose name was Parker. Before Scoop was through with him he'd convinced him to legally change his name to Dr. Painless Parker.

In the sky above there were grand goings-on as well. First, Lieutenant Locklear, the aviator, changed planes in mid-air. Then the Army balloon, filled with photographers, almost had a disaster, one cameraman falling into Maumee Bay. He was soon rescued, but his camera and film were lost forever.

Willard and I were called to the center of the ring to pose for pictures. I saw Ollie Pecord's lips moving and couldn't hear or understand a word he was saying. All I knew was that a towering Willard was standing in front of me. As we returned to our corners, something my father had once said flashed through my brain: "Son, when you find stumbling blocks in your way, use 'em, boy—as stepping stones. If you can't go over 'em, around 'em or under 'em, then goddamn it, boy, go through 'em!"

I didn't know whether I was going to be in a fight or a foot race. Until this moment, Doc had almost convinced me that I'd be able to put Jess out in the first round, but now I wondered. When Willard raised his massive arms over his head, a kind of desperation overcame me and I knew I would have to use every ounce of strength I had—and then some. Not wanting anyone to suspect these emotions, I scowled fiercely and bared my teeth.

I planned to wear Willard down—in any way that was humanly possible. I had to; this moment had taken me eleven long, hard years to reach. Once our gloves were slipped on, we stepped toward each other to shake hands. As Willard moved away I realized I wasn't just fighting for a title, I was fighting for my life.

Clang! Jesus Christ, this was it! For about thirty seconds, neither one of us led. He landed a few blows and seemed surprised when I managed to hook a left to his stomach. I missed a right and a left, and Willard slugged me again. Then I feinted with my left. Willard's guard came down just when I smashed a left hook to the head. He went down. I saw the look of amazement in his face as he scrambled to his feet. I had Jess Willard down on the floor seven times in that first round. No one could believe what was happening. Willard was a groggy mess, his face was red and cut, he was all pink patches and welts.

Ollie Pecord started counting. Reaching ten, he counted Jess out. The crowd went wild; everyone was screaming. Doc was convinced that we'd just won the bet despite Jimmy De Forest's telling him to wait a minute. Willard's being counted out didn't correspond with De Forest's stopwatch.

"There seems to be something wrong with the bell!"

"Shut up! For $100,000 who the hell cares if there's something wrong with the bell! Pecord! Pecord! Raise Jack's hand! Raise his hand! He's the new champ!"

And Ollie raised my hand, grinning. I was stunned. Doc rushed up to me, threw his arms tightly around me and told me to get out of the ring. I did, as people started to climb into the ring. Jimmy told me to move faster. We were by the press seats when Jimmy half turned and saw that the ring was in a state of chaos. Doc, half in and half out of the ropes, was frantically waving me back. Ollie had told him that the fight wasn't over, and Warren Barbour, the official timekeeper, screamed over the confusion that if I didn't get back into the ring I'd be disqualified. The bell rope had, as he called it, "fouled." No one had heard the bell; Willard had been down only seven seconds when it clanged.

So back I went. I'd been champion for less than a minute and had no idea what it felt like. All I knew was that I was once more the contender and that Doc had lost his bet.

Tex O'Rourke, an old trainer of Willard's, some time later blamed the foul-up squarely on Major Biddle's Marines, who had marched in the ring before the main event. He insisted that when the second canvas had been laid for the marchers, a workman must have put the holding rope over the bell, muffling its sound.

Whatever the reason, I was back in that ring just in time for the second round. I had almost wrenched my shoulder punching Willard hard enough to drop him; now I was grimly determined to put him away. I couldn't even understand what Doc was yelling.

Willard was a sorry sight. His face was swollen and bruised. His right eye stared at me glassily and he could hardly talk through his cracked lips. I pelted him with more blows, including a hard left to his eye, partially shutting it. He was becoming bloodier and he spat out a tooth. His defenses were just about gone, and he was staggering with his tremendous arms outstretched as if to keep me at a distance.

All at once he managed to steady himself and landed a left to the chin. I clinched, holding on—it was a pretty powerful blow. When we broke away, I rained blows on him. Twice Jess managed to use short uppercuts in clinches, rocking me. I landed another on his chin. Clang! Round two was over.

By now I was feeling exhausted and my body was throbbing. I couldn't for the life of me imagine going the scheduled twelve rounds. The heat had started to get to me; I felt as though I had no air as I kept sucking it in.

Jess Willard had a worse time of it. He had trouble finding his corner; he couldn't seem to see straight or to hold himself up. Spectators were shouting for Pecord to stop the fight.

When the bell sounded for the third round, my arms felt like lead weights. Willard was now an object of pity, completely at my mercy. He was spent and he made no attempt to fight back. I pounded rights and lefts to the head and the body while he tried unsuccessfully to cover up. He threw a left uppercut, but it was too late. The weaker he looked, the stronger I felt. I knew it was almost over. I hit him again and he staggered, about to go down, when he was saved by the bell. I went back to my corner on legs that felt like rubber. I looked over toward Willard. His face was distorted by a broken cheekbone and he was having trouble holding his head up. I felt sick. I hadn't realized that my inner fury could do so much damage.

I couldn't wait for this massacre to end; I was sapped both mentally and physically. I looked at Willard again—I couldn't seem to take my eyes off him. He was a broken man now, he had nothing left. Willard and his seconds called the referee over and told him that Willard couldn't make it out for the fourth. Ike O'Neal and Walter Monaghan then threw in the blood-spattered towel.

I won. I won. My God, I won! I made it! *I was the new champion!*

Hoots and jeers greeted Jess's decision. Shouts of "Quitter" were heard through the overall noise. I knew it must have hurt. But Willard was no quitter; any man who stood up to take what I had given him was no quitter in my book. Willard had been the people's White Hope. He had "brought back" the title from Jack Johnson. Now, at about thirty-seven years of age, he appeared all washed up. Jess congratulated me and wished me luck and everything that went with the championship. He also mumbled that he'd invested well and had nothing to worry about.

Bedlam reigned. Benches were broken, telegraph poles pulled down. Hats flew into the ring, and thousands—or what seemed to me to be thousands—were tumbling into the ring to congratulate me, to touch me, to tell me off. Bernie and Rickard tried to get my attention at the same time, and I was almost pounded to the floor with all the backslapping. The crowd surged forward, pushing security guards and policemen aside. I was lifted up in the air, hoisted onto a cushion of shoulders and carried to my dressing room. The dressing room itself was so crowded that I had difficulty taking a shower. Everyone stared at me as I dressed. Everyone wanted to shake my hand. It felt swell.

Doc was delirious, but I found it difficult to grasp what had happened. Tex said I was great, that I packed quite a wallop. Now, he said, I had to learn certain things all over again as champion. I didn't know what he meant. (All was not smooth with Tex. He bitterly criticized the United States Railroad Administration, saying that he had gotten reports that as many as 20,000 people had been kept away from the Bay View area because the Government was refusing to place more coaches at fans' disposal.)

We went back to the hotel accompanied by God knows how many persons. Doc and I were interviewed and it looked like it would be an all-night affair. Around ten o'clock I thankfully hit the sack; Doc stayed below to celebrate.

Some said that Willard was ignored after the fight. Allegedly, he told members of the press to leave him alone—and leave him alone they did, after he made a few statements to the effect that I must have had something in my gloves and that we were nothing but a bunch of manipulating gangsters, Kearns being the ringleader. One day, he vowed, he'd write a book and tell all.

We ignored him. He was acting the role of a sore loser who didn't know what he was talking about. He took his defeat bitterly, and some of his hangers-on, for fear of being contaminated by a loser, disappeared. Gene Fowler told me some time later that Jess had dressed himself in his usual ill-fitting clothes and stumbled half-blind along a fence, looking for an exit, when Charles MacArthur recognized him and took him in hand until they found Ray Archer. Archer then drove Willard home. Reportedly, the porches of neighboring houses were packed with women wiping their eyes as if there had been a death in the area. Apparently Mrs. Willard was glad that Jess had lost because it meant they would finally be able to live in peace as private citizens along with their five children. She despised the butchering that went on in the fight game.

That night was to remain vivid in my mind for a long time. I managed to peel off my clothes and flop into bed—where I dreamed the fight all over again. In my dream, Willard knocked me out. I woke up in a cold sweat, confused. I climbed out of bed and stumbled into the bathroom, turning on the overhead light. I peered at my face and saw some small dried patches of blood on it. I felt paralyzed. Pulling on my pants and shirt, I rushed out into the hall. The night clerk was busy. Not realizing I had forgotten to put my shoes on, I ran outside, my heartbeat sounding in my ears. A newsboy was hollering, "Extra, Extra! Read all about it!

"Ain't you Jack Dempsey?" the newsboy asked.

"Yeah. Why?"

I grabbed a paper. There it was, my name in big, bold head-lines. I was the Heavyweight Champion of the World. All of a sud-den, standing barefoot on the street with a newsboy at my side, I felt the full impact of my victory. I had the impulse to yell, Look at me! I did it! but held myself back. I reached into my pockets to give the kid a buck but found my pockets empty. I told him to pick it up in the morning from the room clerk.

"You don't owe me nothin'—Champ!"

18

Daredevil Jack *and the Slacker Trial*

Bets were collected, one way or another. Some people felt foolish for having overestimated Jess and underestimated me. Tom Jones, Willard's former manager, along with Jack Curley, had bet on Jess reluctantly. Jones had helped Jess rise from obscurity to the very top—winning the crown from Jack Johnson. Once on top, Willard sent Jones away, saying his services were no longer needed. Tom Jones felt that Jess was an ingrate. Nevertheless, he bet on Willard, thinking that no one else was good enough to take the title away. He lost $4,000.

Bat Masterson didn't think much of me as champion. (He, too, had picked Willard and had lost plenty.) He wrote that a champion should have bigness and presence, and he gave me six months at most as champion.

I was the World Heavyweight Boxing Champion and didn't have a mark on me. But Grantland Rice dealt me a blow that hurt more than Willard's punches. In his Dempsey–Willard fight article the following day in the *New York Tribune,* he praised my prowess and fighting ability before hitting me hard—below the belt.

> If he had been a fighting man he would have been in khaki when at twenty-two he had no other responsibilities except to protect his own hide.
>
> So let us have no illusions about our new heavyweight champion. He is a marvel in the ring, the great-

est boxing or the greatest hitting machine even the old timers here have ever seen.

But he isn't the world's champion fighter. Not by a margin of 50,000,000 men who either stood or were ready to stand the test of cold steel and exploding shell for anything from six cents to a dollar a day.

It would be an insult to every young American who sleeps today from Flanders to Lorraine, from the Somme to the Argonne, to crown Dempsey with any laurels of fighting courage.

He missed the big chance of his life to prove his own manhood before his own soul—but beyond that he stands today as the ring marvel of the century, a puncher who will be unbeatable as long as he desires to stay off the primrose way and maintain the wonderful vitality of a wonderful human system.

He'd called me a slacker and it hurt like hell because I knew I wasn't. He didn't know about my shipyard work, my substantial donations to the Red Cross or the benefits for Navy Relief. He didn't know about my sending money to my family in Salt Lake or to Maxine. He didn't know how much I wanted to fight for my country. All he saw was the neatly packaged Jack Dempsey that Kearns had sold so well.

In 1918, Grantland Rice had turned down an offer from some big magazine to go overseas as their war correspondent at a dollar a word. Instead, he'd volunteered for active duty. During his newspaper days Grannie had saved up quite a bundle, reportedly $50,000 to $75,000. About to leave for the French battlefield, he had entrusted the entire sum to his attorney with instructions to hold on to it for Mrs. Rice in the event that he didn't return. The attorney accepted the money, blew it and then killed himself. Rice took it calmly, feeling that he had put too much temptation in the man's lap.

Doc told me not to believe anything I read unless it originated with us. After all, we knew how things really stood, didn't we? Don't worry, he said, "I'll set Rice straight on a few things and the whole thing'll blow over."

What he should have said was blow up.

Thousands and thousands of telegrams poured into camp on July 4 and 5. I answered only one of them.

MY DEAR BOY

MOTHER IS PROUD OF YOU AND WISHES
YOU PLENTY OF LUCK. KEEP YOURSELF CLEAN
PHYSICALLY BOY. BE A PROPER CHAMPION.

MOTHER

Offers started pouring in. We accepted a fall tour with the Sells-Floto Circus, and Hollywood beckoned me to come check out her wares. We were virtually swamped with offers, some good, some empty.

The day after the bout, Doc and I picked up $25,000 in Cincinnati for appearing twice a day in a park. Before moving on, Doc signed a contract with the Pantages vaudeville circuit at fifteen grand a week. The one thing that puzzled me was the miraculous disappearance of all the creditors we had picked up along the way.

On my way to Hollywood, I stopped in Salt Lake while Doc went on ahead. It wasn't a good visit. My folks were living in the brand new house I had bought them and talking divorce. While they hadn't gotten along for years, none of us had ever thought they'd think of actually splitting up. I talked to them as best I could, and they agreed to give each other another chance.

While in Salt Lake I bought my brother Joe the taxicab he'd been dying for and spread some more money around to the other members of my family, including Johnny, who was still sick. They needed it more than I did.

In Hollywood I met Doc, who was bursting with good news. Fred C. Quimby of Pathé in New York had approached Doc about putting me in films. It seems he felt I would be good box office. Was Kearns interested? You bet. The contract was signed immediately. It called for $50,000 down and 50 percent of the gross.

My first fifteen-episode serial was called *Daredevil Jack*. I told Quimby I'd have to complete it in twelve weeks because of my upcoming tour with the circus. He didn't know if it could be done, since each episode took approximately one and a half weeks. He told me Pathé was pressed for time and had limited space, but he'd see what he could do. He called Robert C. Brunton, the producer, and explained the problem to him. Brunton in turn approached W. S. "Woody" Van Dyke and asked him to direct *Daredevil Jack*. He agreed. He then asked Van Dyke if it were possible to complete an episode a week. Woody was doubtful until Brunton offered him a $500 bonus for every episode finished in a week. Van Dyke revised his original reaction and *Daredevil Jack* went full steam ahead.

From the time I arrived in Hollywood, everyone made a big fuss over me. My hair was wrong, and my nose was definitely wrong, so they called in Lon Chaney to do a complete overhaul. He put putty on my nose to straighten it out, puttied my ears and pencilled my brows. He put rouge on my face and goo on my head. Everyone stared when I finally walked out of the dressing room.

Daredevil Jack's heroine was pretty Josie Sedgwick; others in the cast were Bull Montana, "Spike" Robinson, Edgar Kennedy, Carl Stockdale and Eddie Hearn. I played a sports star who was to rescue the heroine's life and/or property (with the help of my "daring fists") in each and every episode.

Shooting started every morning at 6 A.M. and frequently continued well past midnight. Van Dyke arrived on the set before anyone else.

I told Van Dyke not to expect much and was surprised to hear him say, "I won't." Woody had the reputation of doing only one take —he didn't give a damn what anyone else's policies were. He sure had his hands full with me; even Teddy Hayes, who was present, admitted that I was a bad ham.

Once everyone had a good laugh when Edgar Kennedy knocked off my putty nose. Two minutes later I accidentally knocked off his toupee and everyone laughed even more—everyone except Kennedy and Van Dyke, who had no time to spare.

Woody Van Dyke taught me how to pull a punch. He had to; I kept knocking the other actors out cold, and the studio's doctor had issued a complaint against me. Pulling punches was a damn sight harder than fighting professionally. I was often ragged at the end of the working day from not throwing punches.

One day Edgar Kennedy and Bull Montana approached me.

"Listen, Jack. Van Dyke's been wondering if you're really that tough, so we have a feeling he's up to something. We've been through a few with him, so keep your eyes and ears open, pal."

Bull and Kennedy were right. Van Dyke was dying to test me, and one day he got his chance in a scene which demanded my taking part in a championship bout (to make enough money to pay off the desperate heroine's mortgage). To make the scene look good, Van Dyke called in some professional fighters, among whom was a Greek who saw *his* big chance. It'd be swell publicity, he figured, if he knocked out the new heavyweight champ. He asked Van Dyke if he could try, and Van Dyke was delighted. But it weighed on his mind. The next day he decided that I was entitled to a fair shake, and he told me what the Greek had in mind.

When the Greek confidently stepped through the ropes into the ring, I snarled, "I hear you want to knock me out! Well, what're you waitin' for?" I dropped my arms and let them hang by my sides. "I'm ready."

He stared at me like a moron. Then he swung at me with everything he had and landed square on my chin.

My turn. I landed a haymaker on his jaw and he went down. The Greek had his moment of glory—flat on his back.

Woody Van Dyke, some time later, got his chance to test me again. He had his crew hog-tie me while I was asleep, then they took turns beating me with feather pillows.

By now Doc and I had agreed on how to split everything, from making pictures to vaudeville to major and minor endorsements. Every time we got paid, Doc'd divide up the cash into two piles, the big one for me and the smaller one for him. Fifty-fifty. It took me a long time to catch on that the smaller pile had the larger denominations.

Daredevil Jack was just about wrapped up when all hell broke loose—from Ely, Nevada. Maxine, in a bad moment, had written a strong letter to the editor of a San Francisco paper declaring me a slacker and insisting I had falsified my draft papers. She insinuated that not only was I a yellow-bellied coward, but that *she* had supported *me* as well as the rest of my family. She also wrote that she had in her possession certain incriminating letters.

Maxine's story was printed in virtually every paper I could name. I was good copy. Doc and Teddy Hayes assured me nothing would come of it. A week passed and the furor mounted. Certain groups were getting ready to tighten the noose around my neck.

Frightened at the snowball effect she'd helped to create, Maxine did a turnabout and declared her initial statement a bit exaggerated, a letter written in a moment of anger and frustration. Her denial was printed, but it was too late.

Before long the pictures taken of me in the Sun Shipyard were pulled out of the files. More fuel. The cry "slacker" was taken up and facts were misrepresented right and left. The original reasons for the Sun Shipyard pictures were ignored; as far as the hawks were concerned, I was a faker and a slacker and I had to be crucified. Some members of the press took up the cry. "Slacker! Slacker!" I heard it everywhere, and when I didn't, it still sounded in my head. It was the last thought I had before hitting the sack at night and the first thought that greeted me when I woke up.

A nervous Pathé shelved *Daredevil Jack*, even though it was nearing completion. They had an investment in me which could backfire.

Grannie Rice had hit me where it hurt, but it was nothing compared with what was to come. Jim O'Donnell, a former war correspondent now with the *Chicago Tribune*, took a personal interest in probing the charges. He wrote:

> Seen with the eyes of twentieth century journalism, the case is loaded with personal spite and tawdry municipal politics and fluent slangwanging in good English and bad, and it is daily stirred to a more acute smelliness by shady newspapers and news agencies which exploit, not news, but rumors and themselves.
>
> Whatever the original merits of the case were, it is now as ugly as sin, and the Maxine Cates angle is the unpleasantest and the one that a self-respecting journalist would be least eager to bear on.

On February 27, 1920, a federal grand jury, influenced by a packet of letters, ordered an indictment filed and issued a bench warrant with a fixed $1,000 bail. I was charged with "unlawfully, willfully, knowingly, and feloniously evading and attempting to evade the draft" on the grounds of dependency. My deferred classification was scrutinized. Before long the U.S. District Attorney's Office got into the act. Charles W. Thomas, an assistant to Annette Adams, the head of the District Attorney's Office, took charge of the investigation. Maxine conveniently disappeared and the muckrakers had quite a time.

Doc was torn with anxiety. He had badly underestimated the situation; I was in a bad light and it was getting worse. If he lost me now, we would both be finished, disgraced. He knew too that I had never forgiven him for the shipyard photo. His exclusive control over the champion was in jeopardy, and he didn't like it.

Doc decided to go for the best. He approached Gavin McNab, a leading attorney in San Francisco who was handling Mary Pickford's divorce. Doc pleaded with McNab to take my case. McNab wasn't sold on either of us, but Doc gave it all he had until McNab relented. He named his fee: $75,000, win or lose, with $15,000 down. Doc was shaken. He told McNab he needed a few days to think about it. But there was really nothing to think about, and two days later we agreed. We were desperate and McNab was good.

I holed up in a hotel in San Francisco and didn't show my face. Teddy Hayes went to Salt Lake to explain the situation to my parents. I had a feeling they would be needed at a later date. My mother was talking divorce again, but Teddy persuaded her to hold off once more, this time for my sake. There was enough going on without the two of them getting a divorce.

Word reached Kearns that Maxine was scared. The matter had been blown out of proportion. Aware that she was a nobody with a past who was accusing the heavyweight champion of the world, Kearns decided to take matters into his own hands without consulting me. He sent Tommy Fitzgerald to Nevada—he knew somehow where to find her—to try to convince Maxine not to testify because a trial wouldn't do either of us any good. She refused to listen, so Fitzgerald attempted to make a deal with her. (Apparently Doc had offered her $25,000 in 1918 if she would leave us alone.) She told Fitzgerald she wasn't interested in any deal. So Fitzgerald upped his offer, and she bit. She was to get the money, go to California, cross the border and stay there until everything settled down. Agreed.

Not trusting any dame, especially Maxine, Doc decided to accompany her to the Tijuana border. He didn't know that he was being tailed by the Feds. As luck would have it, Doc got involved in a brawl, and they were picked up just as Maxine was about to cross the border. She was taken into custody and taken to San Francisco to await the trial. Doc was warned not to tamper with the Government's witness again.

On March 20, 1920, a hearing was held. I pleaded not guilty to all charges. The motions were then submitted on both sides, along with the filing of several exhibits.

In San Francisco a panicked Maxine denied her original story. Her denial was ignored. The trial date was set for June 7, 1920, before Judge Maurice T. Dooling in U.S. Federal Court in San Francisco.

McNab and his assistant, John W. Preston, a former U.S. attorney, prepared their defense after their motions to inspect the record were denied. The jury was selected and sworn.

The Government called its witnesses. Maxine took the stand and told of her nomadic life, of assuming a half dozen aliases and, pressed roughly when cross-examined, of her nocturnal and extracurricular activities.

She confirmed what I had unconsciously known for a long time: My bed had been one of many. Not only had she been whoring, but she had profited from it as well. Then she said that she had given *me* money for support.

My brother Bernie, who was by me, put his hand on my shoulder to hold me down. I glanced at my mother, sitting by my father; her face seemed set in granite.

I remember McNab jumping to his feet and furiously shaking his fist in the air. "This is the first time," he shouted, "since Moses took the laws down from Mt. Sinai, that prostitution is being argued in a court of law as a legitimate means of livelihood." He glared at Maxine and she began crying uncontrollably.

Under cross-examination, Maxine Cates, also known as Maxine

Wayne and Maxine Glasshof Dempsey, couldn't remember how much money I had forwarded to her in 1917. Maybe five hundred, maybe less, maybe more. McNab went through some papers. He shoved $2,000 worth of receipts in her face. If she didn't admit receiving money from me, he'd be more than glad to jolt her memory by producing additional receipts.

Maxine cracked. She admitted that when she had originally attacked me, she'd hoped to get some more money. She was broke and couldn't think of anything else, and I had always been a soft touch.

She stepped down from the stand and McNab called his witnesses. They included my mother, father, brother and sister, and Lt. John F. Kennedy of the Great Lakes Naval Station, who'd gotten special permission from Admiral Moffett to testify. He told how I had wanted to do my bit for the Navy and said that he'd been arranging a release from the San Francisco draft board when the Armistice was declared.

My mother declared under oath that I had been and still was her sole support and that she and the rest of the family couldn't have survived without me in 1917. She told how Maxine had presented herself at the door of the Dempsey house and had begged to be taken in. My mother had taken her in and had even attempted to teach her how to cook and keep house. She counseled her to sit tight until I made good. She told how Maxine, in a short time, had made her life difficult, how Maxine had become restless and had left them.

Doc was called to the stand. He was nervous and immediately became defensive. He was a hostile and uncooperative witness until Judge Dooling set him straight.

McNab called almost twenty witnesses who swore they were aware of my desire to serve my country. McNab pointed out that I had a legitimate reason, the support of my family, that had to be respected.

"This boy has done more here in his own country, in terms of raising money and selling bonds, than the ones who are now crying foul!"

More exhibits were filed—photos, telegrams, checks, letters.

On Tuesday, June 15, 1920, at 10:30 A.M., the jury retired to deliberate my fate. They returned at 10:45 A.M.

"We, the jury, find William H. Dempsey, the defendant at the bar, Not Guilty. John H. Clendenning, Foreman."

I was ordered discharged. I was the happiest man in the world.

The lawyers' fees were met by Tex Rickard and his friend, John Ringling. In addition to the $75,000, they also picked up the press bill at the Continental Hotel in San Francisco. Later, Rickard told me that the total had amounted to approximately $150,000!

That day was the last I ever saw Maxine. She stepped out of the courthouse and out of my life. For a few years I heard news of her from friends who bumped into her from time to time. In 1924, in a fire which destroyed a dance hall in Juarez, Maxine was burned to death, trapped as she slept in the room above.

In Hollywood, *Daredevil Jack* was taken off the shelf and completed, to everyone's relief. With nothing hanging over my head, I decided to look around before heading east. I was young, eligible, a champion—and dames ogled me. I was invited to parties and didn't have to stand on the side and shuffle my feet awkwardly anymore. I was called pal and was smiled at. People laughed with me and wanted to introduce me to their daughters, their sisters, but not their wives. I didn't even have to talk; people were more than willing to do that for me.

Prohibition, the Great Experiment, had been in effect almost a year. In effect, but not effective—at least not in Hollywood. Hollywood, where everyone's next-door neighbor or relative was a bootlegger, was acquainted with a bootlegger or knew a druggist. Noisy, smoke-filled cabarets had given way to speaks and joints. The last American troops were coming home, and Welcome Home parades were to be seen all over.

Once in a while I still encountered hostility, but it was less noticeable among showpeople. They had their own egos to look out for.

Doc, Teddy and I went from party to party, from club to club. Then Doc started going to his parties and I started going to mine.

Once in a while we would cross paths and wave, but I preferred not to see him at all. He was heading us for broke.

Hollywood, to me, was like a circus with countless acts and performers, some good, some bad, still others grotesque. Those who had been around awhile had become local kings and queens, living in their magnificently decorated palaces. Swimming pools were status symbols and new shapes were the rage. Custom-built cars were seen around town, some with footmen as well as chauffeurs. Furs, jewels and blondes were in evidence everywhere.

And there were those who wielded the power of the pen. Gossip columnists were the mother or father confessors of Hollywood, with Louella Parsons ruling from the top of the heap. (As my pal Gene Fowler used to say, "She had the knack of saying the wrong things at the right time.")

I started on a new picture at Hal Roach Studios in Hollywood —when Harold Lloyd, in an accident, blew off his thumb and index finger. All production was stopped and I went back to Brunton Studios. I remember Bebe Daniels, then under contract to Roach, coming into the studio, accompanied by her mother, to have publicity pictures taken with some of us. Bebe Daniels was a pretty girl who had the biggest, softest brown eyes I had ever seen. I liked her on sight, disregarding Doc's warning not to become involved with any women since they didn't mix well with my profession. I asked her mother if I could take her out and she agreed. I walked them to the car waiting outside.

Returning to the studio, I spotted a handsome, dark-haired guy leaning against a pole and vigorously pointing to the departing Bebe. He grinned and smacked his lips, an obvious busybody, probably some out-of-work actor who had nothing better to do with his time. I walked over to him.

"Do you know who I am?"

"Do you know who *I* am?"

"Listen, if you don't stop butting your nose in my business I'll have you run off the lot!"

"Well, in that case, let me inform you that *your* flat feet are standing on *my* lot!"

By this time he was holding in his laughter, much to my annoyance.

"*Your* lot? You'd better tell me who you are if you want to stay on your feet."

"Well, my friends call me pal, but to you I'm Fairbanks. Douglas Fairbanks."

Here I was, telling Douglas Fairbanks off! We got to talking (I had no choice; my "flat feet" were now firmly rooted to the ground) and he told me that his studio was indeed across from Brunton. He was a real charmer all right, and through the years he was to prove a sincere friend. He was a tremendous sports fan and one actor who did his own stunts and acrobatics. He insisted on being responsible for his movies' effects. Fairbanks was a swashbuckling hero to many, but I found him humble. I think he knew everyone from charwomen to heads of state.

Douglas Fairbanks was one of the first to live in Beverly Hills. We found we had a great deal in common, even though he was a Superstar and I was a pug. He wasn't married to Mary Pickford then, but he was working on it—in an old-fashioned way. Once he married her, their house, Pickfair, became the talk of Hollywood. Always generous, Doug offered me the use of their beach house in Santa Monica "anytime."

We even made a film together, with Charlie Chaplin and Jim Corbett, *All Good Marines*, which was one big melee. Naturally, we thought of it as a Classic.

Dead or Alive was my next movie, based on a few incidents in my life. I don't think it was anything to brag about. When it was finished, Doc felt it was time to head back east. Our dough had run out, so it was obviously time to get up another fight.

19

The First Million-Dollar Gate

We left Hollywood, Doc going on to New York while I finished up a circus stint. I headed a show of twenty-five wrestlers and about ten boxers for three or four weeks, grossing ninety thousand dollars, of which I got 50 percent. That was the life. Circus people and circus camps were the friendliest of all. I joked and made up with the clowns and even attempted to put over a chimp-and-champ act, which amused children tremendously since the chimp smoked only the finest Havana cigars.

While with the circus I became emotionally involved with one of the most beautiful, most feminine ladies I had ever met. She was one of the stars of the show, an Irish Italian who had been a big tent performer since she was a child. She had lost her husband and brother three years before and had a streak of mellowed sadness under her glitter. She needed someone, and she turned to me. If Doc hadn't sent one of his boys after me, I think I would have stayed on indefinitely; it was the happiest and most contented time of my life.

I tried to maintain contact with the lady, but she decided that our lives were too diverse, that our involvement had been nothing but a passing one and that I would be happier without her. I couldn't understand what had gone wrong until a friend of hers wrote me a letter telling me she had been paid off handsomely for leaving me alone. Apparently she needed the money more than she needed me. I confronted Doc with what I had learned, and he denied having had anything to do with the matter. I wanted to walk out on him, but I had no proof, no guts and little money (we were still settling some accounts we had run up). I wanted to believe him; I liked Doc, and at this point I sometimes respected him more than I did myself.

It was summer and Doc had arranged a bout with Billy Miske that was to take place in a matter of weeks. Doc had had a falling out with Tex Rickard and was going to be his own promoter from now on. Another promoter, Floyd Fitzsimmons, had helped him arrange the whole thing pretty fast, since Miske badly needed the dough. He was suffering from kidney disease.

On September 6, 1920, I was to defend my title for the first time since winning it fourteen months before. Tickets sold fast, helped by Miske's pointing out that he had never been knocked off his feet and by the curiosity of the fans who wanted to see if I had lost my touch. These two factors led to a paid attendance of a quarter million dollars.

In Benton Harbor, Michigan, where I trained, Tex Rickard came to see me, wearing a disguise. I had trouble recognizing him at first. He knew that Doc wasn't around and he wanted to take advantage of his absence to talk to me. Tex was insulted that Doc felt he could do better without him, and he warned me against Doc, adding that he didn't trust him. "Why, that guy has no heartbeat and no blood. Jack, you just make sure he doesn't do to you what comes naturally to him."

He talked to me for a couple of hours and set me straight on Doc's shrewd handling of money and expenses. I understood what Tex said, but I couldn't bring myself to cross Doc in any way. I was grateful to Doc for everything. As Tex walked out the door, he reminded me never to forget that he was my friend, no matter what. After he left, I found my loyalty to Doc shaken. I didn't know what to do.

When Doc returned and learned that Rickard had been to see me, he was furious. He felt that Tex was trying to undermine his position and warned me against him. I couldn't decide whom to believe.

I had many other visitors while training for the Miske fight, including a gentleman by the name of Al Capone. He was a heavyset man who always wore a white short-sleeved shirt, a wide-brimmed hat and a cigar clenched in his teeth. When he was in camp, no pictures were allowed to be taken and no cameras to be seen. He was impressed with me and offered me money—any amount I named—if I would stage an exhibition at his private club. I refused, but it sure was tempting—especially when he thumbed through his wad of bills and asked if I had ever seen so much money before. I could only whistle. Capone was the kind of guy you either liked or hated. He was a rough customer who wanted to be accepted as a man, not a racketeer.

Capone's office in Chicago was incredible; it seemed like a thousand steps from the door to his desk, which was elevated. I once delivered a personally autographed picture of myself to him. He was to be one of my number one fans right up to and including the second Tunney fight. I remember thinking in 1927 that I was more afraid of who sat at ringside than of who was waiting for me inside the ring.

Twenty-four hours before the Miske fight, Doc threatened to call the whole thing off unless he got Jim Dougherty to act as referee. Fitzsimmons gave in at the last minute. He had no choice. I knocked Miske out in the third round after being unable to land a good one in the first two. When the ref had counted him out, I helped Miske to his corner. I really felt bad for him, but I knew I had done him a good turn by giving him a chance and a share of the purse. Doc and I also had a payday: fifty-five grand, split down the middle—that is, two-thirds for Doc, one-third for me.

Those days I dressed and tried to act like Kearns. Well, not exactly like him, but close. He looked more and more like a prosperous racketeer with every passing day. As champ and manager, we were mobbed on walking into restaurants, theaters and arenas—sometimes when we least wanted to be noticed. I needed some privacy, but inwardly I was afraid of it.

Doc suggested I rubber-stamp my autograph to save time and energy. I refused. After all, it had taken me a long time to be recognized, and if people thought enough of me to ask, then I could comply.

We traveled from town to town, from city to city. For a long time, we had a standing contract with Alexander Pantages and his vaudeville circuit. Whenever I was between bouts or other engagements, I'd play Pantages.

Alexander Pantages was a crusty old Greek con artist, a former saloon porter who had struck it rich in the Klondike. Virtually illiterate, he rubber-stamped his signature for years, but he was no fool. He had a fantastic memory and could tell you who played when, where and how, as well as why, if necessary. He had originally opened his vaudeville theaters on the west coast and eventually built up an entire cross-country circuit.

While playing Pantages, I met Harry Houdini. He was young, with wiry hair parted close to the middle, and one of the friendliest and most sensitive performers around. He'd been Buster Keaton's father's partner and the one responsible for Buster's nickname. He was amazing with his card tricks and stunts, but he never let anyone in on any of his secrets. He was smart, and he knew he was good, so he didn't feel he had to ingratiate himself with anyone.

Once he tried bamboozling Doc into buying his "world-famous" Kickapoo Elixir at a buck a throw. Doc didn't bite, but he said he had something similar in his room. In fact, if Houdini was interested . . . he'd be glad to sell him a bottle.

We worked hard in vaudeville and loved every minute of it. Vaudeville—I remember splintery stages and drafty, dilapidated dressing rooms which frequently smelled of sweepings from a gymnasium floor. But vaudeville had become shaky because of moving pictures. The problem was that the movies, unlike the vaudeville stage, were able to produce "spectaculars," and these "spectaculars" were ruining our business. Nevertheless, theater owners scoffed, the pictures were a passing fad that would never catch on.

Alexander Pantages was good to Doc and me, but he didn't seem to be too well liked on the outside. At least that's the impression I got. One great weakness for very young girls eventually ruined him as well as his reputation.

Doc and I were now doing pretty well in the money department, but at the same time I sensed that my popularity was going down instead of up. Those who had formerly carried a grudge or resented me, still did. The war might be over, but I was still around and, unfortunately, doing well. But while they didn't particularly like me, they still laid out their money to see me fight.

Doc put together my next fight—with Bill Brennan—in the old Madison Square Garden on Twenty-sixth Street. That block-long Garden was by far the best—yellowish-gray with years on the outside, young with enthusiasm and cheers on the inside. It was the center of sports life and entertainment in New York. In it appeared rodeos, balls, circuses such as the Buffalo Bill Shows in which Annie Oakley shot glass balls out of the air, fights, exhibits and conventions.

Designed by the great architect Stanford White, Madison Square Garden was beautiful, with slender arches and a tower upon which rested a magnificent Diana. It had opened on June 16, 1890, with the strains of Strauss's Vienna Orchestra and a ballet. In subsequent years it housed the first auto show, bicycle race, boat show, cat show, dog show, flower show, food show—just about every "first" anyone could think of.

It was also the scene of a famous tragedy. On June 25, 1906, in the middle of a musical comedy, Harry K. Thaw, husband of Stanford White's former mistress, Evelyn Nesbit, walked to a table on the roof garden where White was sitting and shot him three times, causing the frightened audience inside the Garden to rush downstairs and out through the gates.

For the Brennan fight I trained at the Van Kelton Tennis Courts on Fifty-seventh Street at Eighth Avenue. We were having trouble drawing crowds, so Teddy Hayes ran down the street to the Winter Garden and persuaded Al Jolson to come over and help me out. When the weather was nice I worked out in Central Park, the same Central Park that had once provided me with a bench for the night.

Some fight fans believed that Brennan was the better fighter, that he never would have lost our first fight if he hadn't broken his ankle. Others were convinced that he was slipping and that Doc had arranged a set-up. Fourteen thousand people showed up for the fight.

I was booed from the moment I stepped through the ropes. Not only was this going to be a tough fight with Brennan, it was going to be difficult with the fans, too. (I was still the favorite when it came to betting.)

Brennan was a cautious but aggressive fighter. He was ready, and he put up a defense for everything I could do, even jabbing with his left. I felt I was unable to reach him and I knew that this fight wouldn't be an easy one. Brennan had a vicious right as well as a long left which really demolished me. One of my eyes swelled. An ear was torn. I felt I wasn't getting anywhere. Doc obviously felt the same, for he kept yelling, "Now you smack that big bum down!"

By the twelfth round we were both beat, swinging at each other and missing. Then he caught me on my torn ear, but I didn't go down. I swung a left to his face and we fell into a clinch. When we came out of it, I put everything I had into a left to the stomach and a right hook to the heart. Down he went. The knockout was official and I was still on top! Aside from my second bout with Gene Tunney, this bout with Brennan was just about the most closely contested fight I ever had. He came to see me afterwards, as they were stitching my ear back. He said, "I'll get you yet, you son of a gun!" Then he laughed. He never got another chance; he was murdered in New York by an unknown assailant some time later.

The crowd still howled for my blood, so Doc decided to approach the French light heavyweight champion, Georges Carpentier. For this fight Doc had to make up with Tex Rickard. Tex was the only one who could raise the money fast enough.

Carpentier was tall and handsome, a military hero with citations. He had always wanted to be a fighter. At nineteen, he had been the official referee of the Jack Johnson–Frank Moran fight. Georges had fought in every weight division, having won his light heavyweight crown from Battling Levinsky in New Jersey. Fighting me would make him the first man from outside the United States to go for the heavyweight crown in my memory.

From the moment Carpentier's boat docked in the United States, he captured the public's imagination. The woman society columnists adored him. He was so Continental with his accent, his tailor-made clothes, his colorful silk shirts. Georges was exactly what the sports writers wanted, an ex-airman who would, they hoped, do away with the native-born black sheep, the villain—me. He was called the Orchid Man and he never understood why; he was overwhelmed by the reception he got.

While he was generally open to the press, he wouldn't allow them in his training camp on Long Island. No one ever managed to see him on a scale (until the weigh-in) or working up a good sweat. Once Ring Lardner, Frank Graham of the *Sun*, George Underwood and some other newspapermen made it to his camp only to be turned away at the entrance. Lardner was so peeved that the following day he wrote that maybe it was a good thing they were turned away, that maybe Georges had been practising his ten-second nap.

The newsmen appealed to Rickard, who called a press conference and promised to talk to Marcel Deschamps, Carpentier's manager, and to Jack Curley, Deschamps's aide.

My training camp in Atlantic City was an altogether different story. Every character, hanger-on and mug seemed to have made my camp his home. I didn't mind as long as they didn't get in the way. When they weren't watching me sparring, shadowboxing and pulling weights in the ring at two bits a head, they'd be playing gin or pinochle—if they weren't trying to smuggle dames into camp.

Teddy Hayes, my official trainer, and I made a one-reeler for publicity, *A Day with Jack Dempsey*. It showed me at my best, and at this point good publicity was the key.

The bout was scheduled for July 2, 1921, in Boyle's Thirty Acres, Jersey City, New Jersey. Tex had originally had his eye on the Polo Grounds, but when New York's governor tried to impose too many restrictions, the site was quickly shifted with the help of New Jersey political boss Frank Hague.

Once again the fight articles couldn't be signed in New York, so we affixed our signatures to the papers in New Jersey. Doc and Deschamps put up $50,000 as forfeit money. Rickard put up $100,000.

When Doc and Rickard had first gotten together on the proposed Dempsey–Carpentier fight, they had played cat and mouse. Or should I say cat and rat? Each tried to outsmart the other, and Marcel Deschamps, known as the "French Fox," tried to outsmart them both. At first Tex offered Doc a percentage and he agreed. Then, mulling it over, Doc decided that he and I would be better off with a straight fee. It was all right with me; I was to get $300,000. Deschamps readily accepted $200,000 for Georges. Everyone was happy. We had no way of knowing that the gate would surpass $1,250,000. Not taking the percentage was one of the few miscalculations Doc made.

I remember Tex telling me before the fight, "Listen, Jack. The public makes the champion and I'm the public's agent, so tell your loudmouth manager not to underestimate me again."

The publicity started; it was to reach incredible proportions by fight time. Doc, I discovered later, actually encouraged the slanderous attacks on me—anything to insure a big gate. Even kids were tuned in to what was about to happen, making plans to share earphones with those who were fortunate enough to have a crystal set. To them, Georges Carpentier was good ol' George S. Carpenter, some guy who was coming to meet me via Paris.

Warren Brown of the *San Francisco Call* was summoned by Doc and Teddy Hayes to handle our publicity in New York. From the moment he blew into town, there was professional jealousy between him and Runyon. Damon didn't take to most people easily, and Brown just rubbed him the wrong way.

Tex had his share of aggravation. Seems there was a slight problem about the $100,000 he had agreed to put up: He didn't have it. He turned to ace ticket-scalper Mike Jacobs for help. Jacobs knew through the grapevine that this fight would draw well over a million dollars, and he moved fast. He got in touch with the other brokers and speculators, promising them choice seats. Soon Mike Jacobs had raised about $180,000 for Rickard. Tex, not one to forget a favor, thanked Jacobs by giving him exclusive selling privileges for the first twenty rows of all future Tex Rickard fights.

Tired of financial crises, Rickard decided to insure himself by making John Ringling his silent partner. It was one of the smartest things he ever did, and it enabled him to sleep at night. But now he and Ringling were pounced on by the American Legion, several members of the House of Representatives, U.S. Senators and veterans' organizations for spending so much money on a prizefight when there were so many people in desperate need.

Doc chimed in with his sage advice on publicity.

"Rickard, you'll make a million bucks if you listen to me and do as I say. Put a case of booze—Scotch, bourbon, gin—whatever you want, in each newspaperman's room. This way not only will they write, but they'll write good—if they can write at all! I know those guys."

No one paid any attention to Prohibition. Booze poured whenever Doc wanted it to. Many a time his hotel room was stacked on one side with cases of booze and crowded on the other with bookies taking bets, the air in between thick and blue with cigar smoke.

The arena on Boyle's thirty-acre tract was originally slated to hold 50,000 people, then expanded to hold 70,000. Even that didn't seem big enough, so they modified it again. The more it expanded, the more the money flowed out. Rickard now started energetically to solicit ticket sales by mail. Everyone behind the scenes worked frantically as the day of the fight drew near.

Harry Ertle was named referee by Boxing Commissioner Charles Lyon. Tex, Doc and Teddy had wanted James J. Corbett, Otto Floto, Bob Edgren, Bill Brown, Jim Jeffries or Jim Dougherty, but it was soon pointed out to them that the New Jersey authorities were in charge and would select the referee.

The Dempsey–Carpentier fight, besides being the first million-dollar gate, established several records of sorts. In addition to the 93,000 spectators present, there were 700 reporters ready to flash the details of the bout around the world and to the French ships that waited offshore. For France, this fight was like a National Day. Curiously, though it was the first time a Frenchman was fighting for a world title, the bout was not broadcast on French radio. Instead, planes flew above major cities, ready to display red streamers if Carpentier won, green streamers for me. So intense was the excitement that after the fight some planes got their streamers confused, which must have caused a few cases of French apoplexy. French newspapers were poised to print the details; one paper kept an entire column open. A French writer, Gaston Benac, got so involved that he chronicled the bout in many later issues of his paper.

Around the arena were 400 firemen, 600 attendants, dozens of nurses and a fleet of ambulances sent over from the local hospital.

Because the arena was not designed to hold more than 93,000 people, it creaked and swayed. The police and fire commissioners were as shaky as the arena. They pleaded with Rickard to move up the fight time.

As the hour crept closer, I could hear the crowd's roars as they watched the preliminaries. Jerry the Greek, who was giving me my rubdown, was as tense as I was—I could feel it in his hands. He and I felt it wasn't going to be easy; the crowd was pulling hysterically for Georges. They wanted me to lose, even to a foreigner. As the preliminaries drew to an end—maybe I imagined it—I could sense the screaming crowd turning hostile.

Tex Rickard rushed into my dressing room, almost breaking the door down with his malacca cane. I had never seen him so excited.

"Jack! Jack! You never seen anything like it. We got a million dollars in already and they're still coming! And the people, Jack! I never seen anything like the people we got at this fight. High class society folk—you name 'em, they're here. And dames! I mean classy dames, thousands of them!"

He told me how he had climbed to the top of the arena, his arena, and looked wonderstruck on the colorful masses.

He turned to go, then stopped, turned around and said, "Listen, Jack, take it easy on Carpentier. Give the people out there a good run for their money, but be careful. Don't kill him. Don't kill everything." Still the same Rickard.

On his way out he almost collided with Gene Fowler, who was stopping in to wish me luck. They had barred him at the gates—he had misplaced his ticket—until he was recognized by a fellow member of the press and was allowed to pass.

"Hello, Jack. How's my pal?"

"Fine, pal."

"Say, what's the matter, Jack? There are 90,000 people out there waiting for you. It's your big day. In fact, it's your biggest ever!"

"What do you think they're waitin' for? My head, pal, that's what, my head. And if they can't get that, then it's my blood!"

"Jack, what're you saying? Say, you're not scared of going out there, are you?"

"Naw. I just want to get this over with!"

"Sure, pal. I understand."

"Listen, do me a favor. Talk about anything but the fight."

And he did. He was a reassuring sight, with those light eyes twinkling under that cap of his. I knew he realized what I was going through.

Doc rushed in, followed by the press and the usual crew. Gene backed out the door to avoid being crushed. By now I could hear and feel the impatience of the crowd. Jerry worked faster. I shut my eyes.

A jittery Doc walked over to me and spat twice on the ground. "Listen, kid, don't pay any attention to all them stiffs out there. We'll kill him!"

Tex Rickard and I, flanked by two of his associates, look over the proposed site of the new Madison Square Garden.

Accompanied by Teddy Hayes and bodyguard Mike Trent while running on the beach in Atlantic City just before the Carpentier fight.

1921. Congratulating a weary Georges Carpentier after the fight.

1923. Sitting on a Rolls, Doc and I posed for publicity shots in Shelby, Montana. There was little else to do.

Fans line up to buy tickets for my fight in the Polo Grounds. (*The New York News*)

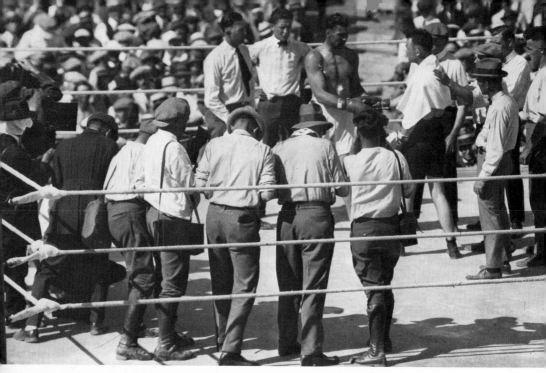

Shaking hands with an enthusiastic Tommy Gibbons before our bout.

Luis Angel Firpo, also known as the "Wild Bull of the Pampas," sends me flying out of the ring head first in our 1923 fight. (*United Press International*)

1924. One of my favorite pictures of myself, taken at a time when I had no worries or cares.

Estelle and I embark on our European tour.

Here I am, acting the part of the Big Hero and showing off in front of the devastated heroine. It was one of those typical scenes found in every one of my movies.

Palling around with Doug Fairbanks and Charlie Chaplin on a Hollywood lot.
(*Courtesy Jim Jacobs*)

Crushing mobs greet me on my way to negotiate for the Tunney fight in Chicago. (*The New York Daily News*)

1927. A stunned Gene Tunney hits the canvas in our Chicago fight. (*United Press International*)

20

Dapper Georges Carpentier

July 2, 1921, was a social event. Anybody and everybody was there: Bernard Baruch, John D. Rockefeller (whom Rickard personally escorted), Henry Ford, some Astors, Jimmy Walker (who tried to get to my dressing room but was stopped), several members of Harding's cabinet, among them Teddy Roosevelt, Jr.; George M. Cohan, Jay Gould, Al Jolson (who had recently gone a few disastrous rounds with me and now sported a proud chin bandage) and many friends. Every newspaperman I could think of was there as well, Tex having slipped something to a few of them before the fight for their help in publicity. Irvin S. Cobb, who was covering the bout for the *New York Times*, wrote:

"The arts, sciences, drama, politics, commerce and bootlegging industry, have all sent their pink, their pick and their perfection to grace the great occasion. The names at ringside would sound like the reading of the first hundred pages of 'Who's Ballyhoo in America.'"

Suddenly, it was time. I put on my maroon sweater and left the dressing room, walking through the crush of bodies toward the ring. It was a muggy day. The sky was strange, giving a distinct silver-blue hue to everything; the air was thick and tense.

I climbed into the ring and disrobed to a chorus of cheers mingled with jeers and cries of "Slacker! Get outta there, ya bum!" It was worse when they saw the American flag sewn on the waist of my white trunks. Several hostile ringsiders threatened to rip the trunks off me. I tried to ignore them. I was in the ring to fight.

Georges climbed into the ring, dapper in a gray robe trimmed with black piping. The crowd was feverishly chanting our names. Those who cheered me argued with those who didn't, and fistfights broke out. Frenchwomen were shrieking in their native tongue for Georges.

Joe Humphreys walked to the center of the ring and bellowed our introductions. "Weighing 188 pounds, from Salt Lake City, Utah, Jack Dempsey!" There was a deafening roar.

Carpentier weighed 175 pounds. The cheers were equally loud. He was thinner than I had expected and chalk white. He looked like a graceful statue. I looked like a street fighter.

Later Georges said, "You resembled a lion, and I had no intentions of getting killed by a ferocious beast!"

Our world championship bout was about to be broadcast on the radio for the very first time with Nat Fleischer and Andrew White nervously manning the controls.

Clang!

Carpentier moved into the ring and circled me with a series of jabs. I took it slow; no use rushing it. I had to study his fighting style.

In the second round Carpentier took the offensive—his only real try for victory. He threw a right to my chin that staggered me. I looked at him with surprise. Could it be that he had been underrated? But he didn't follow through—he had broken his thumb. The crowd was convinced Georges Carpentier was going to win. Every time I made it to my corner, I could hear the shouts, "What's a matter, slacker? The Frenchman too tough for ya? Mebbe yer all washed up. You're soft!" etc., etc.

The third round turned the tide. It was brutal. I threw some blows to the face and smashed one to the stomach, making him cover up. A strange silence traveled through the crowd. When he retired to his corner, I could see Deschamps jabbering to his champion excitedly.

Just before the bell sounded for the fourth, Doc leaned over and whispered, "Go to it, kid. Get him now!"

I rushed in and landed a series of blows. A hard left hook sent Georges to the canvas for a count of eight. He managed to get up, but he was finished even though he was still game. He threw a right which I blocked. With some lefts followed by a right to the heart, I sent him to the canvas. He couldn't get up. He raised his legs but couldn't follow through. The fight was mine. I rushed over to help him up and back to his stool. Blood was flowing from his nose and mouth.

Tex was pleased, as I could see from the way he was puffing his cigar and tapping his cane. He not only had pulled the whole thing off successfully but had also made history with a championship fight that lasted just about ten minutes.

News flashes were cabled to France: YOUR CHAMPION FLAT-TENED IN FOURTH. France's reaction? WE SHALL WEEP IN THE SMALL HUTS.

Doc had collected the money in advance and had given it to the auditor of the Belmont Hotel in New York for safekeeping. After the fight, Doc and Teddy told Warren Brown to stop in New York on his way back to the coast and pick up the money. He did, and he later dropped it off right in our laps.

Kearns and I decided to lay off fighting awhile and dedicate our energies to business, which was fine with me. Besides, Tex felt that I should only fight about once a year. Overexposure or the wrong opponent, he feared, would lead to a small gate. I guess all of us had been spoiled by the million-dollar one. Now he needed time to prepare another ballyhoo buildup.

Doc and I didn't do too well in business. We invested in too many of the "sure" propositions that came our way, including one coal property in Utah on which we dropped about $75,000.

I boxed a few exhibitions and played Pantages, where Doc resumed his old routine. Once, in a Red Cross exhibition, Doug Fairbanks came to the stage and challenged me. He was some thirty pounds lighter as well as being a bit shorter than I was. I held the advantage, so I invited him to hit me as hard as he could while I lowered my guard from time to time. I encouraged him to do his best, or his worst, knowing I could take it. In turn, I would tap him from time to time with an open four-ounce glove. Doug was pretty good. To him it seemed a fairly even match until he realized that in order to hit me he had to get near me, which was the one thing I didn't let him do. Later he told his son, Doug, Jr., that hitting me was like hitting a tree trunk. An exaggeration, but it pleased me because I had a tremendous admiration for his athletic abilities. After our exhibition we remained backstage for a couple of hours, both of us hesitant to be the first to face the overenthusiastic women we knew were waiting outside.

Doc suggested going to Europe. I was all for it. A short while later Doc, Teddy Hayes, Joe Benjamin, Damon Runyon (who was covering the trip for his Hearst paper) and I set sail on the *Aquitania*. By the time we sailed, we felt as though we had been there and back. A bon voyage celebration with enough booze to sink a whole fleet had been laid on, and starlets and showgirls were on hand to kiss me good-bye.

The crossing was rough, and we were relieved when we arrived on terra firma. In London the English treated me like a king. I didn't think I deserved it. Next to them I felt like an unpolished pug, but they didn't seem to mind. We met royalty and nobility. I practised bowing, and I even bought myself a monocle, thinking it made me look quite distinguished. Doc told me it made me look like an ass.

We then went to Paris, with its girls, cafés and more girls. The Parisian government gave me a medal and the French extended their arms to me, despite the fact that I had beaten their beloved champion. One reception led to another. I found myself gaining weight and losing sleep, but I didn't mind it at all. I was having the time of my life!

Rain was the only thing that spoiled Paris, but it didn't stop me. I turned to the intellectual side of the city. I was taken to the Louvre, to Notre Dame Cathedral, to the top of the Eiffel Tower—and on a conducted tour of the Paris sewers.

I saw the giant statue of the Farnese *Hercules*. He was so big and looked so powerful that I was glad they didn't grow like that anymore.

From there I was taken to see the *Mona Lisa*. I was too embarrassed to admit I didn't know who the great Leonardo was.

"Did you know," remarked an American tourist beside me, "Leonardo not only created the *Mona Lisa*, but he also invented the wheelbarrow?"

"You don't say? I'm very well acquainted with the wheelbarrow."

I felt very ignorant among these people who seemed to know so much.

One morning, while the rest of the boys were asleep, I left the hotel and strolled on the Champs-Elysées alone. It felt strange but good. Shopkeepers sweeping their sidewalks exchanged early morning greetings. To them I was just another American face. I sat at a café and enjoyed watching the stream of people passing by. For once there was no Doc or anyone else to tell me what to eat and drink or how to act.

Our next stop was Berlin, where German women tried to tear my clothes off. We stayed at the Adlon Hotel, whose management vowed never to invite me again. Bedlam! Sheer chaos! Even the house dicks were kept busy, for the first time in years.

One evening I was taken to see German women boxers. They were dressed in kilted skirts, jumpers, shirtwaists, short woolly socks and very solid rubber shoes. They were the most savage and offensive athletes I had ever seen. One hefty woman, after getting her jaw broken, still managed a knockout. When we got back to the Adlon I realized that I preferred being a participant to being a spectator.

We returned home exhausted, weak and one step from insolvency. I begged Doc to get me another fight.

21

The Wild Bull of the Pampas

My days seemed to be constantly alternating between boom and bust. For instance, there was that annoying and persistent matter of Harry Wills, who stalked and hounded me from 1922 to 1926. In 1922, Wills's manager, Paddy Mullins, posted a $2,500 forfeit with the New York State Boxing Commission for a Dempsey–Wills fight. Fine with me. But Harry Wills was black in the whitewashed sports world of the 1920s. Most promoters then didn't want to get involved in having to pick a white hope all over again in case Wills won. Even Tex Rickard, who showed interest in public, was inwardly afraid of any kind of racial clash. He had had a bad time of it when he had promoted the Jeffries–Johnson fight and he was going to be damned first before subjecting himself to such aggravation again. Doc didn't want any part of a mixed bout on general principles. Not wanting to antagonize Wills, Tex and Doc agreed, in time as well as under pressure from the Boxing Commission, to accept the Wills challenge and to set a date. On July 11, a contract was signed with a clause stating the date be "set within 60 days after a reliable promoter undertook to stage the bout." This phrasing, which was Doc's doing, enabled him to get me out of the contract.

Despite the fact that the date, place and terms of the contract were blank, Paddy Mullins decided to accept the agreement, banking on our reputations and signatures. When the negotiations were completed, it was agreed that neither Wills nor I would engage in any fights for a thirty-day bidding period.

The Dempsey–Wills fight was doomed from the start. No one would touch it. Commissioner William Muldoon was dead set against it (but nevertheless sided with the Commission). Tex Rickard was informed of high political displeasure, and I was threatened with suspension if I didn't go through with the bout. Paddy Mullins was giving us a mess of trouble, and our hands were tied. We were nervous and irritable. Doc, Tex and I started to take our moods out on each other, causing a good many disputes. Our public press conferences and statements were starting to clash, and I was convinced that not one of us had any integrity left. Doc couldn't stomach Wills and Tex wasn't crazy about Mullins. I felt like the shuttlecock in a badminton game.

As no promoter could be found to stage the bout, the thirty-day bidding period elapsed. Doc then signed me to fight Tommy Gibbons in the little-known town of Shelby, Montana, hoping to show Tex Rickard that we were perfectly capable of promoting me on our own. Because of the dramatic success of the Carpentier fight, Tex felt that I should discriminate and pick my opponents carefully, making sure that I didn't fight too often. Doc, on the other hand, felt that Tex was stalling with his "discrimination crap." So we signed to fight Gibbons. Tex sneered at Doc, declaring the fight was going to be a big, amateurish bust, and added that if I wasn't careful, Doc would succeed in ruining my reputation by matching me with every bum who crossed my path. Doc ignored him—which wasn't too difficult since our guarantee was $300,000.

Those were the days when I really felt for Rickard. He had his hands full with us, and at the same time he was going through personal agonies. It was about then that Tex was accused of having molested some pre-teenage girls who charged him with having lured them into a taxi, ripped their clothes and poured iodine down their throats. The Children's Society rushed in and pretty soon Tex was summoned by the police for questioning. As a public figure who was the object of every crackpot, Tex usually took things in stride. But this episode was pretty ugly and he vowed to fight it. After being questioned, he was released in the custody of his attorney,

J. Irving Lehman. Following the hearing, Tex was held on $10,000 bail. The Children's Society in the meantime had somehow managed to produce seven girls of questionable backgrounds who accused Tex of having molested them as well. It looked like a frame-up, but Tex, unlike many of his friends, maintained his composure throughout the proceedings.

The trial opened. Tex Rickard was accused of having committed second-degree rape. Conviction on this felony meant a long imprisonment.

The girls got up on the witness stand and told their varying stories. As the tales unraveled, one fact became evident: On the day of the supposed attack, Rickard, along with his press agent Ike Dorgan, matchmaker Frank Flournoy and journalist Bill Farnsworth, was in a box at the Polo Grounds watching the Dartmouth–Pennsylvania game. Not only had he been there, but he'd been seen by many who testified in his behalf. Tex was found Not Guilty.

When things calmed down, John Ringling persuaded Tex to take up the reins at the Garden once more.

Meanwhile, Doc firmed up the arrangements for my fight with Gibbons. Shelby, Montana, was a small town that desperately wanted its place on the map. With the talk of oil in neighboring states and fight talk in general, Shelby was gung ho to get itself a reputation.

One day Mike Collins, the fight manager, along with Loy Molumby, a big shot in the American Legion, had stopped off in Shelby, where they bumped into Sam Sampson, owner of the local army-navy store. When Sampson heard that Collins was a well-connected fight manager, he got all worked up and called Shelby's Mayor Johnson. Soon the two of them were begging Collins to do something for Shelby—like arranging a big, well-publicized fight. Collins listened to what they had to say and then called Eddie Kane, Tommy Gibbons's manager in St. Paul. He asked Kane if his fighter would be willing to meet me.

"Listen, Mike," Kane reportedly replied. "You get Dempsey out there, or anywhere, and Gibbons will fight him for nothing. All you got to do is pay Dempsey. What do you think of that?"

Collins relayed this information to Mayor Johnson, Sam Samp-

son and a newly formed committee of interested Shelby businessmen. They liked what they heard and told Collins to get in touch
with us—for whatever price we named—as soon as possible. Collins
wired Doc, offering me $300,000 to defend my title against Tommy
Gibbons in Shelby.

Doc wired back: SEND $100,000 NOW, $100,000 IN A MONTH
AND $100,000 BEFORE DEMPSEY STEPS INTO THE RING, AND IT'S A DEAL!

When the first $100,000 arrived, we headed west and set up
camp in a former beer garden near Great Falls, Montana. Gibbons
was already in Shelby, waiting. While Gibbons was supposedly
good, he was unranked; meeting me was obviously his big chance.
He must have been desperate to risk himself against me for
nothing.

I was joined in Great Falls by my dad and my cousin Don,
a member of the Hatfield side of the family. I trained hard; it was
to be my first defense in two years.

Gibbons, along with his wife and kids, stayed in an isolated
cabin while the press boys, among them Damon Runyon and Grannie Rice, occupied a Pullman car.

On our arrival, word reached us that Mayor Johnson and his
committee were having difficulty raising the second installment of
the guarantee.

Doc raged, "You've got to pay Dempsey every red cent or you
won't see him at all. Don't take us for fools, I warn you!"

The second payment squeaked through. Doc was still jumpy,
and on more than one occasion Runyon told me to shut him up because he was driving everyone nuts. Then the third payment was
stalled. Doc ranted and raved, threatening to cancel the fight. This
didn't go over very well. Frank Walker, an incensed attorney from
Butte, came to us with twenty angry people threatening to tar and
feather us if Doc didn't go through with the fight.

The publisher of the *Boxing Blade* in Milwaukee came down to
look the whole thing over. His impression was that everyone involved was crazy. How could a small town, with nothing to offer
but three rooming houses, one hotel, a train depot and an oil field,
possibly entertain the notion of competing with the great cities of
the east? But the people of Shelby were grimly determined.

When the third payment couldn't under any circumstances be met, Doc agreed, through my persuasion, to take the money out of gate receipts. Shelby's townsfolk were beside themselves; they were in over their heads, having even built an unpaid-for arena. When the monies stalled, the head of the lumber company demanded payment in advance. To soothe the man, he was promptly appointed President of the Dempsey–Gibbons fight, which meant he was now one of the several promoters who had invested in the damn thing and had nothing to show for it but a severe case of anxiety and frustration.

On that July 4, 1923, a total of 7,202 fans paid their way into the arena while another 4,000 crashed the gates. Private railroad cars pulled into town and society and movie stars mingled with Indians, cowboys and local folk. Among them were Mrs. Raymond T. Baker (formerly Mrs. Alfred Gwynne Vanderbilt), Mae Murray, Tom Mix and One-Eyed Connolly, the professional gate-crasher.

The fight itself went fifteen long, grueling rounds. Gibbons turned out to be a fine defensive fighter. He was a perfectionist, not a slugger. For fifteen tough rounds, I couldn't corner him to score a knockout. Even though I was awarded the decision in the end, I felt that this fight hadn't done my reputation or my popularity any good.

After the fight Doc was portrayed as the villain responsible for Shelby's going bankrupt. In Doc's words, "We took in $132,000 at the gate, and that, with the $200,000 I had, saw Jack and me through. Jack and I were not very popular. Jack got away on one of the night specials, but I had to wait an hour or so to clear things up. Eventually I paid five hundred bucks for a special engine to take me to Great Falls." With the gate receipts in his pants.

We had gotten everything in Shelby—from bad publicity to hard cash. Gibbons got nothing but the bout—and $50,000 from motion pictures and a theatrical booking as a result of the bout. Some time later, asked why he fought, he told Colonel Eddie Eagan, then a student at Oxford, "You've gotta eat. I have a big family and I have to support them. I fought Dempsey on a percentage basis and he got just about every penny that made its way through the gate. Sure, I took a chance—and lost. What little money I had was deposited in the bank in Shelby, which went bust. What a mess. I did, however, get a vaudeville contract. I had to compete with trained seals to get enough money to feed the wife and kids."

Oddly enough, the Shelby area began to lose population shortly after 1923. Where it had at one time been sitting on a rich oil field, now both oil and people had disappeared.

While waiting for another fight, I holed up in Hollywood, which was as good a place as any. Doc and I were slowly becoming property owners, having purchased the Barbara Hotel and the Wilshire Apartments in Los Angeles. In addition, I bought myself a house, having grown tired of hotel room surroundings. The house, on Western Avenue in Hollywood, was quite a sight. I listened to everyone's suggestions and spared no expense in putting it together. One Egyptian gentleman, under the guise of cementing a business deal with me, managed to sell me Persian rugs for every room in the house. When he covered the floors, he persuaded me to cover the walls as well. I just couldn't say no.

I invited my mother to come to California to help run the house. She came, but she was miserable. The surroundings were too swell for her simple tastes, and she couldn't get used to my nightly sessions of shooting the bull with pugs and friends who always seemed to be left over at daybreak. Despite the fact that I made sure she had all the luxuries at her fingertips, she decided she would be happier in Salt Lake, where she had her own lovely house. My parents had finally split up and my mother had reached a stage where she preferred to live her own life and not be dictated to by my father or by me.

I had just about gotten over the Gibbons fight when the clamor arose for a Dempsey–Firpo fight. Luis Angel Firpo had proven himself by knocking out Bill Brennan and Jack McAuliffe and doing away with 42-year-old Jess Willard in the eighth round, which demolished Willard's chances for a successful comeback once and for all. Firpo had been a drug clerk in Buenos Aires before turning to prizefighting. Tex Rickard, always keeping his eyes open for new and promising contenders, was impressed by Firpo's strength and stamina and arranged for Jimmy De Forest to train him for championship fighting. By the time we met, Firpo was the champion in Argentina. He was a big fellow, six feet three inches, weighing 215 to 230 pounds.

Speaking to sports writer Hype Igoe one day, Tex said, "Firpo —why, I saw him lay a fellow flatter than a wet flounder. He's the nearest thing to Jeffries I ever looked at. His arms, his neck— I never seen anything like him! He and Dempsey will make the greatest fight you ever seen!" I had met Firpo in 1922 as I was about to sail for Europe. I remember how he marched down to the pier, walked right up to me and kissed me Bon Voyage on both cheeks—much to my embarrassment.

Luis Angel Firpo wasn't sold on meeting me, so Tex told him that he'd either fight me now, while both of us were in top condition, or never. Firpo balked at first, but then he realized this would be his only chance at the title. Doc, back with Rickard again after the Shelby fiasco, managed to get us a $500,000 guarantee. It was a relief; we really needed the dough, and it was obvious to both of us that we needed Rickard. What's more, Doc had gone through tremendous amounts of money after the Gibbons fight and now owed me well over $150,000. Firpo stayed put in Argentina until he got the go-ahead from Tex in New York. Tex, meanwhile, had begun a big buildup for Firpo, called the "Wild Bull of the Pampas" because of his wild hair and Latin fire.

Firpo worked out at the same dog track in Atlantic City that I had used to train for Georges Carpentier. He wasn't too cooperative with the press; he didn't want pictures taken, he hated being interviewed, he insulted various members of the corps. He even insisted he be paid for his training sessions until Tex got hold of an embassy interpreter who helped Tex explain that this was not the practice in the United States. Despite this suggestion, it was obvious that money wasn't the number one priority in Firpo's life; food, on the other hand, was. Even sports writers, who had by this time seen just about everything, were absolutely flabbergasted by the quantities he would pack away. He would stuff himself to the bursting point, pause, ask for more, and then drop off to sleep. Like Carpentier, Luis Angel Firpo made good copy for the papers.

Gene Fowler tried to get an interview with Firpo a few days

before the fight, but unfortunately he picked a day when Firpo and his wife were battling furiously. She threatened to leave him and he shouted for her to leave the jewelry behind. One thing led to another, and pretty soon Firpo was seen charging down the hall after her. Gene, amused, wrote that "the Wild Bull of the Pyjamas was not quite as ferocious as he seemed."

Few, including members of the Boxing Commission, seemed to think much of Luis Angel Firpo. Tex was constantly saying things like, "Take it easy, boys. Watch what you say. You may have to eat those words. When the time is right, and I put Firpo in the same ring as Dempsey, why, the public's goin' to be so anxious they'll be willing to put a mortgage on the old homestead just to buy a ticket."

My training quarters were at Uncle Tom Luther's small place on Saratoga Lake, a few miles from Saratoga Springs. Uncle Tom Luther was quite a character, always walking around wringing his hands, crying about this and that. He was both a walking crying towel and a nervous wreck.

Doc, busy living it up as well as arranging future engagements, wasn't with me very much. Teddy Hayes, on the other hand, didn't leave my side.

One day, while I was training, a young kid fresh out of Columbia University approached me with the idea of getting into the ring with me. He was a cub reporter in the sports department of the New York *Daily News*. His name was Paul Gallico; he had previously been a movie critic but gave it up because of a run of bad movies. Now he was responsible for writing color and "interesting" shorts.

Up to 1923, Gallico had seen only three prizefights, none of them mine. Now, in September, 1923, he decided that the only way to write good color was to become my sparring partner, to see for himself what it was really like to be in the ring with me.

He asked me shyly if I would spar one round with him. Doc was in Atlantic City on a scouting trip, and I figured it'd be okay. Jerry the Greek and Jamaica Kid, my sparring partner, immediately panicked, telling me that Doc Kearns wouldn't approve of this one bit—how did I know this kid wasn't a ringer? I told them to keep their opinions to themselves. I was in charge, and Teddy and I would make the decisions in Doc's absence.

Gallico told me his editor had sent him to spar with me if I'd agree. I couldn't help ribbing him. "What's the matter, son? Doesn't your editor like you?"

I knew perfectly well that this wasn't his editor's idea at all. I also knew that if Doc had been there, Gallico would probably have been chased out of camp. I felt that the kid should be given a chance. He was just too earnest to be turned down. I asked him if he'd ever boxed in his life. No, but he had been an athlete in college. Well, if he was game, so was I. He turned to me and said:

"Look, could you confine your activities to the upper part of my body, because I don't think that I'll be able to take it down there, in the stomach."

"I know what you want—a good punch in the nose!"

"Yes, thank you very much. I think that would be fine."

That's how eager he was.

The "bout" was to take place the following Sunday, and Gallico told me later that he nearly died of worry. In the middle of that week he was assigned by the *News* to a deathwatch, which entailed standing outside Mayor John F. Hylan's home and waiting for something to happen. The mayor was critically ill and Gallico was to stay until there was something to write, one way or another. So poor Paul had plenty of time to worry about sparring with me.

In the meantime, Doc had returned from Atlantic City. He was furious when he heard what was going on.

"Jack, don't be a goddamn fool! Who is this kid? Do you really know? So what if he has credentials? Anyone can get hold of some, you know that. Listen, I don't like the looks of him. He looks to me like a goddamn ringer!"

"Doc, he doesn't look like any ringer I've ever seen. Why, he's as white as a sheet!"

"It figures; just when I leave, someone sneaks in. Jack, call it off, for your own sake. Protect your hide. Listen to me, suppose he knocks you out?"

"Look, I promised him, and that's that. I don't break my word."

"All right, you can do what you goddamn please, but don't take any chances with him. Finish him off quick!"

By noon there were approximately 3,000 people present, no more than usual, but to Gallico the ringside must have seemed packed. He was given trunks, gloves, shoes and headgear. He was then brought to the ring, where he stood outside the ropes with Ray Newman, one of my sparring partners, watching me spar with Farmer Lodge. To frighten the kid and to add some excitement, I knocked Farmer Lodge out cold and, as arranged, he was carried off moaning and groaning. Newman stepped into the ring for three rounds, and then it was Gallico's turn.

Doc acted as announcer and kept glaring at me, hoping that Gallico would change his mind at the last minute.

"In this corner, the Heavyweight Champion of the World, Jack Dempsey." The crowd cheered and whistled.

"His opponent, from the *Daily News* of New York, Paul Gallico." The crowd was quiet. Only a few murmurs could be heard. Someone asked, "Who?"

I came bobbing and weaving toward him and he put out his left—and hit me like a feather. Figuring that wasn't too bad, he confidently began to jab and poke. The next thing he knew, he was sprawled out on the canvas. Doc stood over him, counting. Gallico somehow managed to get up and Doc whispered to me, "Get rid of this bum."

I pulled Gallico into a clinch and said, "Hang on, kid, till your head clears." I gave him a few rabbit punches. Doc, seeing Gallico's eyes spinning in his head, stopped the fight.

The entire thing lasted one minute, thirty-seven seconds, but to Gallico it must have seemed longer. His lip was bleeding and his eyes were glazed. But he had been a sport. And he was grateful; the fact that I'd kept my promise meant a lot to him. The episode helped launch a fine writing career. This stunt, with accompanying photos of him sprawled on his butt, impressed his publisher, Joe Patterson, so much that within a few months Gallico was made sports editor. In time, he had his own column.

Another remarkable visitor was a young J. Paul Getty. Getty was active in the oil business and was so keenly interested in fighting that he had a fully equipped gymnasium in the basement of his house on Wilshire and Kingsley in Los Angeles. I had met him briefly in mid-summer, 1918, while swimming along the Crystal Pier in California. I was a nobody then and he was just a good-looking guy, about my height but slimmer, who messed around with oil. One September morning he walked briskly into Luther's camp and asked to get in the ring with me. We agreed, he got into the ring and, incredibly, he gave me a good, speedy workout. He was a fast and dangerous fighter, light on his feet, and he could pedal both forward and backward. Then overconfidence took over. "Hit me a little harder, Jack. Go ahead, I can take it." And I did, only to see him crumple in a heap. In a flash, he and I both realized that he was better suited for oil.

On September 14, 1923, the gates of the Polo Grounds bulged with people. Mounted cops surrounded the place, trying to keep some kind of order. Mike Jacobs, who with Rickard had been so successful in promoting the Carpentier fight, sat outside, on a borrowed horse, scalping right up to the last minute.

Again the people at ringside read like a Who's Who. The press occupied what appeared to be the first five rows.

Just before the fight, Tex came to see me in my dressing room. "We got another million dollar gate! If you put him away with the first punch, all those people out there won't get their money's worth."

"Listen, Tex. There's one difference between this guy and Carpentier. Firpo is bigger and a slugger. He could kill me with one wallop."

"But, Jack, how is he gonna hit you? He's slow and moves like an old tub. I hate to think of all them nice millionaires going out of here sore at both of us."

"Go to hell!"

The whole fight lasted a total of three minutes, fifty-seven seconds, but those minutes were damn tough ones. Every blow Firpo landed staggered me. He seemed to live up to his nickname as he kept charging and pawing. Nevertheless, I managed to floor him seven times in the first round. But he wouldn't stay down—the lust to kill was burning in his eyes, and nothing was going to stop him. That was evident when he connected with a thunderous left and then a right that sent me flying through the ropes to land on top of the sports writers and their typewriters in the first row. Hype Igoe, who was sitting next to Jack Lawrence, was nearly demolished by my fall, and everyone was yelling. It was pitch dark for a few seconds, then I managed to focus on Firpo's fuzzy form in the ring. Before I knew it, I had been pushed back.

Through the years it has amused me to hear this or that person take credit for breaking my fall and throwing me back as if I were a prized baseball. Igoe was the only one who said nothing while listening to others, including Walter Winchell, George Bellows (who was covering the fight for the *Evening Journal*) and Milton Berle. Even Frank Menke of the International News Service, who wrote all his stories with a pencil, claimed the "honor" of having broken my fall with his typewriter.

I don't remember climbing back into the ring, but I remember seeing about twenty Firpos standing in front of me. I mumbled to Doc, "What round was I knocked out in? What's all the fuss?"

"You son-of-a-bitch, you weren't knocked out! Get in there fast and box this guy. Finish it!"

I crashed a left to his jaw and Firpo went down as if he had been struck by lightning. He didn't move as Johnny Gallagher counted him out—to the roars of the excited crowd. Doc was dancing and my second, Joe Benjamin, almost passed out.

Once in my dressing room, Doc had to fight off the well-wishers. I was in pain, my backside aching from bruised bones. I guess it was a good thing that my fall had been broken by hands and typewriters. All I wanted was to be left alone and to sleep.

The next day I went to see Tex about getting my money before Doc laid his hands on it. I was sick and tired of Doc's picking up the money and spending a good shot of it before splitting it with me. Besides, if I didn't get the dough in my hands now, Doc'd wind up owing me more than he did already. Tex agreed and gave me $550,000 after taking $50,000 for himself. I knew I was in the right. I was scared of winding up in the gutter—the thought made me sweat at night.

That afternoon Doc and I had a falling out, the first major one before our big split. He was furious at me for having gone behind his back to collect the dough. When he heard I'd set up a trust with Hayes's help, he almost went out of his head.

"You damn fool. Why, I could have doubled the dough for you. What the hell's the matter with you? Ain't my advice good enough for you no more?"

It wasn't that. I just wanted my money in a safe place, not spent on tips or cheap dames, and Doc's hands had started to get pretty itchy. While I kept recalling Rickard's warnings, I still disregarded them. As long as I could have some control of the situation, Doc was okay by me.

Inwardly, I was convinced that if Firpo's brain and reflexes had worked faster, if he hadn't stood in the ring flatfooted and perplexed, he probably could have taken the title away from me. He took too long to follow up his advantage. By the time he had realized what had happened, it was too late.

The Firpo fight led to the adoption of the "neutral corner" rule, which stated: "A fighter scoring a knockdown must go to the farthest neutral corner and, if he delays, the count is not to begin until he does." I paid no attention; I wasn't going to fight for a while, anyhow.

I never saw Firpo in the ring again. I remember reading his words in the *New York Times* of September 14, 1923:

"I'm not sore about not winning the Dempsey fight. It was just one of those things. My regular manager Jimmy de Forest wasn't in my corner because he was a friend of Dempsey's. And my handlers didn't protest about the fouls or the time Dempsey was out of the ring. But I don't think it would have made any difference. Damon Runyon and a few other writers said I really won the fight and I think I did, too, but that's all over now."

Just one of those things. Losing, whether you liked it or not, was nothing but an occupational hazard.

22

Estelle Taylor vs. Doc Kearns

Tex Rickard was in charge of building a new Madison Square Garden, to be completed in time for the Democratic National Convention, when his wife, Edith Mae, died. Tex was a man who needed a woman by his side, someone who loved and respected him, away from the sports world. He kept his grief bottled inside and it took him a long while to recover from his loss. In time, Maxine Hodges entered his life and did wonders for his spirits. I remember when he first started to see her; we all kidded him that he'd probably choose to spend his wedding night in Madison Square Garden.

By now Doc and I were definitely not seeing eye to eye. Teddy, my trainer, who'd been with us since 1920 or 1921, was torn between the two of us; we had developed a kind of love-hate relationship that hurt me deep down but I had no way of knowing that this was nothing compared to what was to come. Doc was running faster than ever now, as if he were racing against time itself. His common-law wife didn't help matters; I felt she had hated my guts from the time we first laid eyes on each other. Let him douse his clothes with cologne, I told myself, and go from club to club—I didn't care. His hours seemed to start when mine ended anyway.

I signed another contract to make ten *Fight and Win* serials in Hollywood, this time with Universal Studios, Irving Thalberg and Carl Laemmle, Sr. Universal then was just about the biggest lot in

Hollywood, churning out all kinds of movies, but known for its westerns and such western stars as Art Acord, Harry Carey and Hoot Gibson. One western star, Will Rogers, had been under contract at Pathé as I had been.

Hollywood then was a far cry from the grind factories and rental studios of today. William Fox's studio, now Twentieth Century Fox, had by far the best café, and not only in terms of food. It was a place of seduction—seduction by press agents, by newspapermen and by managers who stuffed you with food and booze. Everything and everyone seemed overplayed.

Dropping names was a favorite pastime, and the names were those of the big stars of the day: Clara Bow, John Barrymore, Buck Jones, Adolphe Menjou, Tom Mix, Dorothy and Lillian Gish, Vilma Banky, Rudy Valentino, Marion Davies, Charlie Chaplin, Norma Talmadge, Fatty Arbuckle, Harold Lloyd and countless others.

Whenever I made a serial, Lon Chaney, who was with Universal, was called in to fix me up as he had before. Chaney had a feather-like hand, unlike Mary Pickford's make-up man, who treated my face the way it deserved to be treated. He was yet to become famous for his scary portrayals in *The Hunchback of Notre Dame* and *The Phantom of the Opera*. In the late twenties, Louella Parsons said that if people ran screaming out of theaters, they had only Chaney and Laemmle, Jr., to thank. Attendance was at an all-time high, forcing some theaters to stay open for twenty-four hours to accommodate the crazed crowds.

One of my favorite two-reelers was *All's Swell on the Ocean*, directed by Erle C. Kenton. It starred me as "Tiger," with Jack O'Day, Hayden Stevenson and Ed Ovey. The story revolved around a homesick fighter who had just completed a successful European tour accompanied by his manager and trainer. Now that the tour was over, "Paree" was no longer gay, so we hopped a boat for home, posing as the ship's entertainment—a magician, a dancer and a musician. We were nothing short of lousy and exposed ourselves as frauds. Things were further complicated by my making a play for the wrong girl. As usual, the closing scenes showed me in the ring, fighting for either my honor or someone else's.

Teddy supervised the production of the serials while Doc

stayed east. He was more at home in New York. In Hollywood he was known, but he didn't have the right footholds. Hollywood was for business—business conducted at either the treacherous cocktail party or the hazardous lunch. This wasn't for Doc. He was at his best in the smoky atmosphere of the speaks.

Those days were nothing but fun and laughs. I was rich and I was in motion pictures. What else was there? The only one who refused to believe I had dough was Pa, despite the fact that I was supporting my whole family, my "entourage" and myself. Sometimes he would visit the sets and look at me as though I were wasting my time. I was making at least $2,500 a week, I owned the Barbara Hotel and the Wilshire Apartments, I drove a white McFarland with monogrammed tires, and I was known in Hollywood from the Mocambo to Ciro's, two top night spots. I was the Champ, but to Pa I was still Harry. I decided to put him straight one day and sat him down in the lobby of the Alexandria Hotel.

"Pa, I'm going to show you something that'll set your mind at ease once and for all." I pulled out five certified checks that I had gotten from the bank and that totaled one million dollars. At first he couldn't believe his eyes; he gaped. I couldn't help grinning at the old man.

"Is that real, Son?"

"Sure."

"Then you're a goddamn fool, Harry. You'd better put it in the bank before someone takes it away from you!"

One day a Mr. Butler of the Butler Rolls-Royce Agency on Sunset Boulevard offered me a deal. He would give me a brand-new Rolls in exchange for the McFarland and a little cash. I consulted Teddy and we both agreed it'd be swell to ride around in a Rolls sedan. We arranged to motor out to Pine Hills, where I was filming, about forty miles west of San Diego. We were running late, so our chauffeur, who had never driven a Rolls before, stepped on the accelerator and we were off in a blur. He drove faster and faster, not realizing how quietly and smoothly a Rolls accelerates. As Teddy and I braced ourselves for the worst, it happened. We crashed; the car spun completely around and then over. We crawled out through broken windows. Teddy, furious, grappled with the driver and I had to pull him away. From then on I drove an open roadster. The luxury of chauffeurs was for Other People.

While I was getting in and out of minor scrapes, Doc went around boasting of how he'd managed to keep dames' skirts and apron strings away from me for the last five years. In fact, as my manager and business partner, he had succeeded in ruining each and every one of my prospects, discouraging me to the point where I was reduced to one-night stands. They were infrequent but safe.

"You don't need dames and all the emotional baggage they carry with them. Prizefighting and dolls don't mix, so lay off 'em, kid."

Lay off them? Why didn't he? Sometimes I thought I would burst. I was annoyed and I fought back by questioning the state of our assets. I asked him for a complete accounting, hoping he'd realize I'd become level-headed. He blew up—"Someone put you up to this!"—and he wouldn't back down from this assumption. Nor would he produce any papers or give me any information.

"Leave well enough alone," was all he'd say.

I wanted my bed and heart warmed by a special woman, not a 2 A.M. bargain. I ached for feminine affection. On days I was free, I strolled down Hollywood Boulevard, invariably accompanied by someone I didn't particularly want around. I think I stared at everyone in a skirt who walked by. Girl-watching was the best pastime in the world, but I wasn't too happy about the "look but don't touch" rule Doc had imposed on me. I wondered if there was something wrong with me. I could have had just about any woman, but that wasn't what I wanted.

One afternoon I saw a sultry broad dressed in chocolate brown, staring at a billboard on Hollywood Boulevard. I walked over to her. She was breathtakingly pretty.

"Pardon me, Miss, but haven't I seen you someplace before?" Boy, was I corny! She gave me the cold shoulder.

"Ahem. Allow me to introduce myself."

"Listen, buster, allow me to tell you to scram before I scream for help!"

I couldn't believe it. Dames! Maybe Doc was right. Maybe they weren't worth it. Who did this one think she was, anyway? I felt mortified and moved away as fast as I could. I turned around to take one last look. She'd disappeared.

While making a western at Universal, Teddy Hayes and I arranged for a gym to be built in the back of the studio. It was to have the works, showers, a ring, rubbing tables, etc. Construction was lagging; Jack Dougherty, Barbara LaMarr's husband, approached me.

"Hey, Jack. Why don't you train with us until your gym is completed?"

"Sure, pal. Thanks."

Turning to Teddy, as if I had become the invisible man, he asked, "How do you think Jack would like to meet a pretty movie star? I hear she wouldn't mind meeting the champ."

Teddy wasn't sold on the idea, knowing how Doc felt about my meeting dames, but I was all for it.

We hopped into Dougherty's roadster and headed for Lansky's pack ranch, where Herbert Brenon was directing *The Alaskan* (1924) for Paramount, starring Thomas Meighan and Estelle Taylor. Dougherty introduced us to Brenon, who then called for his two stars. I shook hands with Meighan and turned to his co-star Estelle Taylor. It was the dame from Hollywood Boulevard! Why did these things happen to me?

She must have been surprised to see me as well, but she didn't show it. I was sunk from the moment I stared into her face. I kissed my composure good-bye. She was beautiful, and I stood there thinking it sure was my lucky day. One thing led to another; pretty soon we were seeing each other virtually every day.

Estelle Taylor, five foot four, hailed from Wilmington, Delaware. As a girl she'd been inspired by Pearl White and Charlie Chaplin. After winning a local beauty contest, doors opened to bit parts and to posing for Harvey Dunn and other artists. Leaving the Sargent School of Dramatic Arts in New York, she managed to land a small role in George V. Hobart's play, *Come-on Charley*. William Fox, a former Union Square nickelodeon operator turned producer, saw her and offered her a contract as well as a screen test. She played in *Broadway Saint* (1919) and one part followed another. Fox cast her as the lead in *While New York Sleeps* (1920) and, satisfied with her performance, sent her to Hollywood where she made *A Fool There Was* (1922), playing opposite Lewis Stone, and *Don Juan* (1926) with John Barrymore, who subsequently became her staunchest supporter.

When I met Estelle, she had just gotten out of a sticky situation with debonair George Walsh, who was going through a divorce. Walsh's wife, humiliated and hurt, had at first named Estelle in the suit but later dropped the charge since Estelle had not been the actual cause of the split. When the divorce came through Walsh vanished from Estelle's life. Because of him, she reaped her share of bad publicity, and shortly after completing *The Alaskan* she broke her contract with Paramount, not wanting to cause them any further embarrassment. In a way, she had done the right thing; rumor had it that Walter Wanger, who had taken over production, had been about to fire her.

I always felt that she appreciated having me around because she was going through a bad period. When we met she was the proud owner of a broken down Willys-Overland which she insisted on parking in front of her duplex on Formosa and Hyland Boulevard, two blocks away from Chaplin's studio. The car was such an eyesore that I bought her a brand-new Buick. Despite the break in her career, Estelle Taylor was the symbol of success for me. She had a Svengali-like effect on me. I neglected training, workouts and discipline.

Poor Teddy was beside himself. Doc knew nothing and was being kept in the dark—for obvious reasons. Every time he called to ask me to lay a rumor to rest, I did, saying there was nothing serious going on. I talked nothing but boxing with him; I even persuaded him to look into taking on Mickey Walker, whose manager had just died. So he couldn't accuse me of not keeping my mind on business.

Estelle Taylor was still married to Kenneth Peabody, a clerk in a wholesale furniture store, whom she had met around 1917. Between Peabody's being kept in a state of ignorance and Doc's not being told the truth (even though all Hollywood knew it), the only way we could get to know each other was behind closed doors. Estelle wasn't exactly the flame of passion; she was delicate and she had a uterine complication which would prevent her from ever bearing children. I didn't care. I don't even know whether I was a good lover or not—all I know is that she made me feel I was the only man in the world.

From the time we met I bought her jewelry, which she insisted on storing in a vault. She even took a few friends, including Louella Parsons, to see her collection. I found this strange, but if that's the way Estelle wanted it ...

When I finally asked her to marry me, Estelle asked Peabody for a divorce. He started the action, and for a time he contemplated a suit against me for damages; he dropped the idea when informed he didn't have a leg to stand on, as he and Estelle had been living apart for a number of years.

Doc made it a point to meet Estelle—and, naturally, he disliked her. Estelle had a razor-sharp mind and tongue and was a good looker; that was just the sort of dame Doc didn't want around me.

Estelle and I discussed my business dealings with Doc, and she insisted I stand my ground and ask him for a complete accounting of our finances. He knew she was behind me, so he stalled while he ran a long and exhaustive check on Miss Estelle Taylor, figuring there just had to be something that would shut up this pushy broad.

I had just about finished at Universal when I married Estelle in San Diego in February. That night I phoned Doc and Teddy, who was training Mickey Walker for him. Teddy answered.

"Congratulate me! I just got hitched!"

Silence greeted me as he passed the phone to Doc.

"The champ wants to speak to you."

"What's doing, kid?"

"Doc, I did it. Congratulate me!"

"Did what? Speak up, I can't hear you."

"I'm married."

"What? What? Who to?"

"Estelle. Hold on, she wants to talk to you."

He slammed the phone down.

I turned to Estelle, who could see I was upset. I couldn't understand what Doc was so mad about. That I didn't invite him to the ceremony? He wouldn't have come anyway. That I didn't ask his approval?

I didn't hear from Doc for a number of weeks and I knew he was really steaming. When I did get a call from him, he said he'd be in Hollywood that night. Teddy rang up Eddie Branston at the Montmartre to tell him we'd all be there.

Estelle and I arrived early and waited. Around nine-thirty Doc walked in, already tight, looking surly and carrying a flask in his hand. Estelle made a face; she didn't touch the stuff and he disgusted her. Doc was antagonistic from the moment he sat down, criticizing everyone and everything at the top of his voice. The people at nearby tables couldn't help staring. He was as drunk as I had ever seen him.

Teddy tried to placate him, but Doc wasn't in the mood to listen to anyone. He shook him off and told him to mind his own damn business. He turned viciously to Estelle and insinuated that he had dug up some information on her which wasn't too nice. I told him to watch his mouth; she ignored him. He moved closer and said that if she was smart, she'd get off her high horse and leave certain aspects of my life alone—or he'd spill the beans. She lost her temper and told him to shut the hell up, that he didn't know what he was talking about and was making a fool of himself. One word led to another and Estelle, furious, stood up, demanded her wrap and, while waiting, told him off. It was an agonizing scene.

In her opinion, Doc was a no-good drunken bum who had outfoxed himself, a lout, a parasite—yes, a parasite. He snarled at her and she shouted that if she wanted to she could produce enough dirt to put him away. Didn't he remember the incident in Tijuana? If he didn't, she'd be more than happy to refresh his memory.

They were at each other's throats and causing a real commotion. Teddy and I tried to calm them, but it was no good. Temperamentally, Estelle was just as strong as Doc. I was afraid one of them would strike the other, when she spun around on her heel and glared at me.

"I'm leaving, Jack. Are you staying or coming with me?"

I went.

Teddy stayed behind and tried to iron things out, but a link had been broken. Doc was too polluted to reason rationally. Teddy asked him why he had to pull such a scene in public.

"Lissen, I don't give a damn where the hell I am. I found him as a bum and I'll make sure he'll go back as a bum. No-good, ungrateful . . ."

Upset, Teddy walked out and came to Estelle's house, seven or eight blocks away. Our front door was wide open, and as he walked in he found our coats and hats thrown carelessly onto the divan. Estelle and I were at war.

"Why did I have to get mixed up with a bunch of pugs? I'm a star, and all I see are flat-nosed pugs sitting around my house and staring. I can't even get decent work. Why, I wouldn't be surprised if your wonderful manager put in a good word for me at the studio. That guttersnipe. I refuse to have anything more to do with him, and I suggest you do the same!"

"Estelle," I pleaded, "hear me out. Doc's been good to me for years. Why, without him, I—"

"That's just it. He's been good for you, but that's over. I'm sick and tired of his pushing me aside and demanding a word with you in private all the time. Who the hell does he think I am? A housekeeper? The maid?"

"Estelle."

"The only thing that s.o.b. doesn't do is sleep in your bed at night, but give him time and he'll do that too. Oh yes, I've met the likes of him before."

"Sweetheart, listen to me, please. Calm down. Doc's not as bad as you think he is. He means well. Everything will work out, you'll see. Maybe if I talked to him . . ."

"Over my dead body. Tonight I talked to him for the last time, and I'm sorry I wasted my breath on that drunken bum. Jack, it's either him or me from now on. Choose."

"What?"

"If he stays, I leave."

"Wait till morning, Honey. Things'll clear up. Please don't put me on the spot."

"I'm waiting."

I felt like dying. Here was my wife asking me to make a decision, right then and there, that would affect my entire life. I didn't know what to do, but I had to do something. I paced around. I thought I saw Teddy quietly letting himself out, but I wasn't sure. Teddy was just about the only person who had really put himself out for me, especially in dealing with Doc. Before making my decision I called Doc, but something in him seemed to have snapped: He was abusive and accused me of ruining our relationship. Fuming, I told him I was going to have nothing more to do with him. There was obviously no other way out; I loved Estelle, and I chose to put Doc out of my life.

Eddie Frayne of the *New York American* and Mark Kelly in San Francisco were among the first to break the story, which subsequently appeared in papers across the country. Other members of the press, not having been on top of the situation, were miffed at having lost out on good copy. Bill Farnsworth wired Damon Runyon, care of Gene Fowler at the Biltmore Hotel in Los Angeles:

WHY DON'T YOU FILE A STORY GIVING LOWDOWN ON DEMPSEY
TROUBLE. WE WERE BEATEN ON OUR OWN STORY. WHY NOT
TRY TO GET BACK SOME LOST PRESTIGE. WHAT'S YOUR
ADDRESS IN CASE GENE PULLS OUT. REGARDS BOTH.

FARNSWORTH.

And this was only the beginning.

Teddy Hayes remained with me as an advisor despite Doc's warning him, "He'll bounce you, you're just one of many." Poor Teddy. Because of his interest in Mickey Walker, his association with Doc and his closeness to me, he was pretty torn apart. Doc, infuriated, kept in constant contact with him. Through mutual friends, Doc threatened me in so many ways that I always avoided his calls. It was tough for all of us, and I suffered more than anyone could possibly realize.

One day Estelle called Teddy, who was staying in our Barbara Hotel, and asked him how fast he could make it to our house. Thinking something was wrong, he rushed over. Estelle met him at the door and whispered, "Come up. Jack wants to see you."

He walked into the room and stopped dead in his tracks with

his mouth open when he saw me. I was lying in bed, my face all bandaged, looking as if I'd been run over.

"Oh, Teddy," she gushed, "look at him. Now he has class. He's had his nose bobbed!"

Teddy just stood there, horrified. I laughed at the expression on his face and told him I was still the same guy, only I didn't look like a pug anymore. He shook his head sadly.

"Jack, you shouldn't have done it. It's wrong, wrong, goshdarn it!"

"What's the big deal? What's it matter what my nose looks like?"

Estelle was beaming. Big deal; it was only my nose, but fixing it had made her happy. I'd recently learned that when she'd first met me she told Louella Parsons that she thought I was one of the ugliest pugs she'd ever seen—that my face was even funnier than the funny papers. Now she'd never be able to say that again. What's more, I'd never have to go through having the putty put on my mug again, either. It had made me feel better too, but now here was Hayes, disapproving, standing before me and frowning.

He felt that this would destroy me in the ring, that my nose would become a target. In trying to preserve it, I'd turn to defensive rather than offensive fighting. No, Teddy didn't like it one bit.

While I went around telling everyone Doc and I had split up and that anyone who had an interesting proposition could deal with me directly, Doc made the rounds telling anyone who would listen how ungrateful I was, how much he'd done for me only to be given a boot in the butt and how I never would have made it to the top without him. He blamed Tex Rickard as well, thinking Tex, behind Doc's back, had influenced me. Doc was convinced that now that he and I had parted, I'd be a soft touch for Rickard.

A pal, Gene Normile, who later became my business manager for a time, figuring he'd do me a good turn, approached Doc and asked him to shake and make up with me. But by this time Doc wouldn't consider it.

"Why, I'll make him walk down a dark alley before shaking hands with that bum!"

Everyone seemed divided in their loyalties. It had become a

sticky situation. Joe Benjamin, my second, alternated between me and Doc, not daring to take the risk of attaching himself to either. The press boys balanced themselves as if they were walking on eggs. Damon Runyon and Gene Fowler felt themselves to be in the most uncomfortable crunch of all. No one was quite sure whether or not our feud was permanent, so speculation was heaped on speculation, and breaths were held for the next byline. In those days, such incidents were really newsworthy; anything that had a tinge of scandal or dirt boosted newspaper circulation even before the ink had dried.

The Dempsey-Kearns Corporation wasn't dissolved formally until 1928 because of lawsuits and countersuits.

I had to get away, so Estelle and I decided to take a combined honeymoon and business trip to Paris, Cologne and Berlin, where I was scheduled to box in exhibitions.

Estelle vomited her way across the ocean. Her dresses remained in the wardrobe and some thought I had left Mrs. Dempsey at home. By the time we arrived in Paris, Estelle was like a worn and ragged toothpick. Nevertheless, the Parisian couturiers managed to make her feel better.

After a whirlwind tour of Paris we arrived in Cologne, where we were greeted enthusiastically. We stayed in the Dom Hotel, and every time we emerged we could barely make it through the lobby. Everyone wanted to see the Champ and his Movie Star wife. Hands reached to touch Estelle, and she could barely see above the well-wishers' heads to call for assistance. Mr. Meyer, the gentleman handling our tour, screamed for everyone to kindly move out of the way, but no one moved. In that jam I was introduced to Germany's fighting hope, Max Schmeling, who looked amazingly like me. We arranged to spar a few rounds together while I was in Cologne. He was good, and I gave him a few pointers, including some on how to get away from the ropes.

"Max, you're gonna be a champ; just you wait and see." He smiled and shrugged. I guaranteed it, and he grinned from ear to ear. Some time later I was proved right.

In Germany Estelle bought everything she laid her hands on, including a 200-pound headache of a dog named Castor, who from the beginning caused nothing but trouble. (We were even sued by a German lady who claimed that she was Castor's rightful owner.) Castor was a dog who could eat from morning till night. He suffered from claustrophobia and had a temper, especially when it came to Estelle. He would have killed for her. Estelle took him everywhere she went, sightseeing, walking and riding. Because of his size, he traveled in a separate car that followed ours; he hated to travel alone, so he bit the drivers I hired. Everyone was talking about the mad Americans and their miserable dog. We moved on to Berlin.

Estelle didn't think it was right for her darling Castor to be alone; she cajoled me into getting him a companion. I approached an ex-lightweight, broken-nosed Lee Moore, to accompany the dog on his daily strolls and to exercise him every morning. Lee obliged for exactly one week.

Early one morning, while we were staying at the Hotel Adlon, Lee arrived to take Castor out. He and the dog were poised at the top of the staircase when Castor spied Estelle in the lower lobby. She looked up and, without thinking, called to him. Hearing his name, Castor took a flying leap down the staircase, dragging a horrified Lee Moore with him. Lee sustained a broken arm, a broken rib, concussion and shock. Estelle got mad and insisted I tell Lee off. I couldn't figure out why.

"Because he called Castor a son-of-a-bitch."

But Moore was the one who told Castor off, and the dog retaliated by destroying the wallpaper in his hotel room. More damages.

We decided to head for home, stopping first in Paris once more. Within a few days, Castor had lived up to his reputation by chewing up a valuable Aubusson rug, along with miscellaneous chairs and drapes. We sailed for the States upon settlement of the suit. The trip back was memorable as well; this time Castor got seasick and Estelle spent the major part of the voyage cradling him in the ship's kennel.

We stopped at the old Morrison Hotel in Chicago, where my friend Leonard Hicks was in charge. I was glad to see him, and we talked over old times until we were interrupted by a porter who wanted to inform us that a monster of a dog had gotten himself caught in the Morrison's revolving doors and become hysterical.

All in all, Castor cost me well over $10,000. Between Estelle and the dog, I had my hands full. My trainer, Gus Wilson, who had accompanied us, couldn't hide his wonder that I didn't chuck it all.

I decided to give Castor away regardless of Estelle's tears. I first approached Runyon, who immediately informed me he was headed out of town indefinitely. I called Gene Fowler, but he had been forewarned and he refused, saying he was tired of seeing his friends die. No one wanted Castor. Eventually, Lee Moore took him off my hands—for a price.

In Hollywood again, we moved from Estelle's duplex to a beautiful Spanish-style home in Laughlin Park on Los Feliz Boulevard, then quite a fashionable area. The house was fabulous; it had an eighteen-hole golf course, a swimming pool, bridle paths and what seemed to be endless oak trees and gardens. We had a ballroom which was used for screening movies and a number of people in help. Estelle decorated the bedroom in various shades of gold and Spanish lace, which wasn't exactly my taste. I imagined how the guys would have held their bellies laughing.

Estelle disliked the outdoors and spent most of her time in the house, reading and having her friends over. Her special friend was Lupe Velez which annoyed me. Lupe felt I wasn't good enough for Estelle and made no bones about it. I told Estelle that I didn't want her in my house; Estelle retorted that Lupe was her friend and that she was more than welcome. If I wanted to get rid of anyone, she said, I should start with the pugs who did nothing but take up space around the house, gaping stupidly at her every time she passed. I told her she was exaggerating. She retorted that I wouldn't recognize a bum if I fell over one. I laughed, pretending it was a joke.

My new business manager was Gene Normile, whom I had taken on shortly after my return. He was shrewd and he had dough of his own, so I felt I could trust him. Nevertheless, when it came to investments, Estelle felt she knew best. One of our first ventures was to invest in our own movie, *Manhattan Madness*, which never paid off. Throughout the twenties, every time I was billed to make an appearance somewhere, or a fight, one of my films was reissued, much to my amazement. *Lothario* was especially big on one of my trips to Mexico City, where pesos were enthusiastically thrown at the screen and at me, causing me to hire police protection.

Hollywood, with all its complexes, was a hard town, but it was good to me. To many, it was a place of disillusionment and embarrassment, as it had been for one Alberto Rabagliati in the years before he was to become a European sensation. Rabagliati was a poor southern Italian who one day decided to enter the much-publicized Rudolph Valentino look-alike contest. First prize was a trip to Hollywood, accompanied by the usual promises of fame and fortune. Much to his astonishment, he won. Fox Studios outfitted him from top to toe, and he was off for Hollywood. Before docking in the States, Rabagliati determinedly practised his bows and his thank-yous—his only knowledge of English.

Arriving at the pier, he strutted down the gangplank, pleased to see a screaming, waving crowd on shore. They seemed to be waving to him. Thank you, thank you, his eyes said. But then he happened to look over his shoulder—and there stood Douglas Fairbanks.

Somewhat shaken, he made his way to Fox Studios, where he was greeted, shuffled aside and forgotten until a well-meaning acquaintance suggested he link himself romantically with some movie actress (good publicity). He looked around, and within two weeks he had zeroed in on one young woman, to whom he sent flowers, fancy candy boxes and hot Latin love letters. The woman was Estelle. And, naturally, she loved the attention this Italian showered on her. I decided to see him and straighten out a few things, but face-to-face I found I couldn't tell him to lay off, nor could I flatten the guy. He didn't seem to understand a word of English.

A few days later he was discreetly advised to focus his amorous attention elsewhere. He shortly found himself another doll—and promptly gave his impending stardom the kiss of death, for the doll was none other than the mistress of one of Fox's big bosses. The one thing we could say about Rabagliati was that he had excellent taste.

23

We Bomb in New Haven

It was 1925, smack in the middle of the decade, when a sour-ness set in. The New York State Athletic Commission, reportedly pressured by Paddy Mullins, declared me ineligible—suspended me from boxing in New York. I had gone to New York to talk to Tex Rickard, who had an ex-marine named Gene Tunney up his sleeve as a possible opponent, and there I was hit with this piece of news. Suspended? For not fighting Harry Wills? I had nothing against Wills.

Muck was heaped on me once more. I might have been on top of the world, but I wasn't all that well liked. In New York some thought I lacked humility, others thought I showed a racist streak by avoiding Wills and still others attacked me for reportedly refusing to tie on a glove for less than one million dollars. In short, the New York I loved had slammed its sports doors on me once more.

My business manager, Gene Normile, told me not to worry, that everything would be straightened out in no time. But he was an optimist; it didn't look that way to me. Doc and I were barely on speaking terms now—but at least we were speaking, if indirectly. He still claimed his percentage, despite the blow-up, and main-tained a thin, irritating thread of communication between us.

Doc had tried to stage a Wills fight for me and had even

scheduled it for that September 4, but the damn thing kept blowing up in his face. Too many people were pulling in different directions. Tex, who admitted the fight would probably draw a million-dollar gate, refused to promote it. Teddy, advising me as best he could, was told by his friend, New York political boss Ed Flynn, to avoid a race controversy at all costs. Estelle, leaning on her Southern heritage, was browbeating me not to fight "that glass-jawed nigger"—which shocked me.

Rickard had placed Wills on the sidelines along with George Godfrey, whom some considered to be even better than Wills. He felt that Gene Tunney, a tough, scientific boxer who was rising fast, really deserved to have a crack at my title. Handsome, placid Tunney appealed tremendously to the crowd, and particularly to women and veterans of war, so Tex was convinced that a Dempsey–Tunney fight would prove the best combination. The more Tex talked about pitting Tunney against me, the less Teddy liked it; he said I'd laid off too long (three years) and that to get in the ring with Tunney would be the end of me. I ignored him and listened to Tex, who had all but sold me on the idea. As Teddy saw it, I could be the most pigheaded person he'd ever met, influenced by my wife, the movies and a fat life. I disagreed. What was a three-year layoff once I got myself in shape? He showed me statistics. I shoved them aside; I wasn't interested in statistics.

But Tex Rickard was, especially in Tunney's statistics, which were getting better all the time. (Tunney had stopped Tommy Gibbons in twelve rounds, where three years before it had taken me fifteen.) The State Athletic Commission, however, refused to let Rickard negotiate with Tunney because of my suspension, so Rickard launched an all-out war on the Commission, informing Commissioners George Brower, James A. Farley and William Muldoon that there was no changing his mind. It was Tunney, yes; Wills, no; and if they didn't like it, he'd take the fight elsewhere (here he was bluffing, since he lacked backing). Farley and Brower were stronger supporters of Harry Wills than was William Muldoon, who didn't approve of a mixed bout at all, like a number of Albany legislators who nevertheless went along with the Commission.

Newspapermen pounced on me, and Gene Fowler, who up to now had defended my position, expressed what he felt as well:

> It is harder to make a match with Mr. Dempsey than to ratify a treaty between the nations. He asks guarantees so vast as to preclude the name of warfare that he excels in. His most dangerous challenger he has avoided for five years, hesitating to risk a title that he capitalizes in the movies. Of such stuff Sullivan, Fitzsimmons, Corbett and Jackson were not made. Mr. Dempsey should relinquish his title or resume his profession by facing the "Patient Senegambian." Patrons of boxing approve the course of the New York State Athletic Commission, and it has at least "called" the champion.

As my theater and film activities were linked to my prestige as a champion boxer, I couldn't afford to be put in the position of the gladiator with the gates of the arena slammed shut. I knew if I took on Wills that tranquility would reign once more between myself and the New York State Athletic Commission. But no one would let me. So the ban remained while Tex Rickard tried to set his oiled wheels in motion.

Despite my troubles with the Athletic Commission, I found New York in the twenties the greatest place on earth. Broadway was a busy patchwork of ever-changing moods, colors and characters. It was a twenty-four-hour town, pulsating with people during the day and alive with blinking lights, laughter and action at night. It was a tough town and, Prohibition or no, it was so wet it was slippery. Jimmy Walker was the mayor, and he resembled a burning stick of dynamite. He was a walking magnet, a former songwriter turned politician who seemingly catered to and cared more about society's goings on than he did about City Hall. Nevertheless, he had the capability of making even the most insignificant issues seem important—no different from most mayors, I suppose, except that Walker kept his priorities prominent in the public eye.

He and I had a mutual friend in Billy Seeman, son of the White Rose Tea king, and Rube Goldberg's brother-in-law. We had both attended Mayor Walker's inauguration and were proud to call him our pal. Seeman's apartment over the Village's Pepper Pot was a popular gathering place (and watering hole) for Broadway mugs,

bootleggers, gangsters, Follies girls, models and the usual assort-
ment of newspapermen, politicians and drifters. They came and
went as though the clock had no hands. There seemed to be a party
every other night, and each gathering of notables was always more
impressive than the last. At least to me; I was still a pug even
though I was the champion. At Billy's the Beautiful People talked
and laughed more than I had ever imagined possible—about everything and everyone. I mingled, on two socially left feet, and absorbed as much as I could.

Seeman had a tremendous sense of social honor even though
he was a playboy. He'd never think of stealing anyone else's girl.
He didn't have to; he knew from the beginning exactly who was
going to be in his bed on any given night. His apartment was frequently loaned to friends for their miscellaneous adventures or mis-
adventures. Every time Walker used it, we'd wait with friends and
then breathe a sigh of relief when we knew he was safely back at
City Hall.

Staying with Billy in those days, when we weren't sitting in
"21", sure beat holing up in some hotel, since anyone who was
interested in finding me did so anyway. I had left Estelle in Hollywood to clear up some matters before she joined me. One morning
Seeman woke me up earlier than usual. My head still felt thick
from the party the night before as I heard him say, "There's an
ambitious young kid out here who's been assigned by his paper
to interview you. He's so jumpy you'd think he was about to interview Coolidge."

I put on my red bathrobe and walked into the breakfast
room where the kid was waiting, pad and pencil clutched in his
hands. He introduced himself as Ed Sullivan. He had been Jimmy
Sennett's assistant at the *New York Globe* before writing sports for
the *Graphic*. I asked him to sit down and he did, righting the chair
he had managed to turn over. I couldn't help grinning, and I told
him to take it easy. The kid seemed to have left his self-confidence
on the doorstep.

"Want some breakfast before we start, kid?"

"Um. No, thanks. I'll wait till you're done—if it's okay with you,
Champ."

I dug into a half grapefruit which rested on a bed of ice in a silver-trimmed crystal bowl. I had just about taken two spoonfuls when I felt the kid's staring. I looked up and saw Sullivan moving his eyes, with undivided attention, from the grapefruit to my mouth and back again with every spoonful.

"Say, you look pretty hungry to me. How about it?"

"Well, um. You see, Champ. I don't think . . ."

I guessed that Sullivan had probably never seen a grapefruit eaten in such a manner and that was why he'd refused to join me.

"Look here, kid. Try some, it's good. Just do as I do, it's not hard even if it sometimes attacks you with a squirt. Let me tell you something, pal. When I was your age I didn't even know that there were people who ate three square meals a day."

This broke the tension and put Sullivan at his ease. By the time the interview was over, he was so grateful it was embarrassing. Years later, when we became close, he confided that he'd almost fainted from fright on that first interview.

When Estelle joined me in New York we moved into a hotel. As Rickard's negotiations were stalled, Estelle and I made plans with theatrical agent Jack Wall for our Broadway debuts in *The Big Fight*. David Belasco was persuaded to become its director, and *The Big Fight* was scheduled to open at the Majestic. I got top billing and $1,250 a week. Estelle got $300 and second billing. She didn't like being second banana, but she figured she needed exposure, especially in the legitimate theater. She scored a small victory when she was admitted into Actors Equity as a full-fledged member while I had to settle for junior membership, which I found absurd, since I was one of the show's heaviest investors.

SAM H. HARRIS and ALBERT LEWIS present
JACK DEMPSEY
and
ESTELLE TAYLOR in
THE BIG FIGHT — a drama of New York life

Estelle was to play Shirley Moore, the heroine, while I was given the role of fighter Tiger Jack Dillon. She was so excited she threw out her corset and bobbed her hair. It meant everything to her. The story revolved around a champion who was tempted by a betting syndicate to throw the big fight for a cool million bucks. It was a typical fight play, set in a Times Square barber shop and a Madison Square arena, and it reminded many of *Ringside*, in which Tex Rickard had had an interest as one of the producers.

Rehearsals were worse than roadwork. I repeated scenes over and over again, trying to get them right. Belasco's stares unnerved me so much that I couldn't even read straight. I found myself dropping as much weight at this as when I was training. In the ring it's the unexpected that makes it interesting; on the stage you always know what's going to happen next. But we weren't sure when Belasco's explosions would occur. He was so impatient and exasperated with me that we feared he'd walk out and leave the show suspended. He shouted for me to speak up, he forbade me to jump around, to swing my arms or to back anyone into a corner. As far as he was concerned, I was the "concrete-laden star of the show."

Before opening in New York we took the play out of town. Word filtered back that I was terrible. We bombed in New Haven. I couldn't wait to hit Broadway and get the whole damn thing over with.

Black-tied stage folk, fight folk, society and bigwigs of all sorts crowded the Majestic Theater that night. Backstage, Belasco was a small, taut bundle of torn nerves, openly cursing at having associated himself with a prospective fiasco.

The curtain went up and the three acts progressed without a major hitch. I didn't think we were all that bad, but Belasco did. He reluctantly stepped forth and made a speech at the final curtain, saying how very gratifying it had been to work with me, that not only was I a great big boy, but I was the best actor ever to hold the heavyweight title. At the end of his speech he decided to make a grand exit by faking a faint and having me carry him off. His performance went over better than the play.

Gilbert W. Gabriel's was one of the first reviews to reach me that night:

They worked up Mr. Dempsey's first entrance with such hurrays and waving of face towels, I almost expected to see him bumping down the barber-shop steps in a golden chariot—like a Radames returning from the wars. He did . . . look exceedingly trim and well-pressed and somehow cute, almost like a cupid blown up to ten times natural size. Out of the upper regions where his head and shoulders reside piped a gentle rather wistful little voice, just the sort of voice that floats across City Hall Park when the newsies and the blackies gather for the spring beginning of the marble season. A voice out of gear with the formidable, fiercely bulging show of a peroneus longus digitorium in the massive limbs below.

It may have been this vocal paradox that Mr. Belasco had in mind when he referred in his curtain speech to Mr. Dempsey as "just a great big boy." It must have been made plain in rehearsals that our Jack would say such a thing as "You cut that out. I'll break your jaw" in precisely the grave, shakey treble the little boy uses in "Strange Interlude." And that you would find yourself wanting, for that voice's sake, to pat him on the head and feed him a peppermint stick instead of booting him on his gigantic gluteus maximus.

Miss Taylor of the movies must have given them a harder time to get ready. She is unfortunate enough to know how to act—badly. There are others and others well placed, for that final fracas in the prize ring, pretty nearly the most real and thrilling representation I've seen the stage obtain.

Though every full house will be a house that Jack built.

Reading Gabriel's review wasn't pleasant, but I wasn't depressed by it; it could have been much worse. Estelle, though, was livid. Here she was, a Hollywood star, and the only review she got was a bad two-liner. I was afraid she'd take it out on me—after all, I had received top billing as well as the larger salary—but she surprised me by taking it out on everyone else. The only one who managed to escape her wrath was Belasco himself, who had, with his final curtain speech, washed his hands of the entire production. The *Telegram*'s Heywood Broun was kinder to her:

> The role of the heroine is played by Estelle
> Taylor, favorably known to all motion picture fans.

It seemed to me that she gave an excellent performance. Her voice is somewhat lacking in variety. But
she was always spirited and at times also moving. . . .
It seems to me that it's no great shakes of a play,
but in many respects a rousing melodrama. . . .

I was not even the lukewarm toast of Broadway and the show
only lasted about eight weeks, during which time we didn't see
Belasco at all. He'd had it with the entire cast and was glad to be
rid of such a piece of tripe. By the end of the run I'd lost $80,000.

I was invited to breakfasts, lunches and dreadful after-hours
cocktail parties at which I had to stare into the same faces I'd
seen at breakfast or lunch. One threesome around town consisted
of Grantland Rice, Ring Lardner and Gene Fowler, founders and
dedicated directors of the exclusive Happy Morticians Club, which
met several times a week to discuss the intriguing aspects of death
and its aftereffects. Rice was the supreme fatalist; with Lardner
and Fowler he would sit around poking fun at death. The high
incidence of those dying slow and painful deaths from bad rotgut
gave them overabundant food for thought while they sat and
drank.

One day Gene invited me to join them. I was confronted by a
rambling Rice and a dour, intense Lardner, who immediately asked
for my thoughts on this prized subject. Not realizing the Happy
Morticians Club was one big satirical jest, I expounded seriously on
my views—whereupon Lardner turned to Gene and said that I'd
put a damper on the entire afternoon, that his time was too precious
for him to become depressed. So much for my one and only invitation! Privately, Gene told me that the Happy Morticians Club
and its interpretation of death were just poking fun at an absurd,
final voyage not unlike a safari into unknown territory. As far as
Rice was concerned, it was "nothing short of laughing at different
aspects of dying from a cut-rate point of view." As far as I was
concerned, they could keep their Happy Morticians Club to themselves—which they did.

Prohibition, and beating it, was the name of the game in New
York. A bottle of Scotch or gin could be bought on Broadway for
up to fifty bucks, depending on the brand and the bootlegger's

mood. Getting drunk was no longer a disgrace—it was a metropolitan pastime. Carrying a hip flask became as common as wearing a belt; it was as important to have booze on hand as it was to have cash. Bookies and some newpapermen couldn't get things done without it. Liquid commerce was one of the most successful enterprises around.

Clubs were big in New York. Among the favorites were El Morocco, Delmonico's, Owney Madden's Cotton Club, The Colony, Coq Rouge, Chapeau Rouge, the El Fay Club, "Legs" Diamond's Hotsy Totsy Club, "21", and Texas Guinan's 300 Club.

Tough Texas Guinan opened her club at midnight on New Year's Eve, 1926, with a "Hiya, Sucker!" Texas claimed responsibility for just about everything that happened after midnight. The paddy wagon became such a familiar sight that Texas greeted the uniformed boys by name and signed autographs for onlookers every time she was hauled in. Never held for very long, she would turn around and open another joint. The hoofers in her floor show were the best lookers in town. Harry Richman and Ruby Keeler gave great performances there. Big time operators, con men and their dolls were a permanent part of the decor. As far as Texas was concerned, they were okay. Society ladies who hung around with the Big Boys were labeled "debutramps" by Walter Winchell. Texas was a pretty smart dame; she greased all palms and took no chances. Nevertheless, she still kept getting busted.

During Prohibition, Federal agents never busted a joint until after they had paid for the bottle or the drink. Bouncers tried to keep their eyeballs peeled for the Feds, but they managed to slip in anyway. One young kid from Philly, Toots Shor, had just started on the job when an agent warned him of a raid. Shor pleaded with the guy, insisting the owners would accuse him of having blown the whistle. He was so convincing that the agent changed his mind —for the time being.

Most people could smell Federal prohibition agents two miles away. Most people, not me. Sitting in a speak with some pals one night, I was dared to give "that knucklehead who just walked in" a hotfoot. Giving the hotfoot was a specialty of mine, and I enthusiastically agreed. The guy waddled in, stood at the bar and ordered a drink. I edged in close to him, then dropped on all fours and stuffed matches into his shoes and lit them one by one. I could hear the snickers behind me. The guy turned to me as I straightened up.

"Do you smell something funny?"

"Naw," I said.

The shoe caught fire just as its owner, Izzy Einstein, notorious undercover prohibition agent now in disguise, was about to make an arrest. He glared at me and announced that I was under arrest for attempted obstruction of justice. The room was in absolute silence. (I could see the headlines: HEAVYWEIGHT CHAMP ARRESTED FOR SETTING PROHIBITION AGENT ON FIRE.) Luckily, Izzy Einstein relented and warned me, laughing now, never to do it again. His partner and associate, Moe Smith, walked in. Moe had at one time run a small fight club on the lower East Side. Izzy knew he'd enjoy meeting me. Did I, Izzy wanted to know, happen to have some more matches handy?

Moe Smith and Izzy Einstein were the best prohibition agents around—and probably the most notorious. They would use their own names and flash their badges when in disguise. They were feared, hated, admired and respected, all at the same time. Some barmen even hung Izzy's picture on the back of the bar to ingratiate themselves, as a precaution—or just for the hell of it.

24

Tunney, the New Champ

Those were days that flowed smoothly, one into the next. Estelle and I were very much in love, and she'd decided to put her own career aside so she could dedicate more time to me. It was good to have her on my side even though Louella Parsons insisted that Estelle and I just weren't suited for each other. Estelle didn't love me as much as I did her, Louella told me, I was only being used as a stepping stone.

Doc was starting to badmouth me more than ever, at the same time hitting me with lawsuits, threatening to attach just about everything that wasn't nailed down. Even Teddy started acting peculiarly and beefed about finances. Being on both sides wasn't easy for him, and I knew he wanted what was best for me. He felt that the one who wasn't getting an even break was me; I had gained too much weight, had slacked off on workouts and had gone to too many parties with Estelle. I reminded Teddy that I was still under suspension in New York State, and he reminded me that this had nothing to do with my not working out.

Rickard was becoming more and more impatient, so I took him aside and told him to go ahead and sign me up with Gene Tunney. Doc, learning what I'd told Tex, came to me one afternoon to inform me that he was still legally my manager and that he was working to set up a match with Wills. I told him that I was a free agent and that I didn't need him taking his cut anymore. The only way I'd keep him on a percentage would be if he agreed to take 33 percent.

"What're you, nuts or something? Who put you up to this, that wife of yours?"

"Listen, Doc, it's either 33 percent or nothing. What's it gonna be?"

He took nothing. From this point on, Doc Kearns fought against me twice as hard as he had fought for me. He resented the fact that I was thinking for myself and he kept insisting that Estelle was going to be the ruin of me yet. I tried to ignore him, but everywhere I turned I'd either be slapped with a subpoena or some strange lawyer would approach me with a deal. Crank calls woke us up during the night and my bank accounts were frozen.

On top of it all, Teddy Hayes and I split when Rickard announced that I would be fighting Gene Tunney in September. I tried to talk to him, but he was on Doc's side of the fence now, and there was nothing I could do about it. In time, Teddy slapped me with a suit as well. It seemed that if I stood still long enough the whole court system would pounce on me.

Through all these problems, I felt I was lucky to have Estelle by my side. I kept telling myself that other people were worse off, especially those who didn't have anyone to help them out of a jam. I talked with Damon Runyon about this, and he agreed wholeheartedly. I remember his telling me that the lonely people were the ones who added the real color to the city's streets, particularly between the hours of two and seven, when the real pulse of the city could be heard. Despite his being surrounded at all times, Runyon was one of those people.

Damon had come a long way since I'd first met him. Once a quiet midwestern reporter, he'd become a chronicler, a real man-about-town (as had Gene Fowler, now head of public relations for Madison Square Garden). Runyon was a swell dresser—to the point of obsession. He'd disappear several times a day just to change his clothes. Changing his shoes wasn't so easy; he had long, tender feet and his shoes had to be broken in before he could put them on. He asked me to break them in, but my size was wrong, so he asked Hype Igoe if he'd mind doing him this favor. Hype, who would have done just about anything for anyone, happily consented.

Runyon was pretty close to Walter Winchell; their friendship ended only with Damon's death some twenty years later. Between the two of them, they saw, heard and did just about everything— except play gin rummy. Long a favorite time-consumer in the fight camps, gin rummy was a source of amazement to Damon. He couldn't understand how we could talk and play at the same time. I tried to give him lessons, but he didn't pick it up until 1940.

Rickard's negotiations with Tunney came at the right time; I had invested in property and now faced getting rid of it because I wasn't working. With Doc on the warpath, Tex had to safeguard any money that wasn't tied down by Doc's writs of attachment. I knew that the Barbara Hotel and the Wilshire Apartments in Los Angeles were going to be on Doc's chopping block before long.

The Barbara Hotel had its share of semi-professional lobby sitters, the most permanent being an ex-wrestler turned popular actor, Bull Montana. He was fond of scaring people away just by snarling. He told some dame that the management had agreed to his making midnight visits to guests' rooms for the sake of good public relations.

Estelle hated to make the social rounds with my friends and preferred having her personal crowd in the house. I guess some of my pals were too rough for her; they usually had no time for compliments and delicate dames. Tom Mix, a former Texas Ranger, rodeo rider and fighter in the Boer War, was one friend who just couldn't tolerate the domestic life I was living. He'd never come to the house but ask me to meet him for lunch at Fox Studios instead. I'd originally met him in 1921 when he came to New York for the very first time since becoming a western star. In 1923, Mix had been my personal guest at the Gibbons fight. He was an impressive guy; watching him make Zane Grey's *Riders of the Purple Sage* with Warner Oland at Fox, I caught myself wishing I could be nonchalant and popular like him. His personal life was more exciting than his movies, and yet he remarked that he would gladly change places with me as long as it didn't include Estelle.

I suppose the grandest parties were William Randolph Hearst's, staged at his 400,000-acre San Simeon along the Pacific Coast. His invitations were so formal that accepting them was like embarking on a Great Adventure. Sometimes his mistress Marion Davies would be there, other times she wouldn't (though her name was usually mentioned). Marion was pretty and somewhat nervous, which caused her to stutter. Word had it that she hit the bottle when Hearst wasn't around. He was a nondrinker, with the exception of an occasional glass of Tokay at dinner. Booze was taboo at San Simeon; even the best-concealed flask was short-lived, for the servants carefully lifted it from unpacked suitcases.

Guests were met by private cars either at the railroad or at the private landing strip and taken to fancy bungalows where they'd be given cards informing them what time meals would be served and who would be sitting next to them—Estelle loved all the pomp while I agonized over what I might say to someone I didn't know. Luckily, Hearst loved the show business crowd, so it wasn't too bad. It would have been a terror to sit next to some foreign diplomat.

Hearst himself was gruff but nice. A candy fiend, he was about my height and weighed around 210. He was athletic, superstitious and an animal lover. Like me, he had a high-pitched voice; unlike me, no one snickered behind his back.

In New York Tex Rickard was having a hell of a time because of me and the still-raging Wills controversy. He'd even tried arranging a fight between Wills and a reluctant but willing Gene Tunney; then Wills demanded so much money that the whole thing had fallen through. Privately, Tex and others had begun referring to Wills as the "false alarm smoke." George Underwood of the *Telegram* was so fiery in his support of Wills that he incited other journalists to jump on his bandwagon and support the Commission's ruling.

When Tex announced that I'd probably be meeting Gene Tunney that fall in Yankee Stadium, pandemonium broke loose. The

Commission, furious, felt that Tex had socked them pretty low, so they met and decided to suspend his license as promoter. William Muldoon was just about the only one who supported Tex. As head of Madison Square Garden, Muldoon said, Rickard was within his legal rights to choose anyone he pleased with whom to conduct business. Tex naturally agreed with Muldoon and pulled back on Yankee Stadium as a proposed site. I didn't care where the bout was held, just so long as it was held.

Rickard had Tunney's verbal agreement, having met with Tunney and his personal advisor Bill McCabe in New York the year before. Billy Gibson, Tunney's manager, was absent from the meeting, but Tunney was so enthusiastic and so eager to meet me that it didn't matter. His word was his bond, and that was good enough for Tex.

Gene Normile and I made a date to meet Rickard in Fort Worth and discuss money. Normile prepared to negotiate for a $500,000 guarantee, 50 percent of everything over a million-dollar gate and 51 percent of the motion pictures (which still couldn't be transported across state lines). Rickard had just come back from Springfield, Illinois, where he'd gone to talk to the governor. Afraid Tunney wouldn't draw, he halfheartedly approached the governor about Wills because of the fuss his people were making in the courts. Governor Small wouldn't stand for a Dempsey–Wills fight and told Tex so in no uncertain terms: He was convinced there'd be a race riot before the first round was over because of the large black population in Chicago. So Rickard gave up bluffing with Wills and listened to Normile, who stated our terms for the Tunney fight.

"Lord, you're tougher than that so-and-so Kearns."

"There's nothing liberal about you either, Rickard. Just how much did you intend giving him?"

"A $450,000 guarantee."

I got up and went to the john, hardly able to suppress my laughter. I really hadn't thought I was going to get that kind of money, and there was Tex saying exactly what we wanted him to say. I eavesdropped.

"Well, Rickard, you're a gambler and so am I. Let me match you on something to see if Jack gets $450,000 or $500,000."

"Okay, Normile, forget it. He gets $475,000 guarantee and that's it!"

"Fine with us. Whaddya say, Jack?" I had just come back into the room grinning. We arranged to see Colonel John Phelan regarding a New York license. We figured that at worst we'd get turned down. Jim Farley and William Muldoon weren't present, but it was just as well. Normile went on the offensive almost immediately.

"Colonel, you're trying to force this man to take on Wills. Well, we signed this article and that article, and all we got to show for it is a bum check. We're not going to be bulldozed by a commission no matter what. If you don't give us a license to fight a New York man, an ex-soldier, an ex-marine, then by God, we'll go somewhere else and you all will be the losers."

"Well, Normile, you're not going to get the license."

"No? Well, let me tell you something. Colonel, I think it would be a good thing if you'd take whatever license you do have, throw it in the toilet and pull the chain. That's all!" And we walked out.

Normile suggested I hole up in Saratoga while he settled a few things in New York. I knew he was mad, but I also knew he was no match for the Commission. I went upstate and he stayed on at the Belmont Hotel with attorney Arthur Driscoll. Within a few days, a man from the license commission approached them.

"You'll never get the New York license unless—have you got twenty-five thousand?"

"Yes, I've got $250,000 in the bank, why?"

"Well, for $25,000 you can get Dempsey's license."

Normile blew his top, but good.

"If that's the way we have to get it, then we sure as hell don't want it. Go back and tell whoever sent you that we wouldn't even give twenty-five cents. Now, scram!"

Normile sent for Tex Rickard the next day.

"Rickard, I want you to transfer this fight out of New York or we're going home!"

Tex knew Normile had to be tough.

"Gene, they'll tar and feather me and run me out of New York if I take this fight away."

"Listen, Rickard. Do you want Dempsey to train right up to the time of the fight and then have no fight? You know the Philadelphia Centennial people want him."

"Let me see what I can do with the people in Philly. And don't say anything. Leave it to me," he said, smiling.

Before long, Gene Normile and Arthur Driscoll hurried up to Saratoga to bring me the good news. I jumped in the air. The fight in Philly was confirmed as far as we were concerned.

That night the press got wind that a story was about to break and were told to stick around. When Normile made the announcement, the writers rushed to the Saratoga Western Union telegraph office where there were seven or eight outlets to New York and only one operator. Hype Igoe, one of the first to get there, was beside himself and yelling, "I have to get this story to the *Journal* if it's the last thing I do!" And he did, with Normile's expert help in handling the wires, thanks to the days when he had been an operator in Butte, Montana.

I rushed back to Hollywood to let Estelle in on the good news. She wasn't as happy as I thought she would be. She'd always hated my being a fighter. Sure, I was a champion, but why did I still have to slug it out in the ring?

I had plenty of time—the rest of the summer—to get in shape, so I decided to start working out on the west coast. Jerry the Greek, who had accompanied me, agreed; he stuck to me like glue despite all the frustrations. Unfortunately, Estelle and he didn't get along. He would bring her candy boxes to pacify her. She felt that he was overanxious about my having laid off for three years. If I got myself back in shape, wasn't that all there was to it? Jerry argued that the layoff would affect my timing, my speed, my skills—and my confidence. He also thought (wrongly) that I'd be afraid of damaging my nose.

"My dear lady, there ain't no substitute for steady work."

"Jack knows what he's doing, just as he always did."

"But he's 31 years old now."

"Jerry, why don't you stick to training him and kindly stop talking so much?"

"Anything you say, ma'am."

I made her apologize to him that night. She might have hated the fight game and its supporting cast of characters, but she had to accept it because it paid for everything. She wasn't doing well in pictures, although she had just signed with Warner Brothers to do *Don Juan* opposite John Barrymore—impressive, sure, but the contract was for only one film. I reminded her that I had stopped collecting from Universal some time ago and that finances were becoming difficult because of Doc's lawsuits.

Seems that everyone I knew was involved in one kind of hassle or another. I suppose my pal Rudolph Valentino could have tied me in terms of being adored, resented, accepted and hated. Rudy and I had known each other from the time we were both with Universal. He was then making *Cobra*, for which he needed boxing lessons. I obliged. Valentino was an intelligent, oversensitive individual who allowed himself to be packaged by Hollywood and didn't like the result. With his slanted eyes, slick hair, good manners and European clothes, he seemed to be every woman's dream— including Estelle's. As far as she was concerned, he oozed charm from every pore. Naturally she ate it up when we became pals.

When we first met, we were both ladies' men. Well, he certainly was, and I thought I was. The big love of his life was the sultry actress Natacha Rambova, who hailed from Salt Lake City. He courted her and managed to persuade her to marry him, which proved to be the worst thing he ever did. She bossed him and everybody around him, and he didn't object. She interfered with his acting and with his films. He was a sap for dames—and no one knew that feeling better than I did. One day he sent Natacha to the French Riviera to visit her mother, who was married to Richard Hudnut. She never returned.

I accompanied him from party to party whenever he was in the mood. I remember him standing awkwardly alone at Pauline Frederick's house. The Hollywood social life bored him, and he found the majority of people he came in contact with shallow. Because of his aloofness, he became the butt of jokes among men who resented him on general principles.

We introduced him to every woman Estelle and I knew, as did his other friends, until he became socially active again. Eventually he and Pola Negri latched on to each other, and he seemed to be all right—until midsummer of 1926, when he was attacked by an editorial, "Pink Powder Puffs," in the *Chicago Sunday Tribune.* The article insinuated that Rudy was a homosexual and said, "Better a rule by masculine women than by effeminate men." It attacked the public's identification with sheiks, clothes and cosmetics. In short, the writer asked, if Valentino was the present day example of a real man, whatever happened to yesterday's?

Poor Rudy was boiling. Once more he felt victimized. He called me, asking me to stand by him whatever happened. I assured him I would and thought no more about it. Valentino felt that he was being attacked because he was a foreigner making a living courtesy the American dollar. America was strictly for Americans, was the way he saw it.

Valentino sent the *Tribune* writer a challenge to meet him, calling him a "contemptible coward." Then he sat and waited while all eyes focused on him.

In the meantime, Valentino persuaded me to call Buck O'Neil, sports writer and boxing authority at the *New York Evening Journal.* Buck was curious about Valentino and asked several leading questions which I can no longer recall, but I defended Valentino as best I could.

"Listen, O'Neil. Valentino's no sissy, believe me. In case you're interested, let me tell you he packs a pretty mean punch."

"Do me a favor, Jack, and cut the crap. I don't buy it and neither does anyone else. Tell you what I'm gonna do. Since the guy is in a spot, allow me to put him in his place once and for all. Tell him I'll take him on if he's willing."

Done. I coached Rudy, giving him every pointer I thought would help in his encounter with hefty Buck O'Neil, which was scheduled for the roof garden of the Ambassador Hotel. By the third round O'Neil admitted that Valentino was no slouch. Valentino floored him. (Many insisted it had been a lucky punch.)

Later, rubbing his jaw, O'Neil remarked, "Next time Jack Dempsey tells me something, I'll believe him!"

Valentino hightailed it to Chicago. He wanted to storm the *Tribune,* but I advised him to lay off or he'd have every photographer there on his back. So he telephoned and was transferred from department to department. No one knew anything about anything. He was wild and he called other newspapers and wire services, trying to smoke the writer out, without success.

He felt the damage had been done; now the public would always have its doubts regarding his masculinity. This incident, along with his mooning over Natacha, drove him to isolate himself from medical attention when he was stricken with peritonitis. Two months after the article's appearance in the *Chicago Tribune*, Rudolph Valentino was dead.

As the summer wore on, Gene Normile became increasingly agitated about the guarantee Rickard had promised us. We knew that Doc would try to collect it, to take his percentage before I had a chance to see the dough's color. It was starting to affect my nerves. Process servers haunted me, and by the time I got to my training camp in Atlantic City, Normile had made sure there were enough hired guards around for my protection.

Word reached me that Doc had said he was "licking me for Gene Tunney," figuring I'd be a wreck by fight time. He sued me for hundreds of thousands of dollars and even got a writ of attachment on the Rolls while Estelle was driving it in Atlantic City. She was forced to get out and walk back to camp, and by the time she got there she was out for Kearns's blood. This didn't help our marriage; Estelle was now complaining that she was feeling the brunt of my mistakes.

One day before the fight, Louella Parsons stopped by to see me. She told me I looked pale and sick, not at all like myself.

"Don't be ridiculous. I just haven't been in the sun."

"I don't believe you, Jack. Even Estelle's worried, and now that I see you . . ."

She looked around my cottage.

"Jack, it's like an arsenal in here with all those guns and things propped up against the wall. And those guards outside! Whatever for?"

I was fully aware that I had more retainers and bodyguards than I could count.

"Well, you see, I've been threatened. I've been out so long that

I guess I'm the perfect target for crackpots. This place is overrun with funny characters."

"So I've noticed." She paused and then asked, "Have you heard from Jack Kearns?"

"Indirectly. Louella, you wouldn't believe what I've been through."

"Yes, I would. That's really a shame. I know how it must be affecting you, and if there's anything I can do, don't hesitate . . ."

"Thanks a lot, Louella, but Doc was never afraid of pen and ink."

Normile decided to ask Rickard for our dough in advance. Rickard agreed. He could see that I was suffering from a dermatitis, brought on by nervous strain, that was causing my skin to crack open. Tex suggested postponing the fight, but I was dead set against it; too many tickets had already been sold and too many people were waiting. Besides, I felt confident I could lick Gene Tunney anyway.

I told Estelle to return to California; she wasn't helping me and was only afraid for me. I trained vigorously, working out every day and gulping down olive oil at night for my digestion. On the Saturday before the fight, a sheriff burst into Normile's West Atlantic City cottage with a warrant for my arrest. Normile and Henry Tobin, a notorious gambler, asked him who the hell wanted me. Addressing himself to Tobin, the sheriff said that he had a body judgment against me and nothing and no one was to stop him from hauling me in. Normile and Tobin didn't need to ask who was behind it.

"What, no bond?" Henry asked.

"Yeah, one hundred grand."

"Come back in two hours and we'll have it for you."

The sheriff reluctantly left and Henry made three calls. In one hour, the dough was in his hands. Normile didn't tell me about it until after the fight. By the time of the Tunney fight, Doc had served me with no less than seven injunctions.

Normile was now afraid to keep the guarantee Tex had advanced us. "I'm going to Philly to stash this dough in a box. You, Jerry and Trent [Mike Trent, my bodyguard] meet me there."

He left us while Jerry searched for Trent. No one had seen him or heard from him, so we decided to take the train to Philly the following day, September 23, without him. When we pulled into the Broad Street Station in Philly, I knew something was wrong, but I couldn't put my finger on it. I felt funny and queasy. Jerry was all over me, not knowing what to do. By the time the train had stopped, I felt my legs had turned to rubber. Jerry leaped off the train and ran toward Normile, who was waiting for us with a hired car.

"Mr. Normile, you better call the fight off!"

"For Chrissakes, why? What's the matter?"

"Look, over there!"

Normile turned in time to see me brace myself against a door. My eyes were shut and I felt fuzzy. It didn't register when he called me, nor did I recognize him.

Normile was worried. "What's the matter, Jack? What is it, kid?"

I opened my eyes and grinned weakly. "It's nothin' I can't lick. Just a funny feeling's all. Here. And here." I pointed to my belly and my head.

"Well, get in the car. Jerry, open those goddamn windows. Let's get some fresh air in here!"

We headed for the stadium, stopping several times so I could jump out and vomit my guts out. I was experiencing sickening heat waves and wondered how many more times I could be sick. I was empty inside and I ached. I tasted the bitter bile in my mouth.

Normile barked at the driver to stop in front of a drugstore. He got out and returned with several pieces of ice which he forced me to chew and swallow. I cursed him.

We finally pulled up to the sesquicentennial stadium, where Jerry and Normile helped me out of the car and held me up. It had started to drizzle. I couldn't stop from retching as I walked. Holding me under my armpits, Normile felt two egg-like lumps and noticed that I had broken out in a rash, but he didn't mention this to me.

I managed to make it up the steps to the dressing room. I

couldn't take off my street shoes for fear of falling down. In the dressing room a letter was handed to me, a beautiful letter filled with love and encouragement from Estelle, sent to me through Louella Parsons. The press jumped on it and asked me where Estelle was. I told them and showed them the letter to squelch rumors of a rift between us. Someone remarked that the letter was good publicity for Estelle Taylor. I ignored this; I was having enough trouble concentrating as it was. Nevertheless, I placed a call and told her to join me as soon as she could. She was having dinner with Jim Kilgallen and a guy named Kopelin Burg. "Darling, I told them to watch your seventh." Seventh? I'd be lucky to make it to the second, the way I was feeling.

Approximately 120,000 people made their way through the rain to see the fight that night, arriving by plane, taxi, train and private railroad car. Tunney had won his light-heavyweight title from Battling Levinsky and now, with 25 victories under his belt, he waited for me. Three-quarters of show business seemed to be there. Tom Mix had chartered a train to bring his friends and mine across the country to see the fight. Politicians were there, mayors, governors, policemen and the chief of police. Top businessmen and society folk found themselves among judges, who found themselves among gangsters.

It was raining pretty hard, and many satin gowns, pumps and hairdos were ruined by the mud. Rickard referred to this fight as the Battle of the Century and was pleased by the turnout. In a way it was his personal victory over all the legislators and commissioners who had squawked so much in New York and made his life so miserable.

I marched down the aisle toward the bright ring, accompanied by my handlers, trainers Gus Wilson and Jerry the Greek. Trent, my bodyguard, was still missing. All I heard was the sound of the rain drowning out the clicking of typewriters and the roar of the crowd. Lights aimed in my face and I sweated, knowing damn well I didn't have my former fighting spark. I knew that Doc was somewhere out there, among the many faces.

The ropes and the canvas were soaked. The rain had made

the air dull and heavy. Tunney followed me, wearing a bathrobe with the Marine insignia on the back. He calmly fixed his own bandages while I fidgeted. When we were introduced, the crowd thundered. Tunney was in fine shape and looked completely at ease, while I felt sick and nervous, half expecting a process server to pop up with another summons. From the time the bout started, I was aware that my body and brain weren't communicating properly. I was heavyfooted and sluggish and felt old with legs that seemed shot. Was this the penalty I had to pay for my layoff—or was it something else?

I knew Tunney was piling up points with every blow, but there seemed to be nothing I could do, though I tried. My handlers were hysterical, sensing I was going to lose the fight. Jerry the Greek shoved smelling salts under my nose and fanned me between rounds, but it didn't make much difference one way or another. Tunney was so scientific a boxer that all I seemed to be able to do was to take his punishment.

I remembered Doc's words, "Pull up your socks, smack the big bum down and let's get this thing over with, kid." Too late now. In the third and fourth rounds I thought my blows had slowed Gene down but I was wrong. I no longer had the resilience to absorb counterblows without letting them interfere with my attack.

What I needed was a lucky punch if I had any hope of keeping the title. One thing I knew for sure: He wasn't going to knock me out!

At the end of ten rounds, through puffy eyes and stinging rain, I saw Gene Tunney's glove being raised in victory. It was over.

I was disgusted with myself—and exhausted beyond belief. Gene Normile sent my congratulations to Tunney, wishing him the best of luck. Tex Rickard couldn't believe what had happened. I had been his number one drawing card and now I was out of the picture. What had been a dynamite threesome was now finished; Doc was managing Mickey Walker, I was a dethroned champion and Tex was out. Well, not for long, he told himself; all he needed was some time to think.

To my surprise, I was loudly cheered as I marched from

the ring, more than I had ever been cheered before. People were screaming, "Champ, Champ!" Could it be that the loss was really a victory? Tunney, the new champion, wasn't exactly crazy about the fight crowd, and he made no bones about it. In the fans' eyes, I was a dedicated pug who loved the fight game and all its grittiness. Maybe they had gotten used to me. Maybe it wasn't all that easy to push aside the love-hate relationship they had for me.

Newsmen crowded my dressing room, clamoring for an interview, a few words, a shot. Once I got to the hotel, Estelle managed to reach me by telephone, saying she'd be with me by morning and that she'd heard the news. I could hardly hear her because of the people crowding the phone.

"What happened, Ginsberg?" (That was her pet name for me.)

"Honey, I just forgot to duck."

The following morning Estelle arrived and was directed to my smoky hotel room, which was filled with the press. She wanted to be alone with me to comfort me, but it was impossible. I had just lost the title, I told her, and I was in a spot; all I could do was cut the interviews short.

"Why the hell did you ask me to join you? You don't need me here," she said, looking around fiercely. "You've got enough people around you. What can I do that they can't?"

"Estelle, try to understand, please. I've never turned the press away, and I'm not going to start now. Please be patient. It'll all be over in a while." She slammed the door as she walked out. I knew she'd be back as soon as she cooled off; I wanted her and I needed her, but my time at the moment was not my own. The last thing I wanted was to vanish from sight and be called a sore loser.

When the majority of the press boys had cleared out, Normile took Jerry the Greek aside. "When did this thing with Jack start?"

"Well, Mr. Gene, you see, it's this way. Every day when Jack is training, he takes some olive oil. Day before yesterday it seemed to make him sick. In the morning Mike Trent gave it to him."

At that point Trent walked in and Normile spun around at him. "Where the hell were you? Why weren't you on the train? You're being paid two hundred bucks a week to keep bums away from Dempsey!"

He said, "I missed the train and took the next one."

"What kind of crap are you giving me?" Normile shouted. "You weren't at the fight or in the dressing room! What the hell; I'll pay you off now."

Gene wrote out a check for $1,000 and handed it to him.

Mike grabbed the check and rushed out the door without saying another word. I looked at Normile and silently questioned him. He told me he was convinced that Trent had somehow been responsible for my illness before the fight. I wouldn't accept it; Mike Trent had been with me too long. So Gene told me that he'd managed that morning to trace two calls from the Ambassador Hotel to the Sherman, where Trent hung out. After the calls were made, the betting on Tunney was laid on even heavier. In fact, in Chicago on the morning of the fight, Frankie Pope and his friends bet half a million bucks on Tunney, causing the odds on me to fall from 3 to 1 (or 7 to 2) to 7 to 5. I didn't know what to think.

Normile wouldn't let things rest—managers never did when their men lost. I thought back to all the rumors in the Willard camp after his defeat; Normile was convinced that he smelled something rotten. Everyone he talked to put his two cents in, including Chicago newspaperman Westbrook Pegler and Gene Fowler. A lot of insinuating questions were asked and too many names were dropped, including Tunney's. That was the last straw. I told the three of them to shut their faces but it was like talking to the wind. They were real sore. Pegler wanted to dig through his files while Normile wanted to clear things up. Considering there was nothing to clear up they could go on forever. Jeez, they were getting on my nerves. It was all pretty outrageous. It was my own goddamn fault I had lost and that was that.

"You know, I wouldn't bet that some mobster didn't have anything to do with your getting sick."

"Listen, all of you, why don't you just lay off? I don't want to get mixed up in the sort of stuff you guys are talking about."

"Isn't that something? The Champ loses his title, and he loses his guts too."

"Will you please let it be and shut up!"

Pegler wasn't satisfied and neither were Normile and Fowler, but they decided to cool it off if that was what I wanted. I sensed I was being humored.

Estelle, meanwhile, felt that the rug had been pulled out from under her. She hadn't cared for the fight game or my friends, even when I was on top of the heap. Psychologically, she found my loss of the championship hard to accept, as did my dad. Mother, too, was sorely disappointed, but she felt that no title was worth the pain and punishment. She had been afraid and had prayed for me the full ten rounds.

Ring Lardner, among others, was reportedly distraught. His great passions in life were Notre Dame and me; he was from Indiana, and to him we represented the midwest. Now he had only Notre Dame left. He cringed at the thought of New Yorkers.

And everyone I ran into seemed to know exactly what had gone wrong.

25

The Long Count

It took a while for it to sink in that I had lost my title. Although I had been cheered on leaving the ring, the forty-eight hours following the Tunney fight were tough. Everyone was talking about me and Tunney, but once the press and the doctor who had changed my bandages had gone, no one but Estelle and Jerry the Greek came to see me. I felt like a forgotten man, an instant has-been. Once I called in some reporters who were standing around outside. They shuffled around awkwardly, no one knowing what to say, so I said it for them. I announced my retirement from the ring. No one believed me.

Tex sent a messenger with a note suggesting I go to California to recuperate. Estelle, Jerry and I packed our belongings and arrived at the Broad Street Station a half hour before the California train was scheduled to pull out. No one recognized me, not even the porter who carried our bags. I must have looked as if I had been run over. The solitary atmosphere of the station depressed me even though Estelle assured me that I was better off being left alone at this point.

We stopped briefly in Chicago, where I was interviewed by some reporters who had gotten word from Tex that we would be passing through. Even they seemed to want to get the interview over with so they could get on with other news. It was difficult to accept this change; I had gotten too used to being in the spotlight.

Leaving Chicago, we headed slowly for California and a private life. When we pulled into Hollywood, no one was more surprised than I was to see mobs jamming the station to greet me, accompanied by a big brass band. Everyone wanted to shake my hand and say a few words to me.

Back home, Estelle resumed her wilting career while I mulled over what to do with myself. Prodded by Estelle, I decided to become a businessman and got a realtor's license. We spent New Year's Eve in Tijuana with Joe Schenck, Baron Long, Gene Normile and others. It was a fun evening and champagne corks popped all night. It turned out to be one of the few occasions when I managed to stop thinking about myself. On New Year's Day, Estelle and I stopped to see the three-year-old gelding I had bought her, Old Kickapoo, named after the famous elixir peddled in vaudeville days.

When I wasn't pretending I was busy, Estelle and I would motor up and down the coast visiting friends. I dreaded the day we'd run out of welcoming friends. In the meantime, I was beginning to receive telegrams from Tex in New York, begging me to make a comeback. I ignored them. He knew I no longer needed the money, but he also knew that I was unhappy out of boxing. It was in my blood. He knew, as I knew, that I was just marking time.

I stopped by a gym in Los Angeles a few times a week, just to look around and work out lightly. I was afraid of getting fat and lazy. Every time Estelle picked me up at the gym, she wouldn't utter a word until we got home. She didn't approve of my hanging around the gym; it was low class, and she wanted me to stay out of the fight game, insisting that my brain would turn to mush if I didn't.

Around the end of January, we went to San Francisco to attend a dinner. On the way I stopped by the *Bulletin* to see my pal Scoop Gleeson, who took one look at me and told me my eyes were yellow and I looked lousy. I told him to quit being a doctor; I felt fine.

February found me KO'd in Hollywood Hospital suffering from blood poisoning. A Dr. Clark operated on my swollen arm and hand, draining the toxins, more times than I care to remember. My eyes were yellower than ever. I was convinced I was going to die because no one would tell me when I'd be discharged. Estelle, distraught, sat in the corridor crying on Jerry's shoulder whenever she wasn't in the room with me. I must have looked pretty bad. Jerry told me that people were speculating on what I'd come down with and were convinced I would never fight again. That first week I dropped about eighteen pounds.

By the end of the month, I was well enough to go home. Estelle played nurse to her invalid. Normile came to visit me, among others, and told me he'd had a minor run-in with Doc. Hype Igoe had begun to write Doc's story and apparently it contained plenty of low blows directed at me. Normile called Kearns and told him to lay off if he knew what was good for him. Kearns allegedly told him to drop dead and to mind his own goddamned business—to which Normile replied that he was doing just that. Further, he warned that if Doc didn't stop, he would produce certain distasteful records of an incident which had occurred some time back in Walla Walla.

"You wouldn't stoop so low, Normile."

"Try me. Listen, ya bum, I can fight as dirty as you, and don't you forget it."

Doc and Hype dropped the project.

Doc and I finally and formally dissolved our partnership in the spring of 1927. He took the Wilshire Apartments while I kept the Barbara Hotel. Doc's legal suits were left pending until they were ultimately settled out of court or dismissed.

Back home I was soon on my feet and looking over my interests, overseeing the Barbara Hotel and meeting with friends for a game of gin rummy or pinochle when I wasn't visiting the gym. At night Estelle and I stepped out.

One day Babe Ruth unexpectedly stopped by to visit. He had just finished making a movie and had some time on his hands while he was holding out for a better contract with the Yankees. What a guy—egg-shaped and boisterous, a connoisseur of booze, food and dames. He and I had met in 1921, and over the years we'd watched each other reap glory and publicity. Walking into the house, he stopped by the kitchen to fortify himself before coming out back to see me. He didn't mince words.

"Listen, Jack. You lost your crown while still on your feet. Sure it's tough, but don't you think you owe yourself and your fans one more crack?"

"No, Babe. I know when I'm through."

"Awright then, sit on your ass and feel sorry for yourself. You know, pal, it's guys like us who just can't back off from the spotlight. We're the ones who got to be at bat, trying for those friggin' home runs until we grind ourselves into the ground. Don't get me wrong. I love my game like you love yours, so don't give me any of your crap. The public is what keeps ya goin'. Look at me—I never felt better!"

"Babe, it's different. You ain't lost nothin'."

"Oh, no? Every time I walk up to home plate, I'm at zero. Zero. Know what that means?"

I'd lost him, but I sensed the point he was trying to make.

"People are asking where you're holin' up and what you're doin'. Pals of mine say that letters are pouring in to sports desks all around the country for you. And here you are, walkin' sideways and bumping into yourself, for Chrissakes."

"Babe, I don't know if I've still got it, see?"

"Well, goddamn it, you won't know till you get out there and try!"

He stayed for a while and we spoke of his homers, which were really getting up there. We also talked of other things when Estelle was out of earshot. Before dark he left, still glaring at me in case I hadn't heard him loud and clear.

Tex had stopped sending wires and started telephoning, word having reached him that I was busy but really didn't know what to do with myself.

"How you doin', boy?" he shouted over the wires. In all the years we knew each other, we always shouted long distance no matter how clear the connection.

"Just fine, Tex."

"You doin' any roadwork and training, or you just playing the Hollywood big shot out there?"

"I ain't doin' nothing special, Tex, but taking it easy."

"Thought so. How'd you like to meet Tunney again? It'd draw a pretty good gate, just like we like 'em, kid."

"Naw. I ain't interested. I'm through with the fight game, Tex. Over the hill, I guess."

"Well, maybe you're right, kid. Maybe Tunney's too tough for you. No one likes to get licked by the same guy twice."

Son of a gun! He was up to his old tricks.

"Wait a second, Tex. Tunney's not that tough. And I ain't no cream puff, you know. It's just that I'm kinda fat and out of condition."

"Well, tell you what, kid. Why don't you start training and we'll see what happens. Maybe I'll arrange for you to meet someone else before Tunney. That way you'll have a fight under your belt when you step into the ring. What do you say, Jack?"

"I'll try, Tex. I'll try."

Smart alligator.

I disappeared into the hills near Ojai, California, away from everybody and everything, including the telephone. Accompanying me were Jerry Luvadis, Gus Wilson, Jim Lyall and Race Horse Roberts. I stayed there six days a week, working like hell, coming home only on Sundays. Estelle, of course, continued to resent my training program. It was just for a little while, I assured her, just to see if I could get myself back in shape. Her friend Lupe Velez didn't help matters by telling Estelle that if I resumed my career, she might as well kiss hers good-bye.

I chopped trees for hours at a stretch, did calisthenics, raced against dogs, jumped rope, carried rocks and climbed trees. It wasn't just a matter of getting into shape, but of training hard to get rid of the flab. I weighed 227 pounds and I plugged away long after fight followers gave up on me. It appeared to be an impossible task, as I was racing against Tex Rickard's invisible clock. He was in New York, looking around for top contender material; I was out west, not knowing when I'd be called.

By June I had trimmed to 205 pounds, increased my roadwork to seven miles and was punching light and heavy sandbags. I moved to Soper's Ranch in the Ventura Mountains, where curious sports writers came to see me. Pretty soon they were writing about me again, but this time in terms of Gene Tunney's being the Champ.

The only sports writer I allowed to observe me at close range was Bob Edgren of the *New York World,* who a few years earlier had accompanied me on a moose hunt, along with Jerry the Greek, Marty Burke and my brother Joe. I felt that Bob had a good eye for boxing; he had been a pretty good amateur fighter himself. After spending three days with me, I could tell he liked what he saw. Returning to New York, he confirmed what I hoped, writing, "Jack Dempsey has come back."

By the time Tex called me from New York, I was ready and I was confident. I told him to go ahead and schedule a bout. I had hardly put down the phone when he called back to inform me that I was to fight Jack Sharkey, a former Navy man, in New York on July 21. He sure worked fast.

Sharkey had already beaten Harry Wills, finally eliminating him from top contender status. Sharkey was later to become champion, but he was determined to try for it now by eliminating me from the picture.

In a way I was thankful that 1927 was proving to be a full year for newsmakers. Around the second week in May, young Charles Lindbergh took off from Roosevelt Field, Long Island, bound for European shores in a small plane named the *Spirit of St. Louis.* Some thirty-two or thirty-three hours later he landed at Le Bourget airfield outside Paris, the first man to complete a transatlantic flight nonstop. We all stopped what we were doing, awed by his achievement. He was a real national hero. He shrank the world virtually overnight. From that moment on, Charles Lindbergh dominated the newspapers.

It was certainly some year. Shipwreck Kelly flagpole-sat for days on end and broke all records. Sacco and Vanzetti were scheduled to be executed, but I wasn't paying much attention, for I was attracted to the "success" stories rather than the "tragedies."

Was it my year as well? Depends which way I looked at it. My marriage was cracking up but my profession was on the mend once more. Rickard arranged for Leo P. Flynn to take over as my fight manager while Gene Normile tended strictly to business. I hadn't had any direct dealings with Leo Flynn since he'd been Bill Brennan's manager some years back, but Tex assured me that Leo was 100 percent reliable, and that's all that mattered. Leo was as tough as a drill sergeant. He was a master of strategy just as Doc had been. He told me what to do from the moment I got up till my head hit the pillow at night. I didn't mind; I needed it.

Estelle and I headed for New York, stopping off in Wilmington, Delaware, to spend the night at her mother's. Her mother had never been too taken with me, and I tolerated her as best I could for Estelle's sake. No use making waves; I had enough problems as it was.

We drove on to New York and checked into the Belmont, where Normile, along with attorney Arthur Driscoll and business-man Leonard Sacks, were waiting for me. I still had to obtain a license to fight in New York and to sign the final articles for the fight. While waiting for these matters to be cleared up, Estelle and I posed for publicity pictures on the hotel's roof till dusk.

Rickard called and said not to meet him in his office, which was swamped by the press. Instead, Sharkey and I were to meet in the Garden's ice skating rink. I arrived to find an overconfident Sharkey waiting for me. He was so cocksure that I avoided speaking to him. Of course, he had all the reason in the world to be confi-dent—I was making a comeback while he was on the climb. Leo told me to ignore him, that his overconfidence was probably go-ing to prove his weakness. I wasn't so sure; Sharkey looked pretty damn good.

After the meeting, Estelle and I, along with my usual entourage, left for Uncle Tom Luther's place on Saratoga Lake. It was just like old Firpo times: I trained till I thought I would drop. Estelle was pretty good about the whole thing. She had made a few friends, and this kept her out of the way. Flynn made me train in secret for a while until I dropped some more weight. Thousands of people were turned away from camp. Balding Tom Luther cried over how much it was costing him per day and complained about the headache the sports writers were giving him. He hadn't changed much either.

Sports writers said I looked good one day and slow the next.

It appeared I'd be going into the ring as an underdog for the first time since my fight with Jess Willard. Tunney's trainer Lou Fink dropped by to look me over and was unimpressed by my workouts. Flynn paid no attention and told Tex to come and see for himself. Speculation topped speculation once more.

While training, I received the shocking news that my brother Johnny had killed himself. He had been on hard drugs for quite a while, unable to kick the habit despite the numerous cures Teddy Hayes and I had arranged for him. In Hollywood he had become friendly with Wally Reid and moved in a fast crowd, spending money like a madman. I had introduced him to all sorts of people, and he felt that he was accepted as Johnny Dempsey—until he realized that in actuality he was only the Champ's brother. He told me to go screw myself, that he was going to be his own person. Now, in a dark moment of desperation, he had done away with himself. I left the training camp to make arrangements and to break the news to my mother and father.

On July 21, 84,000 persons poured through the gates at Yankee Stadium, creating the first million-dollar gate for a non-championship bout.

From the time we first stood in our respective corners, I could see Sharkey sneering. He unnerved me, but Leo kept telling me that if I remembered to keep boring in at his stomach, I'd be all right. He casually mentioned that Doc was sitting at ringside. About two weeks before the fight, Doc had supposedly wired a New York pal:

ARRIVE WEDNESDAY. WALKER READY TO SUBSTITUTE

IF COURTS PREVENT DEMPSEY FROM MEETING SHARKEY.

Sharkey piled up points throughout the fight. I realized I wasn't delivering as hard a punch as I used to, nor were my legs what they had been.

I drove home blows, but they didn't seem to have any effect on Sharkey. He sure was tough; I feared that each of his punches would be my last as he tore into me. By the start of the fifth round, he had me staggering—and believing that maybe old fighters never did come back.

Johnny Buckley, Sharkey's manager, fairly burst with exhilaration as he watched Sharkey pound me. But his fighter began to lose steam in the fifth.

The end came in the seventh round as the crowd, which included F.D.R. and Gene Tunney, stood and screamed. The seventh round was like the fifth except that Sharkey was now more aggressive. I shot in two low punches. Sharkey, instead of claiming foul, turned his head as if to complain to the referee, leaving himself wide open. I delivered a left to the jaw and he kissed the canvas. I was proclaimed the winner; Leo grinned from ear to ear. Buckley's face was dark as I helped Sharkey back to his corner.

Opinions were divided as to whether I had fouled or not. Some thought I had gone below the belt; others insisted that Sharkey wore his trunks high. Even when the fight film was shown in a closed session, the argument remained unsettled. I was convinced that I had won the fight fair and square and that Sharkey should never have dropped his hands to his sides. My left to the jaw was the blow that ended the fight, not the ones to the stomach.

Back in my dressing room, Tex informed me that Teddy Hayes had attached $62,000 of my Sharkey purse for alleged nonpayment of back salary. Knowing it would upset me, Rickard had accepted the summons and held on to it until after the fight.

We left for Wilmington the next day, stopping at Estelle's parents' house once more. Her grandmother, to whom she was very close, was seriously ill, and Estelle insisted on being at her side. Immense crowds gave me a rousing welcome in Wilmington, and that meant a great deal to me.

Nevertheless, those days were strained. Estelle seemed to be undergoing personal anguish, probably due to my return to the ring. She was snappish, nervous and demanding, so I kept my distance. I suggested that she might be better off in California, where she could get some medical advice. She agreed and took a westbound train the following morning. I left, too, but stopped to put in appearances in several major cities along the way. I was mobbed by well-wishers and protected by local police when things threatened to get out of hand. I was riding high again, and it was nothing short of glorious.

In New York, Tex Rickard negotiated the site of the second

Dempsey–Tunney fight. He had been approached by Massachusetts, Pennsylvania, Illinois, Nevada and, of course, New York. The more Commissioner James A. Farley pushed for New York, the more Tex balked. He was unwilling to accept the Commission's proposed $27.50 top ticket price when Chicago was offering $40. Besides, Tex felt there wasn't an arena in New York big enough to hold all the people he expected for his second Battle of the Century. Rumors flew as to which city would be picked. Everyone jumped into the act, including Doc, who said that no matter where the bout was held, he'd transfer his pending suits.

After much discussion and political maneuvering, Tex announced Chicago's Soldier Field as the site. Since it was required that the promoter be a state resident, Tex selected coal dealer George F. Getz for the position while he became "manager of affairs."

No sooner had Tex made the announcement than there was a shrill protest—recalling the old slacker charge—from the American Legion, who felt it was wrong to hold a prizefight in a stadium dedicated to the Great War's doughboys. No one paid attention—certainly not Tex, for whom business was business.

In Los Angeles people turned out en masse to greet me. Their enthusiasm was the keenest I had ever experienced; the railroad station seemed to be one track-to-track carpet of people.

When I got home I was dismayed to find that Estelle was worse. She appeared to be, according to her doctors, on the brink of a nervous collapse. She alternated between crying, laughing and sulking. As the weeks passed she seemed to improve, but I was never certain from one day to another. Deep down I hoped her problem wasn't me. Training for Tunney was out of the question until she was on the road to recovery. Estelle had always been somewhat delicate, and the last thing I wanted to do was leave her alone at the wrong time.

By August Tex had informed me he had well over a million dollars in advance ticket orders that had begun flooding his office three days after the Sharkey fight.

Estelle finally took hold of herself. She realized I wasn't doing either of us much good hanging around and she instructed the maid to pack our bags. We left for Chicago and on the way we stopped in Salt Lake to see my mother, who, for the occasion, invited my father to the house. The two of them were like the grasshopper and the ant, one putting everything away for a rainy day while the other fiddled continuously.

To avoid the crushing crowds in Chicago, we got off at the Oak Park station. I checked Estelle and a nurse into a suite of rooms at the Edgewater Beach Hotel on the North Side. Traveling had made her very pale, and she felt weak at the knees. She said she didn't plan to step out of the hotel unless it was urgent. I spent as many nights as I could with her before getting down to serious training, which was long overdue.

Leo P. Flynn and I stayed at Colonel Matt Winn's house near the Lincoln Fields Track where I trained. My training was off: some days I put everything I had into training, other days I slacked off. Word reached me that Tunney was training nonstop. Both Leo and I hoped he'd go stale, though we knew he wouldn't.

Until a few days before the fight, Estelle adamantly refused to watch me train. "The whole business is nauseating, including the people in it. If I weren't married to you, I'd have nothing to do with you." Nineteen twenty-seven was the year of the first "talkie" and Estelle was frantic over all her lost time.

In camp, Jerry the Greek appointed himself chief food and water tester on my behalf. He wasn't taking any chances (except with himself). As the days passed I found myself becoming increasingly jumpy and irritable. I read and digested every newspaper item written about me and frequently I made the mistake of believing what I read. I just couldn't relax. Even Flynn's know-it-all attitude started to get to me.

At first my workouts were open to the public on weekends with Leo charging fifty cents for parking privileges. One weekend 8,000 people showed up to watch me. In the crowd were hecklers who got out of hand, so Leo decided to keep the workouts private. A cut I had gotten over my eye in the Sharkey fight kept reopening and bleeding. I was afraid the damn thing would never heal.

When certain members of the press insinuated that Estelle

was sicker than I admitted, I begged her to attend some of my workouts. I didn't want anyone to think that my wife's condition was in any way responsible for my strange behavior and sporadic training schedule.

Finally I decided, along with Marty Burke, Dave Shade and Big Boy Paterson, to work out at night under lamps. It was the only way to stop the wild speculation.

Sports writers from all parts of the country invaded both my camp and Tunney's like locusts. On most days a number of them would show up suffering from mild hangovers. Even Runyon was flooding himself with liquids, averaging from twenty to thirty cups of coffee a day. He disliked Tunney ("too slick") and made no bones about it.

Scalpers, including Mike Jacobs, were getting as much as $125 per ticket. The only gripe we heard was from ticket holders who complained they had no idea where the seats were located. Tex had neglected to provide any sort of seating diagram.

Will Rogers and old-timer Jim Jeffries dropped by to see me and wish me luck. Babe Ruth sent me a telegram repeating the advice he had given me when he visited me in Hollywood.

Lawsuits followed both Tunney and me to Chicago. Boo Boo Hoff and New York sportsman Tim Mara loudly claimed that they were due a percentage of Tunney's purse, while a certain B. E. Clements, claiming that he was the possessor of the ill-fated Dempsey–Wills contract signed some time before, was after me with an injunction to stop the fight. I hated going to court to protest the injunction, but I had no choice. A few days later Clements's case was thrown out of court.

Rickard had insured Tunney and me for $100,000 each, even though we were both in perfect physical shape according to the State Athletic Commission physician, Dr. Joseph L. Russell.

A few days before the fight my father showed up at camp and had trouble getting in because no one recognized him. Still calling me Harry, he was told he was in the wrong place. By the time he had convinced whoever was standing guard that he was my father, he was hog wild.

By September 22, I felt I was in far better shape than I had been in Philly. I was stronger, sharper and more confident. No doubt Tunney felt the same way. He'd been guaranteed close to $1,000,000 for the fight—the largest fight guarantee ever paid—while I'd been guaranteed $450,000. I thought Leo had sold me out; he was getting into the habit of making decisions without consulting me. I didn't like it, and I swore to myself that if I won the fight I'd ease Leo out of the picture.

Chicago's Al Capone, to whom I was still The Hero, let the word out that he had enough dough and influence spread around to make sure I would win. Not wanting Scarface to do anything I might regret, I sent him a short handwritten note asking him to lay off and let the fight go on in true sportsmanship. If I beat Tunney, or Tunney beat me, it would only prove who really deserved to be champion. I didn't hear a word in reply, but the next day Estelle received what must have been two hundred dollars' worth of flowers, with a card signed simply, "To the Dempseys, in the name of sportsmanship."

A story made the rounds that Tunney had sent one of his bodyguards to see Capone. He allegedly told Big Al that Tunney was in tip-top shape and suggested that Capone not lean too much toward me. Capone dismissed him.

Just before the start of the fight, there was a last-minute substitution of referees. Dave Miller had originally been selected, but according to a well-connected source, "he was allegedly, while in a Loop restaurant, approached by a few shady characters." Dave was soon made aware of just who "the boss" was. Whatever happened, referee Dave Barry stepped in at the last minute; Miller no longer wanted any part of the bout.

Estelle stayed put in her hotel room during the fight. Later her nurse informed me that she'd locked herself in the bathroom for the first few rounds and stayed there until begged to come out and listen. She collapsed on hearing the decision.

Chicago was jampacked for the event. Extra trains had been put on, and no one was allowed to get near Soldier Field without producing a ticket. Some insisted that two million dollars had been bet in New York alone, with Tunney fluctuating between slight favorite and even money.

People from Rio to Australia waited anxiously for Graham McNamee's fight broadcast. Ringside resembled an opening night. Among the notables were David Belasco, John Ringling, George M. Cohan, Doug Fairbanks, Tom Mix, Mrs. Vincent Astor, James A. Farley, Irving Berlin, Clarence H. Mackay, Doc Kearns and One-Eyed Connolly, the well-known gate-crasher, who'd been expected.

Sports writers included John Kieran, Paul Gallico, Bob Edgren, Gene Fowler, Scoop Gleeson, Nat Fleischer, George Underwood, Ring Lardner, Hype Igoe, Grantland Rice, Westbrook Pegler, Walter Winchell and Damon Runyon. There were countless photographers on hand. And, as at the Carpentier fight, thousands of ushers, assistant ushers, cops, fire brigades, ambulances, nurses and those in charge of Lost and Found were on hand as well.

By fight time the gate had reached $2,658,660—the first two-million-dollar gate.

Our hands were bandaged in our respective dressing rooms with representatives from the rival camp looking on. When it was time, I marched down the aisle toward the ring, accompanied by Leo, Jerry, Gus, Billy Duffy and Joe Benjamin. I wore black trunks and my old worn robe for luck.

Tunney followed a few minutes later wearing white trunks and his Marine robe, accompanied by Jimmy Bronson, Billy Gibson, Lou Brix and Lou Fink.

Joe Humphreys was the announcer. The judges were announced and then Dave Barry called us to the center of the ring.

"Both you boys have received a book of rules of this boxing commission. They are the rules under which you are going to fight. They have been discussed by your representatives for several days at the commission.

"Now I want to get one point clear. In the event of a knockdown, the man scoring the knockdown will go to the farthest neutral corner. Is that clear?"

We nodded.

He continued, "In the event of a knockdown, unless the boy

scoring it goes to the farthest neutral corner, I will not begin the count. When I tell you to break, I want you to break clean. . . ."

He stepped back. "Now shake hands and come out fighting."

I never should have stepped into the ring that night. From the beginning Gene Tunney held the advantage, even though I was grimly determined to win back my title. He had me staggering and leaning against the ropes by the second round. By the third and fourth rounds I was in a bad way, weary and bleeding. I felt flat-footed and I found I was having difficulty breathing. But I wouldn't give up for anything.

Round seven was the round that made the fight, the round I shall never forget simply because it created more than fifty years of controversy. A powerful right followed by a left hook and then by more blows sent Tunney to the canvas with a look of bewilderment on his face.

I forgot the rules. I lost my head and couldn't move as Referee Barry shouted, "Get to a neutral corner!"

I stayed put. The count had already started when I was pushed toward a neutral corner, already having lost valuable seconds. I was the jungle fighter so completely set in my ways I couldn't accept new conditions. I was used to standing over my opponents to make sure that when I pounded them down, they stayed down.

The count stopped and started again at one. At nine, Tunney was up. He then pedaled around the ring, keeping out of my exhausted reach.

"Come on and fight," I told him.

In the eighth round, Tunney was himself and I was floored for the count of one. Round nine saw me staggering to the ropes again, a battered, bloody mess. I could taste my warm blood and my eye throbbed with pain.

When the bell finally sounded at the end of round ten and Gene Tunney was again proclaimed champion, I realized that the time had come to hang up my gloves and leave the ring. I was thirty-two years old, but I felt a hell of a lot older.

The controversy started the minute the fight was over. Some said the actual count in the seventh round had been fourteen;

others insisted that their stopwatches had registered seventeen or eighteen. The question most asked was whether Tunney could have gotten up or not on the first count. I may be prejudiced, but at the time I didn't think he could have.

Now it no longer mattered. Tunney had gotten up and he had beaten me, and that was that. It was the damnedest, most sickening defeat I had ever experienced. I couldn't get out of Chicago soon enough.

26

A Friend Dies–A Marriage Ends

Tunney proved to be a gentleman champion. While he wasn't too crazy about me, he still gave me credit for getting him his million. Actually the purse amounted to $990,445.54, but by giving Rickard his personal check for the difference, he got his million-dollar check. Despite his being the title holder, our names were intertwined for many years. I don't know whether he liked it, or for that matter whether he even cared, but the controversy did keep our names alive for a long time.

Tex was eager for a third battle, insisting he could get me a million-dollar guarantee as well, but I wasn't interested. I was afraid for my eye, having been told that if it was damaged again, it would lead to a permanent impairment and maybe blindness. Tex felt that my retirement was equivalent to a million-dollar loss in gate receipts. He had lost his champion and was now surrounded by many new faces without names. Writers, sensing the loss, tried to generate enthusiasm for the lighter fighting classes. It didn't work. Undaunted, Tex attempted to cash in by investing in motion pictures. He lost a bundle.

Gene Tunney retired shortly after I did, suggesting that his place at the top of the heavyweight division be filled through a competition governed by a board.

The period following the Tunney fight was a comparatively

peaceful one for Estelle and me. The country was in a state of boom: Everyone seemed to have been struck with real estate fever, including me. I sold the Barbara Hotel (valued at $651,000), bought 286 acres of grape land in the San Joaquin Valley and obtained a substantial interest in the Tijuana Jockey Club, which made me partners with Baron Long, promoter James W. Coffroth and Gene Normile, a racetrack man at heart. Normile was still my business manager, but Estelle accused him of acting as my promoter and manager. I reminded her that he, of all people, had nothing whatsoever to gain from me.

I realized that my marriage left something to be desired when we found ourselves in a situation which almost cost us our lives. Estelle and I were having dinner at the American-Russian Eagle Club on Sunset Boulevard, entertaining some friends toward the rear of the room. Nearby Charlie Chaplin was toasting Lily Damita as his guest of honor. Among the other diners that night were the Marquis de La Falaise de la Coudray (Gloria Swanson's husband), directors Harry Crocker and Eddie Sutherland, Colleen Moore, John McCormack and Richard Dix.

The unexpected came when Chaplin, Crocker and I noticed smoke rising through the floorboards near the cloakroom. We immediately alerted the others, and with a minimum of panic we all rushed out into the street, while the owner tried to salvage whatever he could despite our beseeching him to leave. Chaplin found a garden hose and aimed the spray of water, but it was too late. Within seconds a gas leak had generated an explosion which blew the building to bits, leaving us stunned and shaken. The owner was the most serious casualty.

My heart pounding, I turned to Estelle to make sure she was all right. We had missed death by seconds, but she was worried only about her appearance, her face, her clothes, etc. I remember telling myself that I was probably being unreasonable, but a funny feeling stayed with me.

Estelle was no longer the girl I had fallen in love with. She quarreled with some of her best friends and attached herself to new ones. When I was out of town or involved in some tour, she would be seen at the Embassy, the Ambassador or the Roosevelt.

Frivolous and laughing up a storm, she always made sure she was chaperoned by married couples. Through her biting wit and sarcasm she began to alienate many people who knew us both.

One day Tex Rickard asked me to become his partner. I was deeply honored—after all, I *was* a former pork-and-beaner—and we shook hands. He had certainly come a long way since his first promotion some twenty-odd years before in Goldfield. And I always felt that, despite his being exceptionally shrewd and able to size up a situation at a glance, he was also a sucker like me, not able to pass up a "good deal." I guess we were good for each other, in a moderating sort of way. I could take Rickard's word for just about anything.

In December Tex and I, accompanied by his wife, Maxine, and their small daughter, went to Miami, Florida, to promote the Sharkey–Stribling fight. On the way, Tex tried to persuade me to fight the winner. I wouldn't say yes, I wouldn't say no. In Miami he was bombarded with every proposition one could think of, including the creation of a fabulous gambling casino complex with attached racetrack, hotel, marina and sports stadium.

Friends and acquaintances poured in from all over, stopping off in Havana along the way. The Sharkey–Stribling fight had a shaky financial foundation, but Tex wasn't worried. All he needed to do was to sober up some of the sports writers.

On the morning of January 2, his birthday, Tex complained of nausea and a constant pain in his belly. He said he'd been feeling poorly all night but hadn't wanted to disturb us. Maxine called a local physician, who informed Tex that all he had was heartburn or indigestion. So he popped as many antacids as he could find, but the pain didn't stop. Toward afternoon he developed a high fever, and we rushed him to the hospital. Within the hour we were informed that Rickard was gravely ill with complications of peritonitis. He took it calmly and announced solemnly that he figured the odds to be about fifty-fifty. I smiled, but I knew perfectly well he was mistaken. His fever was so high he saturated the bedsheets. The only thing Tex would allow me to do was to keep people away.

On January 4, someone told me that one of the Mayo brothers

was in Havana attending a convention. I got in touch with him and begged him to come to Miami to help Tex. I was willing to pay any amount of money he asked. He gently refused, saying that Tex was no doubt getting top-notch medical attention and that he couldn't do anything more than what was being done already.

I stayed at Tex's bedside for hours on end, desperately afraid he might die alone. He looked so waxen, so drained. Every time I looked at him my heart jumped to my throat. I couldn't eat, I couldn't sleep. The only thing I could do was to try to make him smile.

He reminded me of the time he had first seen me, and chuckled. He told me that I had made him proud through the years, that he was glad he had helped to make boxing respectable. "I still remember the fight with Carpentier as if it was yesterday. You know, Jack, your confidence and mine was the spit that held that darned wooden stadium up." He said I had been more than a son to him— and that did it. When he saw me fighting back my tears, he told me to get out and not come back until I got hold of myself.

Another day he spoke of Gene Fowler, who had handled publicity for him beginning in 1927. Gene had warned Tex that he was an easy touch and that it would show on the expense account. Tex had told him not to worry. One day his accountant, John Chapman, asked where Fowler's vouchers were, only to be told that Fowler was too important for vouchers. A few months earlier, Gene had suggested that Tex take out insurance for $1,000,000, but Tex told him to keep his insurance ideas to himself.

"The minute you insure yourself for a large amount, you croak. No thanks."

On January 6, 1929, Tex Rickard died as I held his hand. I wept like a kid. There was no way I could stop the tears streaming down my face. I bowed my head so no one could look into my face. I reluctantly let go of our last handshake and attempted to comfort Maxine. We hurt, remembering the brighter days as we cried for ourselves.

Tex Rickard, a gambler throughout his life, had made the mistake of gambling with his health—and lost his life. Many thought he'd died leaving millions; others were convinced he had left nothing. Whatever his estate, he had left millions of priceless memories.

Maxine and I made the necessary arrangements for the funeral, which took place in New York. Tex lay in state in Madison Square Garden, where the ring usually stood, while thousands upon thousands of mourners filed past. I choked the Garden with flowers and was last to leave, reflecting on the Tex I had known and loved. I thought, too, about Doc; the three of us had been a powerful combination, and I wondered if each of us hadn't been the catalyst for the others. Could any of us have reached the top without the other? I would never know the answer. All I knew was that I had lost my best friend.

Some wags remarked that it really didn't matter whether Tex went to heaven or hell; he'd probably wind up promoting a match with the other side anyway.

William F. Carey, the head of Madison Square Garden, insisted I carry on with the promotion of the Sharkey–Stribling fight in Miami. For Tex's sake, and in his memory, I agreed. Many were surprised when we turned a potential disaster into a profit. We even managed to donate $5,000 to some charity. In the month before the fight, Carey and Nat Fleischer, who were in charge of publicity and accounts, spent money hand over fist and ran up a $40,000 publicity bill. Prohibition was ten years old and still with us, but that didn't stop the 480 visiting newspapermen from downing $32,000 worth of booze. Even Al Capone dropped by to see how things were going; he'd bet on Sharkey and wanted to be there to collect. He threw a party for the sports writers, and I remember remarking to Fleischer that Capone's tips probably equaled our expenditures.

Now that I was a full-fledged promoter I found that managers were asking outrageous sums for their fighters. At the same time, big money had begun to get tight. Fabulous purses had become a thing of the past.

As a promoter, I became a target of crackpots and publicity seekers; I started to get crank calls and wild letters. Once the Sharkey–Stribling fight was over, fellow promoter Floyd Fitzsimmons and I accepted an invitation from Morris Hotel owner Harry

Moir to stay at his beach house. There Floyd and I experienced what seemed like a bad dream. As we were sleeping, a gunman entered the room, aimed his .38 and fired. The bullet missed me and embedded itself in a wall about three feet from my bed. I feared for my life, expecting to be kidnapped and held for ransom. Luckily, the gunman became scared and fled. From then on I slept with a gun tucked underneath my pillow. (While the incident had been very real, some people accused press agent Steve Hannagan of having staged a publicity stunt.)

In California, Estelle was steaming over my constantly making the news. She felt that because of me and "my friends" we were forced to live under a magnifying glass for all the world to see and, worst of all, judge. She was a social climber who found she was having a terrible time of it even though I was basically out of the fight game. Our communication left much to be desired, and we started leading separate social lives, at the same time denying all rumors of our difficulties.

Because I was traveling more Estelle got the idea that I was deceiving her and tried unsuccessfully to pin the goods on me. I kept reassuring her that I loved only her and wasn't interested in anyone else. But her suspicions flared as her friend Lupe Velez pitted her against me more and more. The reason for Lupe's disaffection for me was obvious: I had taken her out several times before meeting Estelle. I had liked her, but I realized we would never be good for each other, so I stopped calling her. Later I learned that she never forgave me.

By spring my marriage was in a shambles, thanks in part to a story in the New York papers. I was in New York attending a dinner. Afterward I decided to drop by the Fifth Avenue hotel where Gene Normile was staying. Normile was pleased to see me and told me to stick around awhile; he made a few calls and we talked. He mentioned that Joe Benjamin, who was hurting financially, had approached him for a loan a few days before. Normile had refused him, saying that times were tough for everyone, and Joe had stormed off.

While we were talking, Benjamin unexpectedly burst into

Gene's room, accompanied by two gorgeous girls. I had never seen either one of them before. He was loaded and was surprised to see me there. Mustering his courage, he called me a cheap bastard and said I had told Normile not to give him any dough. He yelled that I was nothing but a glorified bum, washed up, through.

Then he began taking swings at me and missing, which frustrated him even more. I tried to get him into a chair, but he resisted, calling me every name in the book. He swung again as I shoved him toward a door. He reeled, tripped over a chair and landed hard against the door, knocking it off its hinges. This awakened some guy next door who immediately called the manager, who then got in touch with the police. When the police learned who was involved, they rang up the press. The following day the headline read: DEMP-SEY AND BENJAMIN IN FIST BATTLE OVER CHORUS BEAUTY.

Joe accused me of catching him off guard. He said I'd been loaded and had made nasty cracks to the two girls he had come in with, being especially abusive to Agnes O'Loughlin, whose mother grabbed a fair share of the publicity as well. Agnes was a dancer with the Whoopee Show, and Mrs. O'Loughlin told the press that I had been a frequent visitor at Agnes's apartment when I wasn't sending flowers to the dressing room.

Estelle was swamped by reporters almost immediately: "Are you and the champ through?" "Did you have any idea he was seeing someone else?" "Has he ever fought over a dame before?"

She remained cool as she answered, "I don't expect him to be alone in New York."

I called her to explain, but it didn't help; I couldn't move her. She gave me hell, saying that I had made a fool of her.

"But, honey, I'm the goat in this. Please try to understand."

"No." She hung up.

Everyone was on my back and I was mad at Joe for doing this to me. The incident marked another downward notch in an already shaky marriage. The more I reflected on our situation, the more I realized that Estelle was grasping at straws. She was getting tired of me as well as growing out of love with me. And I couldn't accept it. It was good that I could keep busy; otherwise I'd have gone crazy.

Economically, I was pretty healthy that year, as was the rest of the country. Experts had prophesied that 1929 would be a good year, and they seemed to be right. Prosperity was growing by leaps and bounds. Attorney Arthur Driscoll suggested I continue with my land investments and acquire some stock as well. Advisors persuaded me to buy on margin. This fascinated me; I didn't have to lay out the entire sum until a profit was realized, which was all right with me. After all, it was a bull market, wasn't it? Seemed to me that most people were buying everything on credit.

Despite the fact that I was somewhat short on cash, I figured that all my investments would pay off within the year.

Several men approached me to become a partner in a million-dollar resort that was being planned for Ensenada Bay in Baja California, to be called Playa Ensenada. The Mexican resort was to have a casino, clubhouses, golf courses, beach and a one-mile pier. It reminded me of the Miami resort Tex had had in mind before he died. I thought the idea was a grand one; critics called it wasteful pretentiousness. I helped obtain a twenty-year concession from the Mexican government and we were on our way.

Late in September, Arthur Driscoll sensed something was wrong. He had stood by me in all my investments, but now he told me to halt everything. Sky-high prices had started tumbling, and he feared I was about to be wiped out. By October, like everyone else, I was unsuccessfully attempting to unload stock. Money was making its way down the drain while we all watched in horror. Arthur told me to hold on to my land investments no matter what, even though I was starting to hurt for liquid cash.

Between the economy's doing a swan dive, my almost worthless marriage and my shaky investments, I had my hands full. I even tried gambling, but it wasn't for me. On top of it all, I was suspended by Actors Equity Association on charges of disloyalty in Equity's attempts to extend its sway over sound pictures.

The New Year bombed its way into my life, wiping me out of approximately three million dollars—and the end was nowhere in sight. I blamed Herbert Hoover for my own miscalculations.

As bad as things were, Estelle and I had it worse. She wouldn't be home when I called, and when I was home we argued over my gambling losses in Agua Caliente. She even accused me of having something up my sleeve every time I stopped in Reno to look over my mining interests. The scenes, with their constant repetitions and tirades, became so bad that I hoped I could reach the point of not giving a damn.

As the days and weeks wore on, Estelle chipped away at me unmercifully, refusing even to sleep with me for one reason or another. I felt like laughing and crying both as I stared at the living room ceiling night after night.

Valentine's Day rolled around and I loaded up with presents —anything to win her over again. It seemed to work; she let me into her bed again. One morning, a couple of weeks later, Estelle woke up and nudged me. I moved closer. She looked me straight in the eye and said, "I've had it. Get out of my life and stay out. I want a divorce."

My heart stopped. I couldn't believe what I'd heard. Divorce? I tried reasoning with her, begging her to reconsider.

"Talk to my lawyers. I'm tired of putting my life on everyone's doorstep. Leave me alone."

I moved into a hotel.

Luckily, I was kept occupied by the Playa Ensenada Hotel and Casino, which finally opened that year to the strains of Xavier Cugat's dance band. Friends and associates from the United States and Europe arrived in private planes, and within a short time the aircraft were greedily vying for space on the new landing field. In addition to the hotel and casino, we planned a steamship company, the Liberty Line, which would run ships from San Diego and Los Angeles harbors to Ensenada.

But by the third week in December we found ourselves in financial hot water. The fabulous resort had already run up expenses of some two million dollars—and was still escalating—while merchants, hit by hard times, presented their bills and demanded to be paid. Despite our grand plans, I realized we were conducting business on a gold-plated shoestring at a time when the showy affluence of the twenties was on its way out. It was only a matter of time, and we all knew it.

The depression, which despite its severity had only begun, had both visible and invisible effects. Everyone was talking about the nine-day, twenty-hour round-the-world trip of the Zeppelin, while we all tightened our belts. My mother dipped into her rainy day savings, hating the very thought of doing so, while my father announced he had obtained a license to marry a certain Hannah Lyle Chapman. He was now 73 years old; the prospective bride pushed 83. I began to wonder about him.

I found it hard to be in the same state with Estelle, as I didn't want to bump into her accidentally. She was out for my hide, and for the first time in my life I had trouble fighting back. Rather than stay in a hotel, I rented a house in Reno, where I had mining interests. I started taking out various women, whereupon the press predicted that each one would shortly become my fiancée. This didn't do my divorce plans or my privacy any good. About a month or so after my arrival, the *Los Angeles Examiner* proclaimed:

> JACK DEMPSEY TO MEET ALL COMERS IN RING
> Reno, Nev., August, 4—Jack Dempsey will be
> back in the prizefight ring within the next three weeks.

They weren't far wrong. I needed money (as everyone else did) despite the trust fund I was unable to touch. In the back of my mind I hoped to make a comeback and to challenge Max Schmeling for the title. Leonard Sacks, who had taken over as my manager, arranged an exhibition tour for me. I boxed forty-two opponents in thirteen cities over a period of thirty days, which earned me over a quarter of a million dollars. It wasn't easy money, though; I was older and I found what I was doing somewhat humiliating. On August 31, in Spokane, Washington, I met five opponents who managed to last some eleven minutes, eighteen seconds over six scheduled rounds. One month later in Idaho, approximately six thousand people showed up to see me put away five more opponents who didn't last much longer than those in Spokane. By the end of the year I had added thirty-one more wipe-outs to my list.

In Spokane both Leonard and I were pleased with my progress. Leonard went on record saying, "I'm positively convinced that by going into training with the right sparring partners, Jack could be ready in six weeks to fight as well as he ever did in his life."

In addition to staging exhibitions, I refereed fights whenever I could. Leonard and I maintained an office in Chicago. One day Iowan promoter Red Henaghan marched into the office, slumped into a chair and started beefing about how lousy business was. He had just blown a bundle and now he was in our office to find out if I'd be willing to help him out by refereeing a bout in Iowa. He felt I was still enough of an attraction to help him get back the dough he had lost; I was to be the insurance for a big gate. I didn't think it was a bad idea, so Leonard talked business as only Leonard could do. Red offered us two thousand plus a couple of round-trip tickets.

"Listen, Red. We know you've got the shorts, and two thousand bucks ain't exactly chicken feed. Because I consider myself a fair man, I'll tell you what I'm gonna do. If you draw a full house, we'll take 50 percent of the gate. If not, then Jack'll do it for nothing. Either way, you'll get a hell of a lot of publicity, see?"

Red enthusiastically agreed. We arrived in Davenport a few days later. That night the arena was bulging with people who had come mainly to see me. After the bout, Red and Sacks were pleased to find that the receipts totalled over $11,000. We settled for the originally proposed deal, two thousand dollars. It didn't seem too bad a way of picking up a few bucks.

Boxing those exhibitions and refereeing were just about the best things I could have done for myself psychologically. The divorce was starting to blow sky high. Some two months after I moved to Reno, my brother Joe, along with a pal, seized Estelle's Rolls-Royce in California. The car, which had been a Christmas present to her, was parked in front of a friend's home in Beverly Hills when Joe and pal jumped the chauffeur, threatening to wring his neck if he made a fuss. Leaving the driver standing helplessly on the lawn, Joe drove the car to Reno. Before I had a chance to straighten things out, Estelle threatened to sue me to get the car back. Since I had completely cut off her garage account as well as the chauffeur's pay, she was convinced I had had something to do with the theft. I told Joe to take the car back.

Estelle accused me of having filed for divorce in Reno, which I promptly denied, though getting in touch with Estelle was next to impossible because she was busy playing a vaudeville circuit in the east. Despite her temporary absence from Los Angeles, I felt uneasy; I was afraid she was sitting up nights thinking of ways to make my life difficult.

On August 24, Estelle Taylor Dempsey declared she was officially filing for divorce in Los Angeles. Lupe Velez, who was now constantly by her side, declared that she was happy for Estelle and that I'd never been good enough for her. Within four weeks I filed in Reno, charging mental cruelty and loss of California residence. Twenty-four hours later, her attorney Joseph Scott filed a counter-suit on grounds of mental cruelty. Estelle, through her lawyer, stated that even if I obtained a Nevada divorce—by default—it wouldn't be recognized in any other state.

The following month I was granted a Reno divorce. I wasn't surprised when Estelle didn't show up; it was better that way. Estelle then announced that she had no intention of recognizing the divorce since I was, as far as she was concerned, a temporary resident. If I was that determined to have the divorce, there was a small matter of property settlement. I had no choice but to settle.

All in all, Estelle did pretty well. She took $40,000 in cash, a $150,000 home, including all paintings and furnishings, and three cars. By mortgaging some property, I managed to pay out the settlement and her fancy attorney's fee. I resented her more than I disliked her. In fact, I would have taken her back if she had snapped her fingers. But she was glad to be free and away from me.

Some time after our divorce, someone approached Estelle for an autograph. Grasping the piece of paper, she saw my name scrawled near the top of it. As she signed, she remarked, "This is the last time that son-of-a-bitch is on top of me." As unpleasant news always does, her obnoxious remark reached me almost immediately. I just had to forget her.

My wallet was hurting, so I kept up my refereeing and the boxing exhibitions, drawing tremendous crowds who convinced me that a comeback wouldn't be a bad idea. I decided to test myself against Kingfish Levinsky, a well-rated heavyweight fighter, although not a top contender. Former fish peddler Levinsky had two big advantages: He was twenty-one and he was enthusiastic. I was thirty-seven and—let's face it—my enthusiasm wasn't what it had once been.

The four round exhibition bout was scheduled for February in the Chicago Stadium. Despite my vigorous training, Levinsky tied me up in every way. He smothered my punches and maneuvered well. Eddie Purdy, who acted as referee, found himself constantly prying us apart. Levinsky was better than I had become, there was no doubt about that. He countered sharply, giving me little room in which to punch. When the bell clanged at the finish of the fourth round, I knew I no longer had any business being in the ring. Even the sports writers who determined Levinsky the winner were forced to agree that I was through.

27

Hannah Williams

Of course it jolted me. At thirty-seven, when most men are at their prime I was finished. But I'd had a long run, and deep down I'd known that it had to happen sometime. In a way I was lucky; I had an opportunity now to learn who were and who weren't my friends.

Wally Beery came to Reno and helped persuade me to take advantage of my prizefight connections by promoting a twenty round bout between Kingfish Levinsky and Max Baer, the master showman of the ring. Levinsky was said to be managed by his sister, Leaping Lena, but his real manager and handler was Harold Steinman, who knew more about the fight game than Leaping Lena ever would. After ten rounds, Max Baer was proclaimed the winner. His manager Ancil Hoffman and I celebrated that night. Ancil was convinced his boy had a chance to gain the title.

For a while I lived from a valise while maintaining Reno as my home base. In that period of my life I must have been linked with everyone in a skirt. Sure I screwed around, and so did everyone else I knew. But I wasn't as intense as the press made me out to be. One woman, Follies dancer and film actress Lena Basquette, almost got me into hot water. She was said to be my ex-trainer Teddy Hayes's girlfriend when she decided to take up with me. She was a beautiful woman, and I was flattered. She denied that there was anything serious between her and Hayes, and I took her word for it. Teddy, Joe Benjamin and Doc Kearns were, to put it mildly, still unfriendly, and Lena's tilt in my direction did little to restore peace.

Louella Parsons introduced me to Lena Basquette in an attempt to help me get over Estelle. I publicly denied I was seeing her, telling the curious that the lady in question was a wealthy Argentinian named Miss Rosita. We laughed about it, but I must have been a prime blockhead. Instead of being discreet and going to remote, intimate places, I was taking her to fashionable night spots. The more I took her out, the more Teddy Hayes stormed. He was probably calling me every name in the book. Lena and I were together for a while in Reno, until I had to leave for scheduled appearances on the Pantages circuit. Some years later, when Teddy and I made our peace, I learned that one day she had told Teddy that she was on her way to meet Louella Parsons and Doc Martin at the Cocoanut Grove. Instead, she hopped the first plane to Reno to join me. After Lena and I had simmered down, she returned to Teddy, who no doubt loved her very much.

Nineteen hundred thirty-three marked the repeal of the Noble Experiment. Prohibition was over. Jimmy Walker was out of City Hall in New York, and Franklin Delano Roosevelt was in the White House. About seventeen million people were unemployed. Apples were being sold on New York City street corners for a nickel. Those who had pawned their radios stood outside radio shops listening to *Amos 'n' Andy* or Ed Wynn, the Texaco "Fire Chief." Laughing with the comedians was an effective escape from the grim realities and hardships of the day. Child labor was abolished and the average worker took home about fifteen dollars a week—if he was lucky enough to have a job.

I was now shuttling between New York and California, still living out of a suitcase, as if I were running from myself. New York was better than ever as far as I was concerned. Sardi's, La Hiffs's, Leon and Eddie's, Dinty Moore's, "21", Billingsley's Stork Club and Perona's El Morocco were catering to the well-heeled or the well-connected, while the Childs Restaurant chain advertised, *All you can eat for 60 cents*. Not surprisingly, I saw a good many well-known persons stuffing themselves in Childs before boozing it up in the night spots.

The Stork Club's Sherman Billingsley was, in my opinion, the epitome of the good host. Low-keyed and somewhat remote, he was a self-educated man whose style of one-upmanship was to brag that he had even less formal schooling that I had. He was a great gift giver (for promotional reasons) and never felt the need to advertise. Walter Winchell was a constant customer, faithfully holding court at Table 50. Among his frequent tablemates were J. Edgar Hoover, who used to take in the room in four directions at once, and Damon Runyon. When Damon later lost his voice because of cancer, he still used to sit in the Stork Club, scribbling busily.

Speaks had shuttered and many first-rate bouncers and saloon keepers had opened legitimate places. Toots Shor, who had worked for Owney Madden (who had a piece of the fight action in New York), had by this time not only opened his own joint but established the reputation of being able to drink even his best customers under the table. Toots was a good friend who also seemed to know every dishy babe in New York. I remember the time we sat together in the Paradise Restaurant on Forty-ninth Street and Eighth Avenue in New York. Abe Lyman, the orchestra leader, was playing there that night, and sitting with us was Nils T. Granlund, formerly Loews Theaters' general press agent, who had a piece of the joint. Nils knew more women than Toots and Don Juan put together. Every time some beauty walked through the door, she'd make a beeline for him before anyone else. That night, musical comedy star Hannah Williams, known for her rendition of "Cheerful Little Earful," walked in and sat down with us. Small, light-haired and very pretty, she was early for a date with Lyman, so she decided to sit with us until he finished. She dazzled me; by the time Lyman was ready to join Hannah, I informed him that his twosome had become a threesome. He wasn't too happy, but he saw no way to get rid of me.

In those days it seemed that every time I was in Hollywood, someone wanted me in New York, and vice versa. Woody Van Dyke, who had become a top director since the days of my *Daredevil Jack* serials, telephoned me from Hollywood and said he needed help. He was refilming *The Prizefighter and the Lady* for Louis B. Mayer, starring Myrna Loy, Primo Carnera and Max Baer—and he needed me. Apparently he was having a tough time with Baer and Carnera, who were at each other's throats, and Jess Willard, who was just standing around. All of them were only slowing down production. He asked if I could do anything to keep them in line.

"Well, Woody, nothing short of knocking them all out—ha, ha!"

"Jack, I'm serious. Mayer's already giving me hell for lost time and Myrna's getting nervous. I'm asking you to do this as a personal favor."

"Okay, you just tell me what to do when I get there."

By the time I arrived Woody had it all figured out. To make sure I stuck around, he gave me the part of the referee in the picture. Woody wasn't kidding when he said he had his hands full. Carnera was oversensitive and wouldn't cooperate, while Max played practical jokes on pretty Myrna, the only woman in the cast. For once her loveliness didn't help her at all. Max once wired her chair just as Van Dyke hollered for quiet on the set. It *was* quiet, until Myrna sat down. She shrieked and we howled, while Woody glared and threatened to send our heads rolling. With all the shenanigans, I felt bad for Willard—he seemed so ill at ease. Once, as he looked at the cameras, he remarked, "You know, I feel kind of pathetic." Of all people, he was the one who really needed a good laugh.

For a while everything was calm and we worked on the picture, having no idea that Myrna was plotting revenge. Somehow she had learned that Max had a horrible fear of mice, so she had bought a lifesize mouse which not only squeaked but leaped into the air. One day, in the middle of a scene, Myrna opened her eyes wide and gasped, pointing to the floor. "A mouse!" she yelped. Max turned deathly white and almost fainted dead away; then he jumped into Primo Carnera's arms and hugged him tight, clutching his neck and almost choking him. Myrna laughed loudest of all. From that moment Max laid off, and the rest of the filming proceeded without a hitch.

In addition to my role in *The Prizefighter and the Lady*, I played the lead in *Mr. Broadway*, a film about a former pug turned ambitious Broadway producer. I was the only one who thought the film deserved to be a box office smash. It wasn't. While the movies were interesting, I preferred live audiences; at least you knew from the very beginning whether or not you were laying an egg.

Now that I was actively involved with Max Baer, I handled his vaudeville bookings in between his fights. He was a natural performer, not a ham like me. He loved every minute before the footlights. Toward spring, manager Ancil Hoffman informed him that he was to take on Max Schmeling from Germany.

I remembered Schmeling from my European tour. He was pretty good then, and I wondered if he still was as I drove to see him at his training camp at Lake Swannanga in New Jersey. I went a one round exhibition with him, stayed for dinner, and then returned to Baer to tell him that Schmeling was good. But Max was confident and trained hard. (By the end of the tenth round of the fight, it was clear that Schmeling had trained harder.)

Despite my constant traveling, I found myself making more trips to New York than ever before. Love had come into my life again, and this time I wasn't going to make any mistakes. Hannah Williams was still married to bandleader-aviator Roger Wolfe Kahn, son of banker Otto Kahn, though they weren't living together. Hannah had plenty of admirers, including Abe Lyman and bandleader-crooner Russ Columbo, not to mention me. I didn't want to figure too prominently since the last thing I wanted was to be cited in Hannah's divorce case.

When we dated I made sure we were not alone—at least early in the evening. Later, when all the wags had gone to bed, it was a different story. She was a Pennsylvania girl, one of three sisters, who had started singing and dancing on stage at four years of age. She had a strong but not overpowering personality, and she was unusually unselfish. For the first time in a long time, I didn't compare a woman to Estelle. As the months passed and 1932 became 1933, I came to the realization that I wanted to marry her. She accepted me and said she was going to Reno to file for divorce from Roger Kahn. He was, she said, impossible to live with because he was always "running home to mama." Divorce wasn't a novelty to Hannah; it would be her second.

Hannah arrived in Reno with her sister Dorothy, who was then married to jazz trumpeter Jimmy McPartland. I stayed out of the picture. Dorothy kept Hannah company while she was establishing residency, and I waited nervously. Russ Columbo flew in shortly after she arrived, convincing many that he was the one she would marry once she had her divorce. After signing the final papers, she changed and disappeared to a dude ranch with Columbo. Later, when everyone was thrown off the track she met me.

Few recognized us as we drove into Elko, Nevada, accompanied by friends who had driven from Salt Lake for the small ceremony. I registered in a hotel under the name of Mike Costello while Hannah registered as Jane Gray. Hannah looked beautiful as Justice of the Peace A. J. MacFarland married us. Hannah said she was the happiest girl in the world and proclaimed to the press who had discovered us, "I'm through with show business. I'd rather be a wife and mother and take care of my husband than be Greta Garbo." I was walking on air; ambition, at least, would never rear its ugly head. Hannah was going to be Mrs. Jack Dempsey, which was the way I wanted it.

I was surprised when Estelle sent her best wishes via the press: "I wish them much happiness. I hope they will avoid the little things that caused the split between Jack and me." At the time it was like rubbing that last bit of salt in an almost healed wound.

We honeymooned at my small ranch in Reno, then we joined Max Baer and his wife at his place in Roseville, California.

Hannah and I got along as though we were really meant to be together. She shared my interests and accepted my friends as Estelle had never done. Before long, Hannah found that she was pregnant. That threw me. Sure, I wanted a kid, but that idea of being a father scared me. What if it were a boy? Would I name him after me? Would he suffer because of me? Seven months would tell.

On July 14, 1934, I wired invitations to a baby shower in the Stork Club. Everyone thought the idea was cute. But in actuality it wasn't so cute. Some time back, a certain journalist had brought one of Adolf Hitler's men, Putzy Hanfsraengl, into the club, causing a great deal of fuss. Jewish members thought it insulting and gentiles were irritated, so together they formed a committee to decide

how the Stork Club could show the public it had not meant anything unfriendly or offensive by admitting Hitler's man. What was
needed was a neutral, fun occasion. After some discussion, they
decided that a baby shower in our honor was not only cute but
would serve the purpose.

Hannah couldn't make it that day, so I took over, collecting
everything from mechanical rabbits to silver diaper pins. Max Baer
was there, and Gene Tunney ribbed me about the possibility of producing female triplets. He and his Polly had just had a boy, and
Gene seemed to fit the role of the proud father perfectly. I was
still uncomfortable but relieved—I admit it—that I wasn't the one
to have to check into the hospital.

Living with Hannah as she became heavier wasn't easy. She
felt clumsy and undesirable, and she was having a tough time that
was made worse by my continual absences. In the first quarter of
the new year, I worked as a referee and did promotions in twenty-
two states and two foreign countries. We lived in the Hotel Navarro
on Central Park South those first two years, along with my mother,
whom I had asked to stay with Hannah for a while. That turned
out to be one of my biggest blunders. Unfortunately, Mother, now
in her early eighties, disliked Hannah intensely and constantly compared her with Estelle, whom she had liked very much.

Once, returning home from a long trip, I was met at the door by
Hannah, upset and agitated, while my mother sat on the sofa with
her face grimly set. I ran to Mother, thinking she had had some
sort of an attack. I asked her what was wrong, and she only shook
her head. I turned to Hannah, who burst into tears. I didn't know
what to think.

"Will someone please speak up and tell me what's going on?"

Neither of them said a word until I had repeated the question.
Finally my mother spoke up while Hannah glared.

"Son, Mother wants to go home."

"What? Mother, you have everything at your fingertips here.
We want you to stay. Why on earth would you want to leave?"

"I'm not happy, Son, I'm just not happy."

"Hannah. Mother."

In 1934, Hannah and I introduce Joanie to her first camera lens.

Out on the town with my two favorite girls, Barbara and Joan.

Once again I turn to mining as I attempt a comeback. (*United Press International*)

Here I am posing with the one and only Babe. (*United Press International*)

1941. Charlie Johnson and Minneapolis Mayor Hubert H. Humphrey greet me on one of my War Bond Drive stops.

Here I am with President Lyndon Baines Johnson. (*Official White House Photo: Yoichi Okimoto*)

Deanna and I in my Broadway restaurant a few years after we got married.

Greeting my old pal Judge John Sirica shortly after he appeared in the national spotlight. (*Capitol & Glogau*)

1970. Joe Frazier, Jack Sharkey, Georges Carpentier and Gene Tunney join countless others in wishing me Happy Birthday in Madison Square Garden. (*Courtesy Ed Basist*)

"Don't, Son. It's not necessary. I know when I'm not wanted. I'm just an old woman who will join the Good Lord shortly."

"What the hell is this?" By this time I was raving.

"I'm so hungry all the time. Hannah won't give me anything to eat and she treats me bad."

Hannah jumped in. "That's a lie and you know it! All you have to do is pick up that telephone, tell them who you are and what you want, and they'll send it up—just as you do for everything else."

"You know I can't manage."

Instead of seeing the situation clearly as a power play on my mother's part, I put the blame on Hannah, who began crying again. I would have looked into my mother's face for the truth if I had had any brains. Hannah looked up through her tears and called me a beast, reminding me that she was pregnant and that allowances should be made for nervous tension. That calmed me down somewhat, and I apologized as my mother silently shuffled out of the room. It finally got through to me that if I wanted this marriage to work I'd have to listen to Hannah instead of jumping to conclusions. A few weeks later my mother decided to go back to Salt Lake City. The conflict between the two women hurt me like hell.

On August 4, 1934, Hannah Williams Dempsey gave birth to a beautiful little girl. We decided to call her Joan for no specific reason. Leaving the hospital, I rushed through the lobby of the Hotel Navarro shouting, "It's a girl, it's a girl!" as everyone turned to look at me and grin. Gene Tunney was one of the first to send me a congratulatory wire, saying he regretted that the proposed 1954 bout between his son and mine would obviously have to be canceled.

About the time Joanie was born, boxing was legalized in Washington, D.C. Goldie Ahern, a matchmaker and a client of a young attorney named John J. Sirica, obtained the first license under the new law. District Commissioner Melvin Hazen, a member of the Riding and Hunt Club in Washington (which housed a big arena), got together with Goldie, and the two of them decided to promote a bout with me as referee. I agreed and went to Washington. When the fight was over, I took one-half of the gross gate—about $1,500. By the time Goldie had paid the fighters, there was very little left. But at least he paid them.

Goldie introduced me to his Italian-American attorney, John Sirica, who was no slouch himself when it came to boxing. Sirica and I hit it off from the beginning. He wasn't really making it as an attorney; times were tough and money was tight. Many times, when he hovered over a low, I'd invite him to join me to boost his morale. He once stayed with me in California for almost a month. On several occasions he remarked that perhaps the law wasn't for him, that maybe he'd be better off at some other job. I wouldn't hear of such a thing, and I sent him clients whenever I could. Considering the mugs I knew, it wasn't difficult to find someone who needed help to get out of a jam. Good friends never let me down, and I'd be damned if I'd let Sirica down. One of the proudest moments of my life was when he was appointed a judge by Dwight Eisenhower. The haul had been long and hard, but in the end it paid off handsomely.

Everyone seemed to be getting married for the first time while I was on my third—which I hoped would be my last. From the time the baby was born, we found living in the Navarro a bit cramped, so we moved to an apartment on Central Park West.

Once we had moved from the hotel, Hannah seemed very happy. She was a good mother who doted on Joanie, and Joanie was getting prettier with every passing day. Things were peaceful and I made a point of trying to be home more often.

Shortly after Joanie greeted the world, an old man arrived in. New York by train, carrying a battered valise from which the sleeve of a shirt was hanging. Looking around, he found a traffic cop and asked, "Will you tell me how I can find my son, Harry, the champion?"

"Champion of what, Pop? Listen, I'm busy. I don't know any Harry the champion."

"Please, everyone knows him."

"Harry who?" He turned to another cop who had walked over. "Jimmy, I think I've got a live one on my hands."

The old man insisted. "Harry. Jack."

"Listen, Pop, which is it, Harry or Jack?"

"Well, to me he's Harry, to you he's Jack."

"Jack Dempsey?"

"Yes."

"Christ! Why didn't you say so?"

Hannah and I were surprised when my father presented himself at the door, accompanied by a New York policeman who suggested we keep the old man in one place, before getting my autograph and leaving.

I was glad to see him. He stayed a few weeks and then announced that the city was too much for him, and he returned home to peace and tranquility.

Max Baer was keeping pretty busy. In June, 1934, he demolished Primo Carnera for the title and in June, 1935, he proceeded to lose it to Jimmy Braddock. Max was raring to reclaim his title so Ancil Hoffman quietly arranged a bout with the Brown Bomber, Joe Louis. Mike Jacobs, former ticket broker turned promoter and general manager of the Twentieth Century Sporting Club, formally announced the match between Baer and Louis with ten percent of the gate receipts going to Hearst's Milk Fund charity. The fight was to be the most significant mixed bout since the Great White Hope went against Jack Johnson some years back. Max was very unhappy about this matchup and didn't want to go through with it, but I told him there was no way he could back out. I had my seven percent to protect, as well as Max's reputation.

He trained, but his heart wasn't in it. Surprisingly, however, he did a turnaround the night of the fight. He exuded so much confidence that we couldn't help staring. "I can't wait to get into that ring. This fight'll be kid stuff. I ain't worried. Pow! Smack! Why, I'm as cool as you, Jack!"

Max confidently marched to the ring and climbed through the ropes into his corner. Joe Humphreys stepped forward and acknowledged huge applause before introducing Baer and Louis. By the end of the fourth round it was over by a knockout. Max was right; he shouldn't have gone into that ring.

Arthur Brisbane, known for his splashy page-one columns in the Hearst papers, later wrote that a gorilla could lick a heavyweight or three prizefighters at one time. I sent Brisbane's column to Baer, who wasn't amused.

Before long, journalist Dan Parker came around to interview me, and I found myself discussing gorillas with him for an entire afternoon. When Parker left his eyeballs were coated, but he nevertheless devoted an entire column to the subject. I had agreed with Brisbane. The entire ludicrous matter raised a lively debate in fight circles. Gene Tunney got involved: "The gorilla grabs something and tries to crush the life out of it. A Dempsey left hook landing on the stomach would tear the animal in two." Gene claimed that a man has twenty-four ribs while a gorilla has only thirteen. Later, *Time* magazine, hand in hand with the *Encyclopaedia Britannica,* found that a gorilla has thirteen *pairs* of ribs, one pair more than a man. Mercifully, the entire gorilla vs. man controversy gradually died down.

When Joanie was about fifteen months old and Hannah was pregnant again, we started getting late-night calls from some tipster who warned us that our little girl was in danger of being kidnapped and held for ransom. Remembering what had happened to Lindbergh's kid, I wasn't going to take any chances, so we packed some bags and went to Atlantic City. It was the time of the elevator operators' strike, and we were glad to be leaving the city. Once we got to Atlantic City, we put Joanie under guard. In those days, Atlantic City was nice, but Hannah became cranky and complained about the humidity. She wanted to return home, where she said she felt more secure.

On August 28, 1936, Barbara appeared in Polyclinic Hospital, just as her sister had two years before. A cheerful baby like her sister, Barbara looked just like Hannah. People couldn't believe that an athlete like me couldn't produce an all-American boy, but I didn't care. My two beautiful girls were joys to me.

It was obvious now, more than before, that we needed a larger apartment, so we leased fourteen rooms at the San Remo on Central Park West. It was a beautiful apartment with windows overlooking the park. Hannah tried her hand at decorating, and pretty soon it took shape. By the foyer there was a cork-and-bamboo-lined bar, and in the living room hung enlarged George Bellows etchings and a family portrait. Between the servants and the rent, I explained to Hannah, I would have to accept more out-of-town engagements than before. She understood.

In the late thirties I acquired Max Waxman as my business manager. Normile had become heavily involved in racetracks while Sacks had confused friendship with business and was accomplishing very little. We parted good friends, but I needed and was lucky to get a fox like Waxman, who personally handled my bookings, personal appearances and general commitments, leaving me free to think about establishing some stable line of work in New York. What I wanted was a restaurant—a gathering place for sportsmen, fight men, journalists and celebrities—just as others before me had wanted a saloon. Scouting around, I finally signed a contract with Louie Brooks to build me a Jack Dempsey restaurant on the site of the old car barn across from Madison Square Garden. Jake Ruppert, the beer man and sportsman, was backing Louie's end, so money was no object. Halfway through razing the car barn, Ruppert abruptly backed out, leaving Louie stuck—but not for long. He approached Jake Amron for help. Amron was the successful owner of the Hollywood Restaurant and the Flanders Hotel, one of the sharpest and most dapper men around Broadway. Louie Brooks explained his predicament to Amron and asked him to come into the business deal as operator and part owner. This was a polite way of asking Amron to fork over some dough to save the place from fading into oblivion. Amron was all for it, and pretty soon I proudly saw my name both vertically and horizontally in neon lights. In time, Amron took over a major portion of Brooks's share, leaving him with a token ten percent.

We planned a grand opening in March, 1935, with publicity to the point of saturation. We got in touch with press agents Murray Lewin and S. Jay Kaufman of the *New York Mirror* to help us make up a comprehensive guest list. If I'm not mistaken, the total number of guests wound up topping 2,500 people.

I played the grand host while Hannah circulated beautifully. More people came in than went out, which caused a severe shortage of space. It was so overcrowded that new arrivals had to push their way in.

I spied my father perched on the mezzanine, motioning and waving to me. Wondering what he was doing, I decided to see for myself. There he was, clutching an old-fashioned clicker in his hand, a half-empty bottle of whiskey by his side.

"Hey, Pa, what're you doing?"

"I'm countin' how many people are walkin' in through that door of yours. Sure, my fingers are all tuckered out, but someone has to make sure that Jewish partner of yours don't take advantage of your good nature, boy." He shifted his eyes.

I grinned at him and said, "Pa, it's all free. No one's shelling out a dime. Amron and I are in this thing together, so you get those thoughts out of your head. Pa, it's our opening night and it's all free—for publicity, get it?"

"Now you tell me. Here, get me off this thing before my ass falls off."

The restaurant turned out to be successful. Pretty soon it had developed a loyal following, and there wasn't one night when some celebrity didn't show up.

The biggest problem was keeping drunken pipsqueaks away from me. Every time they boozed, screwing up their courage, they'd try to punch me in the nose. As a general rule, whenever this occurred either Max Waxman or some pal would escort these mighty men out. On one occasion it got so bad that I had to hightail it out the side door.

The men who did push-ups or practised their shadowboxing on the sidewalk made me think back to a certain night in 1931, when I was scheduled to take on three opponents in an exhibition fight in Winnipeg. Because of the unruly crowd, Ernie Fliegel, who was with me, hired guards to protect me, stationing one of them outside my dressing room door with orders not to let anyone pass. Every time Ernie or Waxman passed him, they were struck by the strange expression on his face. Finally, Ernie asked him what was the matter. The guard answered that all his life, as far back as he could remember, he'd wondered how it would feel to get hit by Jack Dempsey. Ernie, amused, told the guy to come into my dressing room where I was warming up with Jerry the Greek, with Waxman looking on. Ernie prodded the guy into repeating his wish, and I scowled playfully and hit him on the chin. Down he went—out cold —while Jerry gave way to hysterics, hollering, "Christ, it'll be a lawsuit! Jack, how hard did you sock him?"

He chased me out of the room while he splashed water on the guy. Ernie and Max ushered Jerry out as well while they calmed the guy down. Knowing I had to face him sooner or later, they invited him to breakfast the next morning. That night I couldn't sleep for listening to Jerry pacing the floor above me. Morning dawned and we all sat waiting tensely for the guy. Amazingly, he was still crowing about how thrilled he had been to get knocked out—why, he'd even tell his grandchildren about it! We all breathed a sigh of relief.

Some time after I opened the restaurant I was approached by Jess Willard, who asked me to give him a job. He was down, and I was the only person he felt he could turn to for help. I was more skeptical than flattered, but I decided to give him a try. At that time we carried Jack Dempsey's Special Label Whiskey, "the whiskey with a punch," so I gave him a job as a liquor salesman, promoting our liquor. (Now that Prohibition was a thing of the past, salesmen were making good money.)

When word got around that Willard was going to launch the whiskey in an advertising campaign, the press, along with their cameras, jammed themselves into the restaurant.

The ad called for Jess to walk over to the bar where the barman would say, "Well, well! If it isn't Jess Willard! What'll you have, Jess?"

"A Jack Dempsey Special Label on the rocks, please."

We went through it several times until it sounded natural. Then came lights and action as the lenses zoomed in on Willard.

"Well, well! If it isn't Jess Willard! What'll you have, Jess?"

"I'll have a Johnnie Walker Black Label on the rocks," said Jess.

After Willard had been on the job awhile, he began to stop by the bar quite a bit. I recall the time the bartender asked Jess if he wanted a Jack Dempsey Special Label. Unfortunately, Jess was overheard saying, "Jack Dempsey Special Label? That junk? No thanks."

Jess Willard wasn't with me for long the first time, nor was he with me for long this time. But I'll say one thing for Willard—in his own unique way, he tried.

Once the restaurant had caught on and was running smoothly under Amron's supervision, Waxman arranged bookings for me once more. At times they were back to back, and I found myself hopping off one airplane or train and onto the next. As long as I had the energy, Max booked, even though I was running myself into the ground.

Around this time I acquired the Dempsey-Vanderbilt Hotel in Miami Beach. That, as an investment, proved less than profitable. I was sued by just about anyone who could think of a reason. If someone so much as slipped on a tacked-down carpet, or swallowed something the wrong way, I was in trouble. Money was short, and suers were obviously plentiful. It was one big headache.

The more I traveled whistle-stop, the more Hannah complained that she was being left alone. Insensitive or not, that didn't stop me, though it was starting to lead to arguments, at times in front of the children.

On one trip I stopped in Dayton, Ohio, and holed up in the Biltmore Hotel to fight off the grippe. A Dayton pal who owned a local clothing emporium, Dave Margolis, called me to say that a woman named Miriam Cessna had gotten in touch with him and asked for my number. She wanted to give me her father's personal regards. Dave figured that I knew Mr. Cessna, of the airplane Cessnas, so he gave her my telephone number, even though I took no calls.

Thirty minutes later Miriam Cessna rang me up and rattled on excitedly about my soon-to-be-scheduled appearance at a civic group's fund raiser. In honor of my presence, she wanted to donate a plane for the inevitable raffle—on the condition that I make the presentation. I agreed, and she went on and on, not letting me off the phone. I wanted to get rid of the dame, but short of hanging up on her there was nothing I could do but listen and hope she'd run out of steam. After all, a plane was a plane.

When she didn't show in Dayton, I forgot all about it. But when I got to Chicago, there she was. She stood up at a charity affair and donated a Cessna, and everyone made a big fuss over her. The people were touched and grateful, and she reaped plenty of praise and appreciation. In Minneapolis she donated another plane, then she did it again in St. Louis and Salt Lake. By the time I reached Denver, Miriam Cessna had not only given away six planes but had fallen for me as well.

I was beginning to feel closed in; I couldn't go anyplace or eat anywhere without the woman waving and batting her eyelashes at me before moving in like gangbusters. If she'd been pleasant, I might not have minded, but there was something about the woman that I didn't like, though I couldn't seem to pinpoint what it was. I called Margolis in Dayton.

"Listen, pal. You got me into this mess, now help me get rid of this dame." While the last thing I wanted to do was to antagonize her father, Dave just had to get her off my back any way he could.

So Dave hired a dick named Rose who ran a thorough check on the woman while she went on donating one Cessna plane after another. It took a while, but Rose finally came through. The Cessna aviation family had no Miriam. This Miriam Cessna had no planes. She was an impostor. I kept out of sight until she lost track of me, but it took a hell of a long time.

Something else that took a long time was the elimination of legislation prohibiting the interstate transportation of fight films. Despite prizefighting's having gained general acceptance in forty-seven states, there were still those who opposed it as a dangerous sport. Everyone seemed ready to ignore the serious mishaps that occurred in such other sports as football, polo and skiing.

In May, 1939, I appeared with Gene Tunney, John Reed Kilpatrick, various sports commentators, boxing and athletic commissioners, broadcasters, attorneys and a theater owner at a hearing before the U.S. Senate Subcommittee on Interstate Commerce. The subcommittee was comprised of Senator Ernest Lundeen of Minnesota, who acted as chairman, Senator Edwin Johnson of Colorado and Senator Warren Barbour of New Jersey, who had been the official timekeeper at my Willard fight. Barbour had urged the elimination of the legislation which forbade the transportation of fight films. The interstate commerce obstacle had been created in 1912, when Congress reacted to the uproar and racial prejudice that resulted when Jack Johnson beat Jim Jeffries and kept his championship title.

I was glad when the Senate called me to testify; I really couldn't understand why it was a crime to transport the fight films the public wanted to see. Besides, the films were being bootlegged anyway.

Not one witness opposed the passage of the new bill, which was finally enacted in 1940. Both boxing and I had taken giant steps.

28

In Coast Guard Uniform

Newspapers reported rumblings of another war. Day by day we worried as Hitler became more and more of a power, a menace none of us quite understood. On September 1, 1939, war began formally with the German invasion of Poland. Speculation ran high on how much time would elapse before the United States would have to get in there and fight. Selective Service called, and all men of fighting age responded. I was now forty-five years old. I wanted to serve, to do something constructive, but I feared being turned down. Max Waxman advised me to sit tight.

A few months into the new year I opened a headquarters for the National Sports Committee for the reelection of Franklin Delano Roosevelt (who was to win easily over his opponent, Wendell Willkie). Roosevelt and I knew each other, but we were more acquaintances than friends. In 1922, in a letter to his 1920 running mate, Governor James M. Cox, he wrote:

". . . except for my legs, I am in far better physical shape than ever before in my life, and I have developed a chest and a pair of shoulders on me which would make Jack Dempsey envious."

When Cox showed me the letter I was pleased; I liked and admired Roosevelt, who many a time had sat at ringside. He was heard more on radio than any other personality; his running for office provoked heated rivalry between newspapers and radio.

Roosevelt was the first President to be seen on a blurry invention called television, for which I paid eight hundred bucks.

Not only was Roosevelt a great man carrying an oversized burden of worries, but he was also a prankster and a practical joker. When a friend, Wild Bill Lyons, expressed a desire to meet the President, I obtained an appointment and went to the Oval Room of the White House to speak to Roosevelt.

"Mr. President, I have a pal who is just tormenting me to meet you. Fellow by the name of Wild Bill Lyons. You may have heard of him."

"Is that so? Well, Jack, you can bring Lyons here to meet me on one condition."

"What's that, sir?"

"I've never seen anyone being given a hotfoot, and I've heard that you're pretty good at it, Jack. What about showing me how you do it while Lyons is here?"

"Anything you say, Mr. President."

A few days later I showed up with Wild Bill standing nervously by my side. His hair had been greased down and his shoes shone like mirrors. We walked into the President's office and Roosevelt leaned forward to grasp Lyons's outstretched paw in his two hands.

As Wild Bill stared and jabbered about what a great honor it was to be in F.D.R.'s presence, I dropped down, stuffed matches into the soles of his shoes, and lit them one by one. Smoke curled up as Roosevelt clasped Lyons's hand tighter. We all wondered how long Wild Bill could maintain his composure in front of the President of the United States. The matches caught and Wild Bill, no longer able to control himself, yelped, "Please, please, Mr. President. Let go of my hand."

"Why, Mr. Lyons, whatever is the matter?"

Roosevelt wouldn't let go at all until Wild Bill yelped, "That goddamn son-of-a-bitch Dempsey just gave me a hotfoot!"

The President released his hand, and Wild Bill jumped about five feet in the air. By the time the fire in his shoe had been put out and it was all over, our bellies ached from laughter.

I had just returned from a barnstorming tour as referee when my home life began to fall apart all over again. Hannah and I had now been married seven years, and maybe the seven-year itch had set in. She had made no public appearances except for the musical *Hooray for What!* in New York with Ed Wynn and Kay Thompson and a few radio shows with me. Now she wanted to go back into nightclubs. I couldn't help it; I exploded.

"What about your wanting to be a wife?"

"I would be if you were ever home."

"I'm home as much as I can be. How do you think you'd be living if I didn't bust my ass to earn a living?"

"Don't give me that. You've got the restaurant and God knows what else!"

"Listen, Hannah. I've got to fulfill these engagements and then I'll be home so much you'll get tired of seeing my face."

"Sure. I've heard the tune before and I've already read the book. Did it ever cross your mind that the girls need a father?"

"How about a mother? Do you think your working at night will do them any good?"

"More good than being on the road like you."

Hannah was unhappy, and I stubbornly refused to accept it. She had, I felt, everything but patience. She was listening to people who didn't approve of my traveling. And she was throwing away our hard-earned dough on outrageous bills and telephone calls. When I asked her to cut down on spending, she laughed.

"You're not getting any allowance this month."

She slapped my face, cursed and left the room. I was tempted to hit her but got hold of myself before cornering her in the bedroom.

"What do I have to do, lock you in until you promise to behave?"

"Get the hell away from me, you, you—"

"You must take me for a goddamn fool."

"That's an understatement."

"I'm leaving this house," I hollered. "I don't want you here when I get back."

"Don't worry. I won't be."

Before leaving town I cut off her checking account, partly because I wanted to make sure she wouldn't go away. When I returned, it was as if nothing had happened. If anything, Hannah and I seemed to have rediscovered the missing physical spark. It was crazy.

Three weeks later, while in Detroit on Mother's Day, I was informed by attorney Moses Pelakoff that Hannah had filed for legal separation on the grounds of incompatibility. I was stunned and tried to get in touch with her. For the first time I was really afraid of losing my little family.

Hannah got custody of the two girls with the provision that I could visit them whenever I wanted. I asked her to give our marriage one more chance, and she said she would consider it. At least that was a step in the right direction. I missed her, and I longed for my girls. Maybe it didn't show, but I wanted to be a family man; I realized now that my family was the only thing I had that was of any real value to me.

On July 1, 1940, I had my last professional fight. Some time before I had refereed a wrestling match involving Cowboy Lutrell and had given what in his opinion was a bad decision. Now the grudge between the insulted wrestler and the boxer (me) was to be settled.

Nat Fleischer acted as referee for the bout. I hadn't been in the ring for eight years, and I was too old to be in the ring, but my ego was bolstered when the fans cheered me even though Lutrell was a popular guy. I felt as if I were twenty-five years old again. The fight itself proved interesting, and in one minute, thirty-eight seconds of the second round I blasted Lutrell out of the ring with a left hook. Fleischer, undaunted, continued to count Lutrell out even though Lutrell was no longer inside the ropes. I was buoyed with success. I hadn't lost my strength. Maybe, if we went to war, the Armed Forces would consider me after all.

First, however, there was that matter of putting my personal affairs in order again. That sure took some doing. I vowed to change my lifestyle, to be with Hannah more instead of burning up telephone wires. I loved her and I wasn't about to lose her. It touched me deeply to see Barbara and Joan cling to me every time I had to leave the apartment. I begged Hannah to have a heart.

We finally reconciled in 1941, and for a while everything was better than it had ever been. She was by my side through laughter and tears. Some of those tears were shed on the steps of St. Patrick's Cathedral, at George M. Cohan's funeral. I looked around and realized that we were no longer the boys we had been. Runyon, Fowler, Winchell, Sullivan—they were all big names now. We were all either fatter or thinner, with sparser and grayer hair. And we had all gone through a hell of a lot. Someone remarked that Cohan would have appreciated the fact that he was now only minutes away from Broadway.

I remained in New York for quite a spell. The restaurant was a gold mine. Like many other spots, it had become a gathering place for our men in uniform. Max Waxman, in the meantime, had developed into a pastrami freak. He would sit in the restaurant and wait for the deli man from around the corner to bring him his overstuffed sandwich in a brown bag. Then he would wolf down that precious sandwich while customers stared. Many must have wondered if there was something wrong with the food they were eating.

We were beginning to enjoy prosperity again, with the advent of the cocktail hour, the invention of television, and the boost in nightclubs. Theaters were selling out while big name stars went on the road in support of bond rallies. Religious attendance went up and morale climbed. Nightclub comics no longer told Adolf Hitler jokes.

Then the laughter stopped. On December 7, 1941, the Japanese attacked Pearl Harbor. Now it was no longer a European war but a World War. Defense industries called for workers and assembly lines churned day and night. People started collecting scrap metal, rope, bottles, tin cans—anything that could be used in the war effort. People were gung ho in an all-out effort to help. The Stage Door Canteen opened with notables in the kitchen and notables waiting on table. Lynn Fontanne became the finest waitress anyone ever saw.

Everyone was doing something, and I decided that the time had come for me to enlist. Hannah didn't take my announcement well at all. She was listless and lonely while I spent time at benefits or at the restaurant. I told her to invite some friends up, which she did, but her best friend still seemed to be her sister Dorothy. Everyone must have been drinking more those days—since I came across a number of empty bottles around the house. I never suspected that it could have been Hannah.

One morning, Max Waxman accompanied me downtown to Whitehall Street, where we joined some three hundred men filling out enlistment papers. Despite Max's being in his middle fifties and pretty stocky, he was as determined as I was to get into uniform. I filled out my papers (signing up as a buck private) and then took the physical, which I passed. Max's military career ended the moment he stepped on the scale.

Technical Sergeant W. E. Kelly signed me in that day. As usual, the press had gotten wind of what I was up to, and that night my picture was splashed all over. Less than twenty-four hours later, the U.S. Army informed me that because I was overage they couldn't take me. Unless Congress passed a law raising the age limit, I could forget about obtaining a waiver. I couldn't believe it! I felt better than ever and was probably stronger than many of the boys who were being taken. I had passed the physical, held $75,000 worth of defense bonds, and was probably more anxious and determined to serve my country than the average man, because of the humiliation I had gone through in 1920.

I sat in my restaurant debating my next course of action when Bob Edge, a sportsman acquaintance, walked in wearing the U.S. Coast Guard blue and white. I told him what had happened, and before I knew it I was being sworn in as first lieutenant in the Coast Guard. This was one of the most gratifying moments in my life.

Informed that I was to referee a fight for a bond rally in Denver and other cities, I spent as much time with Hannah and the girls as I could before leaving. Hannah was now more determined than ever to face the footlights and the crowds. We had bitter arguments over this—arguments that made the children cry. She was tired of sitting home and playing the role of solitary wife and busy mother; she wanted to do something constructive with her life, and I stood in her way. Now that I'd enlisted, I'd probably be away from home more than before. She wasn't about to go stale waiting for me while I constantly carved out new careers for myself. The more she crabbed, the more annoyed I became, until I blew my top and told her to go ahead and do whatever made her happy, just so long as she didn't neglect the girls. If she wanted to be on stage so badly, there was nothing I could do about it. I think that was one of the last times I saw her smile; I left feeling somewhat better.

Returning from the Coast Guard tour, I was sent to the Manhattan Beach Training Station, where I reported to Commander Arthur G. Hall, Commanding Officer Captain G. U. Steward and Lieutenant Commander Herbert F. Walsh.

I was put in charge of the physical fitness program. My job was to see that four thousand recruits quickly got into tough physical condition. Every day I put the men through two or three hours of calisthenics, six miles of clocked roadwork and gymwork. Aiding me was a staff of fifty, including boxers Marty Servo, Nathan Mann and Lew Ambers, wrestler Bibber McCoy and Spike Mooney of the Ohio State football coaching staff, who acted as my personal assistant. In addition to general conditioning, I taught essential principles of self-defense, using such weapons as hard rubber knives for slitting the enemy's jugular veins and arteries. At the same time I stressed the importance of bringing in prisoners alive whenever possible.

I felt strongly that those men who guarded our long coastline, our docks and our shipping facilities had to be tough—able to meet any emergency. Being respected and looked up to by so many fine young men gave me a strange and powerful feeling. I was proud of my uniform—but I was uneasy holding a new automatic rifle; it was a far cry from Pa's old rusty one.

The men couldn't help calling me Jack when the big brass wasn't around. Otherwise they would act stiff and formal, fooling no one. A few of the officers pulled rank on me, but I disregarded them and took commands only from my immediate superiors.

Both officers and enlisted men were required to take instruction in Japanese, German and mathematics for navigational purposes. I found that I was no better or worse than I had been in grammar school, which wasn't saying very much.

That Coast Guard uniform of mine was like catnip to women. They loved me in it, and that made me feel like a young bull again. They winked and threw me engaging smiles without getting much in return. I was no longer in a smiling mood because of Hannah. She had started making the rounds of nightclubs, being seen with certain men I wouldn't have given two plugged nickels for. As the cliché goes, I was the last to know.

Friends advised me to open my eyes if I wanted to save my marriage. What could Hannah be doing that I didn't know about? I didn't mind her visiting friends or having friends in, just so long as she was a proper mother to Joanie and Barbara. Nevertheless I was stricken with jealousy, so I hired Ned Peterson from the Universal Detective Agency to do some snooping for me. Pictures began arriving of Hannah in this nightclub or that, looking like she was having the time of her life. When Ned showed me a photograph of Texan Benny Woodall and his sister, with Hannah apparently sitting on Benny's lap, I saw red.

On November 22, 1942, I was part of a raiding party on our apartment. Busting open the door, I found Benny Woodall fully dressed, his shirttail hanging out, asleep on the couch, his shoes and tie in the bedroom. I might have killed him if I hadn't been held back. For some time I had had the impression that Hannah's friends ran for the back door whenever I showed up. I saw them as an intrusion on my privacy and that of my wife. Frequently I was rude to them. I couldn't help it; I was just too insecure to rest easy, leaving a beautiful wife at home while I traveled. Seeing Woodall asleep on the couch was more than I could take.

I had had it both with myself and with Hannah. It was clear that we weren't suited to live together without getting at each other's throats. I obviously wasn't marriage material, and it was high time that I accepted the fact.

I established residency in Scarsdale, and arranged to keep the girls out of sight, not allowing Hannah to see them until the whole unpleasant matter was settled. Then I filed for divorce, charging adultery (the sole grounds for a New York divorce at the time), naming Benny Woodall, with whom Hannah had been acquainted since 1940, as correspondent, and citing Lew Jenkins as well. Hannah filed a countersuit.

As the case went to court, my private life once more lay open in the papers. At the onset, Arnold Koch represented Hannah, while

Arthur Driscoll pleaded my side. In May of that year, Hannah suffered a nervous collapse in her suite at the Hotel Navarro. Doctors and nurses were summoned to her side, which annoyed my lawyer who opposed any adjournments.

Once Hannah was feeling better, she took the stand and lashed out at me. Under oath she stated that I had slapped her around and made her bloody, and that I had put a gun to her head and threatened to pull the trigger. Driscoll chained me to my chair with his eyes. He knew that I had never laid a hand on her.

She brought up the unpleasant episode between her and my mother, swearing that I had taken my mother's side, and that when she had pleaded with me to understand that she was pregnant and that allowances should be made for nerves, I had turned on her and shouted, "Go get yourself an abortion." Furthermore, she stated, the elder Mrs. Dempsey had contributed to the breakdown of our marriage by constantly comparing Hannah to Estelle Taylor. That I couldn't deny.

She insisted that out of the seven years we'd been married, we had really been together for only three.

Benny Woodall got on the stand and swore that there wasn't anything between him and Hannah. He considered himself nothing more than a family friend. He recounted his version of what had happened on the night of November 22. That evening, Benny remembered, he'd been invited for dinner with his sister and Dorothy, Hannah's sister. As the meal was about finished, his sister was called to the telephone, where she was informed that one of the children had taken sick. She left, and a short time later Dorothy went to the pharmacy to pick up a few things for Hannah, who wasn't feeling too well herself. Woodall stayed behind as he still had a few hours to kill before he caught his streetcar. Aware that Hannah wasn't feeling well, and knowing she kept jewels in the apartment, Woodall decided to stay at least until Dorothy came back. He waited, propping himself on the couch with his newspaper. That still didn't explain the shoes and tie in the bedroom, even though it seemed to explain everything else.

Both Hannah and Woodall denied every single allegation. Hannah, when asked, even denied she'd ever been drunk in her life.

At one point she asked for the courtroom to be cleared before smearing me with every vicious name she could think of. She told the remaining members of the court that I was a slob whenever I was home and that I walked around in my undershirt in front of the kids. I couldn't believe what she was saying. She seemed a totally different woman telling of a mortifying life with some brute. I didn't recognize her and I didn't recognize me. Her attorney had her up there fighting as hard as she could. Nevertheless, she appeared to be on the verge of another collapse.

Between Hannah's testimony and Woodall's, I would have been shredded if I hadn't produced my own witnesses. Testifying in my behalf was our former cook, who referred to Woodall as the "automobile man" since he was "always identifying himself as Mr. Dodge, Mr. Ford or Mr. Packard"; another witness, bantamweight fighter Louis Salica, said he'd watched Woodall and Hannah get pretty chummy in a restaurant. At this point the incriminating nightclub photograph of Hannah was presented in evidence.

My star witness was Harry Goldman, prizefight photographer from the Bronx, who told how he used to drop by the apartment to say hello to Hannah and ask about me. One night, he said, he had too much to drink at the bar in our apartment and fell asleep in a chair. He woke up at dawn and saw Benny Woodall, fully dressed, asleep by Hannah in bed. Moreover, Goldman stated that Hannah had told him in 1941 that she had given Benny presents, including an overcoat, some shirts and a watch.

On a couple of occasions I didn't show up in court because of Coast Guard assignments. When I was there, however, my entire body ached; it was all I could do to hold back the tears.

After days that seemed endless, Justice Mortimer B. Patterson granted me a divorce from Hannah and awarded me sole custody of the girls. Hannah's new attorney David Tepp (she had let Arnold Koch go) immediately filed an appeal to protest my getting custody.

Losing both the girls and the verdict was a bitter blow for Hannah. She sobbed and had to be helped from the courtroom. For a second I was tempted to rush to her side and to hold her close. I wasn't in such good shape myself; I felt as though I'd absorbed a worse battering than I had ever had in the ring. Not only had I lost my wife and my home life, I now found myself in the awkward position of having to be both mother and father to my little girls. Despite what Hannah and I had put each other through, I vowed to do my best to look out for her. After all, we had had some good years together, and she *was* the mother of my daughters. I guess I felt she deserved more breaks in life than I had given her.

Soon afterward my mother died. She had been my last refuge for strength and courage. She died of old age, among her own in a Salt Lake City hospital. Her attending physician, Dr. Pendleton, was amazed at her fortitude: On her deathbed she playfully threatened to punch him in the nose if he didn't stop fussing over her.

It was hard for me. I had never been one to prepare myself for anything but prizefights. I remembered with sadness how afraid the girls had been of this tiny woman who for some reason was usually able to get her way with their big father. Once one of them had greeted her so enthusiastically that she had fallen over, much to the little one's horror. What they couldn't realize was that they would never meet a more gentle or courageous lady than their grandmother.

In the mid-forties, while I was still in uniform, Amron persuaded me to join him in acquiring the lease of the Great Northern Hotel in New York. That sounded pretty good to me, having recently given up the Dempsey-Vanderbilt in Miami. I needed a place in New York where I could hang my hat. That place turned out to be the Great Northern's penthouse.

At about the same time, I unveiled in the restaurant a James Montgomery Flagg mural depicting my championship fight with Jess Willard. I had commissioned Flagg to do it and was very proud of the result. The only other work of his I had ever seen was his famous "I want you" recruiting poster.

Victory bond drives were taking place all over the country. U.S.O. was spending $100,000 a month for servicemen entertainment at the camp shows, while Eddie Cantor's Purple Heart circuit played to capacity audiences in hospital tours. I participated in several tours, showing off with some shadowboxing while the more talented members of the troupe sang, danced or performed skits. I helped raise funds for the fight against polio, associating myself with the Kenny Institute while touring military installations.

With all my dashing about, it didn't occur to me that my two young daughters needed me just as much in my off-duty hours as anyone else. Sure, I called them every night, but this was no substitute for my being with them. When I saw them I gave them spending money, which they promptly let run through their fingers, despite the watchful eye of their governess Anne Gallagher, the housekeeper and Gene Fowler, who used to drop in and keep me posted.

Living within their allowance was out of the question; they weren't any great shakes in terms of money management—just like their father. I loved them and worried about them, but there was a war going on and, rightly or wrongly, I felt I had no time to play governess when I could afford to hire one.

Radio announcer and cameraman Harvey Twyman accompanied me on a tour of the Pacific theater, snapping pictures of me with young men in uniform and sending the photos to local papers back home. Every time I stopped in a new place I'd be recognized, and young soldiers would ask me to sign letters home and autograph books, articles of clothing—even skin if nothing else was handy. Some of those boys never got to see American shores again. If my presence gave them even a flash of home, that was good enough for me.

On the way to Okinawa, I stopped by one of the Coral Islands to say hello to United Press war correspondent Ernie Pyle, who was also on his way to the Ryukyus. We spent a day or two together. He was misty-eyed as he said good-bye, telling me he would probably never be seeing me again. I told him not to be ridiculous; if anyone was going to make an exit, it would probably be me. Ernie Pyle was right: He didn't make it back home.

As we approached Okinawa's mainland, we kept our eyes peeled for the enemy. When the ship stopped and the motorboats and rafts starting filling up with men headed for shore, my superior officer pulled me aside.

"Jack, you stay here with me."

"Sir, I trained these boys and they look up to me. Thanks, but I go where they go."

"But, Jack. . . ."

"Sir. This means more to me than you can know." And I was one of the first to step ashore.

From Okinawa, I toured Australia, the Coral Islands, Thailand, Ceylon (where I was stricken with some Asiatic disorder) and Calcutta, where I did some refereeing before feeling too sick to continue. I was sent home to get medical attention for my sores as well as my rusty belly. When I checked in to a New York hospital, I felt somewhat better though I looked pretty lousy.

In April, 1945, Franklin Delano Roosevelt suddenly died, leaving all of us in shock. People cried in the streets and the nation was plunged into mourning. We worried how we would end the war without him. Harry Truman, gentle but tough, was sworn into office while we held our breath; changing horses in midstream made us uneasy.

In May the German armies surrendered and on August 6 the United States dropped the atomic bomb over Hiroshima, followed shortly by another over Nagasaki. At 7 P.M. on August 14, 1945, the Japanese officially surrendered. The war was over.

Celebrations went on day and night. Broadway traffic stopped, and people were dancing in the street and jumping on car hoods. Radios blared music and news from open doorways, shops and windows. Everyone kissed and embraced his neighbor; we all felt like brothers in a great big family. I'll never forget Broadway that day. It was my street and I belonged there. I was warned of being trampled. So what? So was everyone else, and it felt great!

Broadway made such an impression on me that day that I approached my partner Jake Amron, who was still basking in the restaurant's war profits, with a proposition. I wanted to see my name up in lights on Broadway. Amron listened and agreed it wouldn't be a bad idea. Amron pulled a few strings, and before long my name did go up, on Forty-ninth Street and Broadway. For a while Amron and I kept the original restaurant as well, but the one on Broadway became such a success that we decided to concentrate on the new one and give up the old one, though it wasn't even ten years old.

I had barely taken off my Coast Guard uniform, having been honorably discharged in September in Long Beach, California, when I was called back to participate in a whistle-stop war loan drive for the Treasury Department, hitting seventeen major cities in about five weeks. Among those I teamed up with were my young attorney friend John Sirica, Gene Autry, Hubert Humphrey and Lyndon Baines Johnson.

Autry was a popular country and western star I had met in Hollywood in 1936 when he was under contract to Republic Studios. He looked pretty sharp in his Air Force uniform—as I hoped I did in my uniform. On the drive, Autry would invariably be the m.c. while I stood beside him and suffered through something like this:

"Ladies and gents. When I was five years old, this man here was the heavyweight champion of the world. Why, I remember asking my folks . . ." Autry meant well, but I finally asked him to cut it out because he was ruining me with all the young babes who were probably thinking how well preserved I was for an old coot!

Halfway through the drive Lyndon Baines Johnson joined us and proceeded to get mad at me because I was holding everyone up by signing autographs. As he steamed, I told him:

"Listen, pal. I haven't been champion now for almost twenty years, and believe me, if people still remember me and ask for my autograph, then the least I can do is to find time to give it to them."

Some years later, at his presidential inaugural, Johnson thanked me, saying I had taught him a valuable lesson. (It seems he'd gotten some member of the press corps mad for the same reason.)

In Minneapolis, on the last leg of the drive, I was welcomed by Mayor Hubert H. Humphrey. He accompanied me to Ernie Fliegel's 620 Club along with promoter Charley Johnston. Fliegel's club was one of Minneapolis's favorite restaurants, and the crowd was so large that day that I had to get up on my toes while standing on a table to get the attention of the people there to buy bonds. Humphrey and Johnson stood beside me. After having met so many mayors on the drive, being with Humphrey was refreshing. He was an attractive politician who didn't try to hustle anyone.

The war loan drive over, I was once more a busy civilian, dividing my time between New York, where I had my business, and California, where I had my girls.

In April, 1946, Rear Admiral Ed H. Smith, Commander, Third Coast Guard District, awarded me a citation that read: "For outstanding performance of duty as Director of the Physical Training Program of the U.S. Coast Guard and later as Morale Officer for Coast Guard Personnel, June 1942–October 1945." The applause, at this stage of my life, was the most heartwarming I'd ever received.

When I spent a long stretch in New York, Gene Fowler would write to try to convince me to set myself up in business on the west coast because he was running out of companions. "I drink them to death or worry them to death." By this time he was fifty-six years old; I was fifty-one.

One day Estelle Taylor, accompanied by her agent Bill White, dropped by Gene's house to discuss a book she wanted to do about me. As far as I was concerned, she could write anything she liked as long as it didn't encroach on my life. Despite all her ambitious intentions, she never followed through on the project. Gene liked Estelle and found her quite pleasant—despite her disapproval of his habit of eating cake and drinking whiskey at the same time.

New York in those postwar years was in a state of euphoria with that venerable institution, the American Dollar, conspicuous once more despite the shortage of some goods. The Stork Club and El Morocco still held their own, but the Copacabana, Zanzibar, Diamond Horseshoe and Latin Quarter were starting to pack them in as well. Toots Shor summed it all up: "Any bum who can't get plastered by midnight ain't really tryin'."

Toots Shor, with his amusing remarks, had turned out to be a good pal. Sometimes, looking at him, I would be reminded of a night in Philadelphia in 1930. An acquaintance, Jack Kelly of the Philadelphia Kellys, had organized a sports night and invited me to attend. Since Toots was from Philly, I invited him to come along—and was surprised to see him hesitate.

"Come on, Toots. You can show me some of the sights, pal."

In the end, he agreed reluctantly. I felt I knew the reason for his hesitation; he had left Philly broke, a street fighter and a bum. I sensed that this was bothering him as we pulled into the station, and I grabbed him by the arm as we stepped onto the platform. If he needed a pal beside him, I was there.

The crowd cheered my name and asked for my autograph. All of a sudden, a few of Toots's old pals spotted him standing with me and started yelling, "Hey, Toots, Toots." Later he told me he would never forget the sensation he felt that night. It was as if I had given him the courage to face again the city he'd been so eager to leave.

Between my New York friends and my out-of-town pals, I think I was out more than I was in. I hadn't been a bachelor in a long time, and now that there was no war, and I had no sticky entanglements, I planned to find as much pleasure as I could.

John Sirica, who was practising law in Washington, used to like to meet me in New York. We would invariably wind up at some club, usually the Stork Club, El Morocco or "21". One night we went to a smallish nightclub because John was acquainted with the organist Ethel Smith, who was performing. As we walked in I heard my name stage-whispered from table to table. Just before the show began, a thin young man wearing a tux engaged Ethel Smith in conversation.

"Jack, who's the skinny kid talking to Ethel?"

"I think his name is Frank Sinatra."

We didn't pay much attention to whether he was good or not; after all, we'd come to hear Ethel.

I spent November and Christmas with my two girls in New York, buying them practically everything they saw. Women. Young or old, they really didn't change much. Christmas and New Year's over, I took the girls home to California and decided to stay there awhile.

Shortly after my arrival, Joe Schenck, then chairman of the board at Fox, called and asked to see me.

"Jack, how well do you know Dr. Harry Martin?" (Doc Martin was medical director at Fox and Louella Parsons's husband.)

"Doc Martin? I knew him pretty well. He's a swell guy, except when he hits the bottle. Luckily, Louella reminds him when he has an operation scheduled for the next morning. Why?"

"Well, Doc's been bragging to Harry Brand [Fox's publicity director] and me how he was the greatest barroom fighter of all time and how he once KO'd you."

"No kidding."

"No kidding. Naturally, we're not only skeptical of his skill as a fighter, but we're convinced he's lying. Now, Jack, if you're willing to go along with us, we'd like to show Doc up. What do you say?"

"Sure," I grinned. "I'm game. Shoot."

"Okay, listen carefully. Harry doesn't think his bluff will ever be called. So the next time you see him—make sure we're with you —say, 'Christ, you're the barroom fighter who knocked me out!'

"Now he knows it's a lie, and he knows you know, so he'll have to come clean."

I couldn't wait. When the showdown finally came, I went so far as to name the joint in Chicago where he had supposedly knocked me out. Martin stood up and puffed out his chest. Instead of being put in his place, he pointed to Brand and Joe and said, "Hah! Didn't I tell you?"

I stayed in California for a few months before I began speaking to boys' clubs and refereeing again. I just couldn't keep away from the ring even though I wasn't fighting. Since I didn't really show my age, I disregarded it altogether.

On one trip to Denver I was honored along with journalist Bob Considine, who was at that time writing Babe Ruth's story. Everyone was proud of Considine; the Babe's story was sure to be an entertaining and an inspirational one.

Just before the dinner, while sitting in my suite at the Brown Palace Hotel overlooking Mount Evans, I was disturbed by a loud rap on the door.

"Come in." An old man walked in and stared at me.

"Are you Kid Blackie?"

"Yeah, I'm Kid Blackie. Who are you, old-timer?"

"I'm W. H. Lehr and you owe me a buck twenty-five cents.

You ran out on me without payin' for your pictures and now I'm here to collect."

I looked at Lehr closely and decided it just had to be a joke.

"Why, you old son of a gun. I thought you'd forgotten that one. Besides, the pictures were no good," I said, thinking backwards fast.

"Oh yes they were, and here's a copy of 'em just to show you how good they were."

He showed me the pictures and then burst out laughing, seeing the expression on my face. All of a sudden his face clicked. Lehr had been a photographer in Victor, Colorado, way back in 1914 when I blew into town (via the rods) for a fight with the Boston Bearcat. In his shop window Lehr had put up a sign offering nice, glossy photographs for a buck and a quarter. Without a dime to my name, as was the usual case, I walked into the shop thinking it wouldn't be a bad idea to have photographs of me in a fighting pose. Explaining to Lehr that I was broke, I promised to pay him out of my purse. He agreed and took the pictures. That night, carried away by my knockout of the Bearcat, I hopped the first convenient freight out of town, forgetting to pay Lehr. Now, more than thirty years later, here was Lehr standing in front of me, asking for the buck twenty-five due him. Once the finances were settled, Lehr and I reminisced about what he considered the good old days—and I considered the hungriest days of my life.

On Washington's Birthday the following year, my father died in Salt Lake, like my mother, of old age. He was 92. I never learned —or even cared—what happened to his second wife. I didn't attend my father's funeral because I wanted to remember him as he had been, before all the arguments, the whiskey and the disillusionments. He had hurt my mother for too many years. Deep down, I knew I had tried to be a good son to both my parents.

Now that memories of the war were fading, people once again directed their energies to boosting Hollywood and sports. In the boxing world, many speculated on the future of Joe Louis just as they had done with me years before. Louis, about to engage in a controversial title bout with Jersey Joe Walcott, was starting to show rust, and many felt his mental and physical timing was slow. I agreed, remembering how my own reflexes had been the first to go. The more people talked about Louis, the more I thought about myself and how everything had changed—not necessarily for the better or the worse, just changed. Louis had been champion now for ten years, but he was a different Louis than the Louis who had fought Baer and Schmeling. One of the things I respected about Louis was that he was much more of a gentleman in the ring than I ever was.

Doc Kearns was getting into the news, still up to his old tricks, now attempting to propel Joey Maxim to the top. I pretended not to pay much attention to Kearns, but I devoured every item printed about him—as I'm sure he did with me. In recent years we had reestablished a flimsy contact, but it threatened to snap each time he attempted to finagle me. Nine out of ten times he'd still manage to leave people holding the short end of the stick, and I wasn't going to be one of them again. As a rule I always looked for and found good in most persons; with Doc, I didn't even bother to look. Perhaps I would have felt less bitter toward him if he hadn't claimed exclusive credit for my success and still continued to speak of me in condescending terms after so many years.

We were well into summer when Babe Ruth, the greatest slugger of them all, died after a courageous but losing battle with cancer. Babe had made his last appearance wearing his soon-to-be-retired number 3 uniform in July, on the silver anniversary of Yankee Stadium. Unable to make it to New York to say good-bye to my old pal, I nevertheless felt a terrible void. Gravel-voiced Ruth had been on the rise at the same time I had been, and now he was gone.

In Hollywood I turned movie producer while intimate friends smirked. My first undertaking naturally had a sports background which we hoped would reach the growing sports-minded audience. We followed that fiasco with a film called *The Big Wheel* (1949), starring Mickey Rooney and Ellye Marshall. It was the first in a proposed annual series to be done over the course of five years.

Anyone who might be put on film was approached, including Joe DiMaggio, who just wasn't interested. DiMaggio was, unlike me, a very private individual.

In 1949, Hank Greenspun, a Las Vegas friend, was indicted

by the federal government for violating the Neutrality Act by taking certain war matériel out of the country, destined for Israel. Reading of Hank's indictment, I rushed to Las Vegas and told him to pack a valise; I was taking him to Washington to see if I could do anything to help clear up the matter.

I admired Hank's spunk and courage. At first he balked at the idea of going to Washington, not wanting to get me involved. He protested that it was a matter for the State Department, even though he felt he was being used as a scapegoat. Everyone was being ultracautious about antagonizing the Arab nations either officially or unofficially. I ignored Hank's arguments. In Washington I looked up almost everyone I knew, with the exception of President Truman, who had enough trouble. I felt as though I was carrying a red-hot coal.

When Attorney General J. Howard McGrath informed me that the United States couldn't lean one way or the other, I understood that there was nothing I could accomplish. I attempted wading through more red tape but backed off when the State Department clashed with the Department of Justice over Hank. I felt bad, not being able to do more, but Hank Greenspun was grateful that I had tried.

29

Deanna

I was still traveling around the country refereeing, visiting the men in hospitals, talking to boys' clubs and organizing charity drives when I wasn't in my New York restaurant or at home in California.

Jake Amron and I had been partners in the restaurant business for over fifteen years when he decided that he had grown tired and wanted out. I understood how he felt. Running the place had been in his hands more than mine while I fulfilled commitments around the country. Amron, not wanting to leave me holding the bag, approached Jack Amiel, who owned the Turf Restaurant on the corner and was pretty well known in the restaurant field. Before long, Amron had sold his share to Amiel. Amiel reminded me a lot of Amron, though Amron seemed to have a tenacity all his own. Underneath it all, I really didn't care much who my partner was, just so long as he knew the things I didn't.

On January 30, 1950, after a cross-country refereeing and good will trip, I flew into New York to be guest of honor at the Boxing Managers' Guild Dinner at the Hotel Edison. I had been voted the greatest prizefighter of the half-century in a nationwide poll of sports writers and sportscasters conducted by the Associated Press. Jack Kearns was to be one of the other honored guests, which evoked mixed reactions for me. But I recognized what I had to do and say at the dinner, for it was the first time in years that we would be together in a public spotlight.

271

That night, before the dinner, the telephone wouldn't stop ringing. Reporters called, asking this question and that, and women called. How they found out where I was, was a mystery. One even sent me a bunch of flowers with a card saying she'd meet me after the affair—without signing her name.

As I entered the hotel ballroom I was crushed by autograph seekers, more than I had seen since the 1920s. It was as if the years had somehow dropped away. Thunderous applause greeted me when I walked in, with 1,200 people standing to welcome me.

I spotted Gene Fowler seated at a table with a pitcher of beer in front of him. I walked over to Gene and said, "This is partly my dinner, partner, and where I sit my old pals are going to sit—with me, on the dais."

He refused. "Jack, I guess I've known you longer than anybody in this room except Kearns. You may have been a tramp once, but you were never a bum. You get yourself up there. Your old pal is sitting here, pretty proud of you."

As I was about to leave Gene, someone sat down next to him. Always the gracious host, Gene pushed the pitcher forward toward the man.

"How about a beer?"

"Never touch the stuff."

"Funny, I just began drinking it myself." I could swear I heard him muttering that it was just his luck. . . .

This honor was the greatest thing that had happened to me in a long time. I was touched that the sports writers and sportscasters had thought me worthy of such distinction. There had been so many fighters before and after me that I wondered how they could really pick a best. It was difficult enough to compare any two of us.

As I listened to the presentation, my mind raced back to Firpo, Gunboat Smith, Bill Brennan, Willie Meehan—all greats and none of them with me on this occasion. Then I glanced to my left, and there was Kearns. I guess he had always been there, even after we broke up. After the presentation, I pushed my chair back and stepped to the podium. Thanking everybody for the honor, I spoke words which had been a long time coming.

I will be grateful to Kearns all my life for making me a champion. Kearns told me I was the greatest fighter in the world and I believed him. He told me I was a terrific puncher and I believed him. He had me breaking doors with punches.

On the morning of the Jess Willard fight Kearns came to me and said he had bet $10,000 to $100,000 I'd win by a knockout in the first round. He told me I was going to knock out Willard. I believed him.

Gentlemen, Jack Kearns made me a million dollars.

To this Jack Kearns replied, "This means more to me than Maxim winning a dozen titles. Everybody has always known my heart belonged to Dempsey."

At long last, we shook hands. As of that night, I forgave Doc for a lot of things—even though I could never forget.

Damon Runyon was the one writer I sorely missed. On this night of tribute, his presence was the one I'd have appreciated most. He had, in pain and silence, passed away some four years before. My loss of him as a friend was something I couldn't bear to talk about; he had been like my mirrored conscience for so many years. As I had realized so long ago, when I lost Tex Rickard, the pain was worse for those who were left behind. Friendship between two people was a precious gift; if I appreciated my friends more than the next guy, it may have been because I didn't have any real ties or roots of my own.

I recalled how I had looked up to Rickard, how I had loved and admired him as a man. Nowadays, if two men were fairly close pals, gossips would speculate and insinuate until the friendship changed footing or soured. I was sure Tex Rickard wouldn't particularly have liked this new world, which was changing its expressions and its tastes from day to day.

Even Madison Square Garden wasn't the same. Once, after participating in a Ringling Brothers Barnum & Bailey Circus gala opening performance with Emmett Kelly, Sr., for the benefit of the New York Heart Association, I walked outside and tried to see things through Rickard's and Ringling's eyes. Ringling, who had ultimately paid for my slacker trial and had been a backer for Tex's Garden and many other ventures, would have been sorely disappointed at what had become of his dream. Cops on horseback were now curbing people while taxi drivers honked their horns and pedestrians shook their fists and raised their voices to add to the din. Motorcycles roared while street vendors peddled junk. Only the smell and feel of excitement itself was familiar.

Television was really catching on now, and it had the same effect on me that talking pictures had had in the twenties. One of the funniest things I remember doing on television was appearing in a boxing skit with Bob Hope. I hadn't put on my ring togs in a number of years, and Bob confessed that he hadn't either. (He had once apparently been an amateur fighter in Cleveland.) While I wore four-ounce gloves, Bob's soft gloves were of suitcase size.

In 1952 I was called to Fort Lauderdale. John Sirica had finally decided to take the big plunge and wanted me to be his best man. The day before the ceremony, John was as nervous as a cat. He had met Lucy Camalier some five months before and had fallen head over heels in love with her. We stayed up the whole night talking; by dawn, he had finally managed to calm down. I, on the other hand, had become a nervous wreck.

Everyone I knew was either getting married or getting divorced while I was still trying to be both parents at once, even though the girls really didn't need me anymore. Hannah had remarried, and I had breathed a sigh of relief, hoping she would at last find what she was looking for.

On one of my frequent trips to Chicago I was approached by the warden of the Cook County Jail, who asked me if I would talk to the inmates. I had never been in a penal institution, and I felt it would be a worthwhile experience. Handclapping and cheering greeted me as I stepped through the gates. For once the warden had no control, and for once he really didn't care. The inmates were glad to see me; each and every one wanted to speak to me and to touch me. One big gentleman, who seemed to have more privileges than the others, drew near me.

"Hey, Champ. It would give me a great honor if you would allow me to give you a shave."

I looked into his face, saw his expression and agreed. It was his way of thanking me for coming. I was put into a makeshift barber's chair and draped with towels, while my enthusiastic barber stropped his shiny straight razor vigorously. Then he lathered my face and placed the blade by my Adam's apple. Gazing at me with a strange light in his eyes, he stage-whispered, "How would you like your throat cut?"

"Why, any way you want, son," I said, my voice even higher than usual. For a moment no one spoke, and then he smiled and proceeded to shave my face.

The men plied me with questions on all sorts of subjects, ranging from the long count to women. Thousands were present to hear me stress the importance of keeping on the right side of the tracks—now that they knew what the wrong side was like. Holding a grudge through life was pointless, I told them, and I cited several instances from my own experience. Summing up, I pointed out that a sense of humor, enthusiasm and perseverance were the essential qualities a man needed to get ahead. They were the qualities that I felt had helped me.

By the end of the day, after having been shaved, after having spoken and sparred with some of the inmates, I was bone-tired but glad I had accepted the warden's invitation. But it wasn't until a few years later, when two prosperous-looking gentlemen walked into my restaurant, that I realized that my visit had made an impression. Identifying themselves as former inmates of the Cook County Jail, they informed me they had since made good. One was head of his local chamber of commerce, while the other had just applied for a patent for an invention, and they had stopped by just to thank me.

That meant a lot to me; I seemed always to be thanking people more than I was being thanked. Except, of course, by women.

In the twenties and thirties they had been dames and broads to me; now they had become women. (There were still very few ladies around.) Estelle Harmon Spencer Auguste of Palm Beach was a woman as well as a lady. She was also stinking rich. I had been introduced to her on one of my tours, and in time I became so infatuated with her that I thought I was in love again, even though it was a far cry from the passionate obsessions of the past. One night, influenced by the moon, the palms and her, I proposed. She accepted.

From that moment I felt as though I had a noose around my neck.

A few days later she announced to the *Miami Daily News* that she had inherited some $35,000,000 from her banker husband and that she was going to marry me. None of my friends took it seriously, and hers ignored us altogether. I might have been a celebrity, but I wasn't fancy or well-bred enough for them.

In March of that year, Hannah, who had recently been divorced from Tommy Monaghan, was seriously burned when her cigarette ignited a mattress and fire broke out in her hotel room in Los Angeles. Nearly overcome by the smoke and heat, she had staggered outside where the police picked her up and took her to the Santa Fe Hospital. I rushed home to California. When we walked into the hospital, I told the girls not to make any statements. The fact that I was with my daughters didn't mean much to the press, but the fact that I was visiting my ex-wife did.

No matter what, Hannah was still the mother of my daughters and a part of my life. I took care of her hospital bills, paid for some plastic surgery and suggested she come to live in my home, where she could look out for herself as well as her daughters.

Up to then I had felt that the girls were in good hands when I was away. I had depended on my long-time buddies, Willie Bernstein, who seemed to enjoy his role of official protector and substitute guardian, and Gene Fowler, who kept his antenna up. Willie was there all the time and thereby kept my mind at ease, as did Gene.

Nevertheless, a mother was a mother, and Hannah at this stage of the game had nothing to lose and everything to gain. She was touched and she agreed. When she was discharged from the hospital I took her to the best women's shops and outfitted her with everything she wanted. The whole thing must have overwhelmed her, for two weeks later she packed a bag and moved away without even bothering to let me know.

By this time, Estelle Harmon Spencer Auguste and I were through. She had realized what I had suspected for some time, that I was not the man for her. We parted on good terms and I never saw her again.

Following these brief but unnerving interludes, I resumed my work as referee, hitting many cities before resting up in Chicago.

One week after I had checked into the Morrison Hotel, I had a totally unexpected visit from Bill Tate, my old 1919 sparring partner, who was now aged and in failing health. I was pleased to see him and asked him if he was still putting good men away. He laughed and told me he was now a night watchman in Chicago—and afraid he was going to die.

"Don't be ridiculous, Bill. You've still got plenty of good years in front of you. Now, is there anything—you name it—that I can do for you, Bill?"

"Well, the only thing I ever wanted in life was to spend the rest of my days workin' a farm, but I ain't got the money."

"Forget the dough, Bill. You can mortgage the farm to me. You look around, see what you like and I'll handle everything. Since I'll be out of Chicago for a couple of weeks, take your time and when I come back I'll sign the papers and we'll close the deal. How does that sound to you, Bill?"

He bent his grizzled head down and burst out crying, burying his shiny black face in the largest handkerchief I had ever seen. Embarrassed, I patted him and told him I wanted to see smiles, not tears, from now on. He nodded his head and we shook hands.

I didn't give the matter much thought until a week before I was scheduled to be in Chicago again. Having heard nothing from Bill for a couple of weeks, I tried unsuccessfully to reach him by phone, letter and wire. Concerned, I called some friends who sadly broke the news that Bill had passed away. Life in the end had been fair to Bill; he had died clutching hope.

Everything seemed to happen too fast in the fifties. Suddenly my daughters were both married. They were beautiful young ladies now, but I still regarded them as little girls. It threw me when I learned that Barbara had been smoking for years; but there was nothing I could do.

Now they had new men, young ones, in their lives—which didn't make me happy one bit. I was shaken and suffered from an idiotic jealousy that I tried to hide. I encouraged all of them to look to me for financial help, which they did. This, in addition to my continued presence, was suffocating their marriages and finally caused domestic rows and resentment. I supplied them with more groceries and more homemade preserves than their already groaning cupboards could hold. Presenting myself on their doorstep, fully laden with packages, whenever I was in town, gave me confidence that I'd be welcomed with open arms.

If they had stood up to me from the first and acted like mature adults instead of children playing house, everything might have turned out better than it did. I was wrong and I was at fault, but in the end, so were they.

Around this time, Tonopah, Nevada, celebrating its sesquicentennial, invited me to be guest of honor at a dinner. I had fought Johnny Sudenberg there in 1915 and was eager to see him as well as some of my old friends who were still there. Stopping in Las Vegas, I persuaded Hank Greenspun and Wilbur Clark to accompany me as my guests.

We checked into the Mizpah Hotel and waited upstairs in our suite for the welcoming and reception committee. Before long the phone jangled and we left the room to meet the committee in the lobby. On the ground floor, we walked three abreast toward the group, Hank sandwiched between Wilbur and me. One young lady from the group rushed up to Hank (who strongly resembled me), grabbed his hand and stared into his face, barely managing to say, "Oh, Mr. Dempsey. I'm so very thrilled! I've waited years for this great honor!"

Wilbur and I were almost doubled up with laughter, but the woman ignored us. Hank, thinking fast, did the only thing he could do under the circumstances: He leaned forward and kissed her noisily on the cheek. The woman turned crimson and breathed, "Wait'll the girls hear about this! Oh, Mr. Dempsey."

That night the dinner was a huge success, but I couldn't help wondering what the lady's reaction had been when I was introduced and gave my speech.

My restaurant on Broadway was doing better than ever, and I tried to spend as much time there as I could between my frequent trips to the west coast. In New York I lived out of suitcases and hotel rooms again, having given up my penthouse in the Great Northern Hotel. Urged by several advisors, I had sold my California house and purchased an apartment house complex in Santa Monica around the time Joan and Barbara began to need me less. Now I was a landlord again—for the first time in a long spell—but I didn't make the mistake of meddling with the management. I put my brother Joe in charge.

My apartment in Los Angeles wasn't exactly the biggest apartment I had ever seen, but it suited me just fine. One day, while I was sitting in the dining room playing cards with my pal Willie, the phone rang (interrupting a very crucial hand). Willie jumped up and answered it.

"Champie, it's Walter Kane for you."

I had known Walter, who was now working for Howard Hughes, since 1922, when I was playing the Pantages and he was at the Orpheum working with Dorothy Aubrey.

"Hiya, Walter. What can I do for you?"

"The boss wants to see you."

"Right now?" I asked, seeing a winning hand going right down the drain.

"Well, as soon as possible. Why don't you meet me at my house on the Strip and we'll take it from there?"

"Fine. See you in a short while." I hung up and looked at Willie.

"Maybe Howard Hughes wants to do your life story, Champie. Jeez! I can see it now . . ."

"Now, Willie, get hold of yourself and don't jump to any conclusions. Come on, let's get out of here."

We had barely arrived at Walter's house when Howard Hughes strolled in, looking as if he had just been outfitted at a rummage sale. He was, from the time we'd occasionally double-dated way back when, the worst dresser I had even seen.

Not wasting time on social amenities, Howard patted me on the back and spoke.

"Jack, you know something? You drew more money from boxing exhibitions than today's fighters are drawing from real fights. In fact, you were and still are one of the most colorful personalities I've ever met."

"Why, thank you very much, Howard." I still didn't know why I was there.

Hughes then turned to Walter and told him to take us to

Deborah Kerr's for lunch. Still in the dark, we accompanied him to her house, where other guests were already seated, among them lovely Jean Simmons, whom Howard liked very much. Evidently he hadn't scored with her, so he was willing to do anything to make her happy.

When I greeted Jean, she said, "Jack, I can't tell you how thrilled I am to meet you. I've always enjoyed fights and when I was a little girl, my father used to take me with him whenever he could."

As she spoke, she stared at me, making me squirm in my seat.

"You know, I just finished filming *Guys and Dolls*, and oh, you must see it. Will you?"

"Sure." I had obviously lost my tongue.

She then proceeded to describe the movie's fight scene, getting to her feet and showing me how she threw her punches. In a playful mood, she threw a bad right and I, going along with the gag, lay down on the rug.

All in all, it turned out to be an entertaining afternoon with a gracious hostess, swell food and nice people. It also accomplished absolutely nothing.

A few months later, when *Guys and Dolls* was released, Jean Simmons was interviewed and asked, "How come you fought like a professional in the film?"

To which she replied something like, "I knocked Jack Dempsey down flat while sparring."

Reading the article, I thought she was cute, but Willie felt that no "dame" was going to say that about me and get away with it! A couple of days later, lunching at Ciro's, Willie spied Jean Simmons with attorney Greg Bautzer. Before I could stop him, Willie had made his way to their table.

"How do you like that! Jack Dempsey slips on a carpet in Deborah Kerr's house on purpose, and you say you knocked him down. Why, when he sees you, he'll punch you right in the nose! Fair's fair, and that means a rematch!"

Bautzer, who apparently lacked a sense of humor that day, looked poor Willie square in the eye and reportedly said, "If Jack intends to do what you say, he'll have to deal with me first."

In Chicago I had become associated, through George Florey, a local public relations man, with the DeVry brothers, founders of the DeVry Technical Institute, as Director of Student Welfare. This was very gratifying to me; I had always enjoyed talking and listening to boys who were still learning and charting their course in life. The DeVry Institute was a fine school, though I put out more in terms of time and energy than the contract and salary covered, after shelling out 25 percent to Florey.

It was about this time that I was approached by former fly-weight fighter, now promoter, Bobby Manziel to referee a fight in Monroe, Louisiana. I had met Bobby a while back, but I hadn't seen him in quite a stretch, so I agreed to do it. When it was over Bobby and I reestablished our friendship, and before going home I reminded him that if he ever needed me again, all he had to do was holler or wire.

Some months later he wired me for the money to buy a very promising oil lease. It wasn't that much, so I sent it to him. Before long, I received another wire: WE'VE HIT THE JACKPOT. OIL. COME DOWN.

I couldn't believe it; it was the only money I'd ever loaned which seemed likely to be paid back.

Everything was running smoothly until Edward Mike Davis, a friend from Denver whom I had introduced to Manziel, filed suit against Bobby, contending that:

> On December 15, 1956, he had delivered to Manziel his personal check for $6250.00 in payment for an undivided one-sixteenth of seven-eighths working interest in a tract of 1,261.15 acres in Marion County, subject to payment of a proportionate part of the cost of drilling, completion, and equipping of any wells subsequent to Well No. 1. . . .

> Bobby Manziel executed and delivered to Davis an assignment of the one-sixteenth in the "40 acre tract" that claimed to be the only interest Davis had in the operation because of his failure to timely execute certain options which would have permitted participation in drilling of wells *other* than the one said to be represented by the December 15 check.

Despite the impending suit, Bobby and I discussed plans for a large athletic arena. Just as everything seemed to be coming to a head, Bobby suddenly died. Now I began to worry, knowing the focus would turn to me. My association with Bobby Manziel had been based on a handshake; I now found myself in the awkward position of being a key witness to "certain transactions as well as a party to litigations"—since Bobby had given me an interest in the deal.

Edward Mike Davis prepared himself for battle with Manziel's estate by hiring a distinguished firm of attorneys, as did Manziel's family in defense. As often happened with legal suits, it was a long time before the case came to court.

In 1956, George Florey and Bill DeVry asked me to meet them in a projection room at N.B.C. Studios in Hollywood, where they assured me I would see something really interesting. Sitting in that tight little room with the two of them was starting to get to me, when a loudspeaker blared: "Jack Dempsey, Jack Dempsey? Are you there? This is Ralph Edwards, and *This Is Your Life!*"

It turned out to be some night. The first guest from my past was Roy Stubbs, with whom I had attended Sunday school in Provo when I wasn't working. I remembered we both wore trousers that were at least six sizes too large. Then came Johnny Sudenberg, my old opponent in Goldfield and Tonopah, followed by my brother Joe, whom I had seen the previous week, and Fred Fulton, whom I had put away in eighteen and three-fifths seconds back in 1915. I was really glad to see him; his hands still looked like they packed a pretty powerful wallop. Joe Benjamin, my old friend and sparring partner, greeted me next, and I remembered the time I'd nearly demolished him in the hotel room.

Edwards introduced one of my old vaudeville partners, my daughters and my grandchildren, after surprising me with Georges Carpentier, who had been flown in from Paris, and Luis Angel Firpo, the former Wild Bull of the Pampas, who had come all the way from Rosario, Argentina. After the show we all went to the Hollywood Roosevelt Hotel, where I was officially presented with the gloves I had worn for the Carpentier fight and the shoes I had worn for Firpo.

Seeing Georges that night really excited me. I felt deep affection for this fine and gentle Frenchman for many years. Up to the day he died, his path and mine crossed many, many times, but never so unexpectedly as on this night.

I found Firpo broader and more effusive than ever. Shortly after the show, Firpo invited me down to Rosario to be his guest at a celebration. I agreed happily. When I arrived I was so beat that he had someone show me to my room at the ranch. I had barely unpacked when I heard a great deal of noise outside. Opening the windows, I saw what seemed to be hundreds of people running like crazy, back and forth, setting up tables and umbrellas and dressing large steers. I didn't know what was going on; I climbed into bed and dozed for a few hours.

Later, sitting with Luis, I asked him, "What's all the commotion outside?"

"Commotion? Oh, that's nothing."

"Nothing? Why is everyone running around?"

"Because of the small party I'm giving in your honor."

"Luis, tell me, how many did you invite?"

"The whole town, my friend."

I never saw a party quite like that one; it lasted one entire day and night. It was great, and Firpo's friends were among the most colorful, warmest people I had ever met.

Not wanting to impose on my host, I made plans to leave a few days later. As Firpo took me to the plane, he draped his massive arm across my shoulders, thanked me for coming and handed me an envelope, telling me not to open it until I reached New York. I agreed. In New York I forgot about the envelope until the next day, when the maid drew my attention to it as she was sending my suits to be cleaned. Ripping it open, I found, in large denominations, twenty thousand dollars, with a note stating simply, "Just a small token of friendship and appreciation from one old friend to another . . ."

We had fought so long ago, yet it seemed like yesterday. I found it hard to believe that even the Dempsey–Tunney fight was celebrating its thirtieth anniversary.

I had now been around for a hell of a long time, but women,

seeing me as Ripe and Available, began to zero in on me more than
ever. One of them, vivacious, blonde, cutie-pie Mamie Van Doren,
was really out to snag me (or so I thought), bending Willie Bernstein's ear every time I was in town or about to be. Mamie, whose
interesting name had apparently been given her by a film studio,
had the most burning ambition I had ever come across. Intense in
everything she did, she flattered me and unsettled me at the same
time. Chasen's, the Mocambo, Mike Romanoff's—none was too good
for beautful Mamie. She loved the press and, naturally, she loved
the limelight, much to my discomfiture.

Another very energetic lady was Elsinore Machris in Palm
Springs. Elsinore, a lovely, older, philanthropic lady, was a neighbor
of Dave Margolis, my good pal from Dayton, who had bought the
Howard Manor Hotel from Bob (the Millionaire Sportsman)
Howard and his wife, former actress Andrea Leeds. Shortly after
he acquired the hotel, Dave and his wife Annabelle persuaded me to
become associated with them and their operation, which was probably one of the best moves I ever made. The two of them helped me
unwind after many a strenuous trip. Dave, who had always known
everybody there was to know, was a big hit with Elsinore. She always managed to know I was in town the moment my plane
landed at the airport.

One day she approached Margolis. "Dave, I would like to
throw a big, beautiful party in honor of Jack Dempsey in the
Howard Manor. Naturally, I'll take care of everything."

"That's very nice, Elsinore."

"Yes, I know, and since you're a friend, I'd like to tell you con-
fidentially that I would very much like to become Mrs. Jack Dempsey, and I want you to encourage him and help arrange it. You're his
best friend, so see what you can do."

"Elsinore, I don't think . . ."

"Tell you what. For a wedding present I'll present Jack with a
check for $1,000,000, and if you make it all possible, I'll give you
$50,000 or five percent."

"Elsinore, I can't do that. A party is one thing, but . . ."

"Yes, you can."

Elsinore's bash was a party to end all parties. She invited two hundred fifty people, including the cream of the movie and publishing industries, as well as members of government (which necessitated security all around). It took a virtual army to supervise the affair. The guests, regaled by music from top bands, drank magnum upon magnum of imported champagne that flowed through the night and well past daybreak.

From the moment I appeared, the victimized guest of honor, I felt uncomfortable. I knew I had to refuse gracefully her offer of matrimony. My anxiety further increased when Joanie and Barbara took me aside and inquired, "Daddy, just in case, what are we supposed to call Elsinore? Mother, Elsinore, or what?"

"What do you mean? Why, just call her Aunt Elsinore!"

The party was written and talked about for days. I thanked Elsinore profusely, but I didn't bite, even though it is said that every man has his price. For quite a while afterward, every time I saw Elsinore on the street I would trot the other way rather than confront her. If I stayed away long enough, I hoped, she'd focus her attention on someone else.

Toward spring I left California for New York once more. Having grown tired of my usual hotel, I switched to the newly opened Manhattan, which was closer to my restaurant as well as being in the heart of the theater district. The Manhattan was slightly different from other hotels in that its lobby was situated on an upper level. Taking the escalator up, I spotted an extremely attractive woman working in the jewelry shop. She was blonde, but for some reason she reminded me of Estelle Taylor (which was both good and bad).

Since I had booked to stay in the hotel for a month, I decided to check her out. The next day, walking across the lobby to pick up my mail, I saw her again. For the first time since I could remember, I felt shy about approaching a woman. I returned to my room, rifled a drawer and came up with a pair of cufflinks which I deliberately bent out of shape and put in my pocket. I then left for an appointment with the hotel barber.

The shop was located on the mezzanine, which gave me a fine view of the lobby. From the mezzanine I could observe her, but she couldn't see me since she never looked up. Later I approached the counter holding the bent cufflinks in my hand. She looked up and smiled; my palms sweated.

"May I help you?" she inquired in a strangely accented voice.

She was as lovely up close as she had been from a distance, maybe lovelier. I wondered where she was from, narrowing it down to either Cuba or Europe.

"I was wondering if you could repair these cufflinks for me."

"No, we don't do repairs. I suggest you take them back to where you bought them, sir."

The woman was definitely Cuban, so I lapsed into what I considered to be my best Spanish: twelve and a half words mixed with a very fluid pig latin. She looked at me blankly and then answered in real Spanish, informing me that she was European—and did I by chance speak Italian as well as I spoke Spanish? I laughed, knowing perfectly well she sensed what I was up to. I could tell she found me amusing, which was all in my favor.

"What's your name?"

"Deanna. What's yours?"

I realized she had no idea who I was, so I told her my name was John L. Sullivan. She bought it. Not being capable of carrying on small talk for more than a minute or two, I told her I had an appointment and had to leave. We said good-bye, and I knew I had made a hit.

What I didn't know was that the moment I walked away, the bell captain rushed over to her and said, "Do you know who you were talking to?"

She said that she certainly did. I was none other than John L. Sullivan, probably in town for business. The bell captain laughed, informing her that I wasn't John L. Sullivan but Jack Dempsey, a name which meant nothing to her. He told her exactly who I was and that I was the heavyweight champion, to which she reportedly replied, "Isn't he kind of old?"

I didn't see her the next day or the following one. The sales-girls told me that Deanna was the owner of that shop—and of one in another hotel as well—and came in whenever she pleased. I went back to spying from the balcony until she returned the next day.

"Hello, Deanna."

She nodded and turned away. What was the matter with the woman? I tried again, and with blazing eyes she turned to me and snapped, "Why did you tell me your name was John L. Sullivan? Look here, sir, I don't care who John L Sullivan is, and I don't care who you are. No doubt you had quite a laugh at my expense!"

"You're angry with me."

"No, I'm not. I'm never angry."

"Well, would you like to have a cup of coffee with me to show me you forgive my joke?"

"No, thank you. I never have coffee with anyone I'm not properly introduced to."

"You want to be introduced, do you? Well, let me see what I can do." I looked around and motioned for a bellhop, who whizzed to my side and performed the introductions for a buck.

"Well, how about it?"

"No, Mr. Dempsey, thank you very much."

"Why not?" I was right when I thought she reminded me of Estelle; she was just as exasperating.

"I don't know if you'll understand this or not, but I just opened here and I don't feel that it would be very nice having a cup of coffee, or anything for that matter, with a man I just met in a lobby."

"But I'm—"

"I don't care. All I know is that no is no."

All I knew was that I was starting to want her, so I didn't let up until she finally relented four tries later, probably against her better judgment.

Coffee led to lunch and lunch led to dinner. I really liked her, but I was cautious, making her tell me all about herself and her daughter, who was then visiting an aged grandmother in Italy. Deanna was separated from her husband, who refused to give her a divorce. He had a girlfriend who was putting pressure on him and, having no intention of marrying the girlfriend, he wouldn't hear of a divorce.

Our courtship took place in Sardi's, Toots Shor's and the Stork Club. As I got to know her better, I took her to my restaurant, where the regulars gave her the once-over.

Fortunately she understood that I had to travel more than I stayed put. As the months flew by I tried to spend as much time with her as possible. At the same time I denied to the gossip columnists—and sometimes to myself—that I was involved with any one woman. I had fallen in love again, and while it was completely different from all the other times, one thing was the same: I was scared.

In the interim, Deanna's husband had broken off with his lady friend and had found a woman he wanted to marry, which paved the way for Deanna's divorce. This development made me very happy; dating a still-married woman was making me uncomfortable.

On Thanksgiving, Deanna flew out to Los Angeles to meet my daughters. Hannah happened to be visiting Barbara, who had two kids and was soon to be divorced at twenty-one years of age.

The girls and Hannah took to Deanna well, so on New Year's, 1958, when the clocks chimed midnight, I proposed to her, hoping with all my heart I wasn't making another mistake.

I asked Deanna to get a divorce now that her husband was willing. She flew to San Diego where she hired a taxi to take her to Tijuana. Once she had contacted the attorney and presented the necessary papers, it was only a matter of a month until the divorce was final.

Since Tijuana was so convenient, and was one of the few places where I wouldn't be easily recognized, I persuaded her that we should be married there. At the airport I was pounced on by an eager reporter who wanted to know where I was headed. I told him that I was going to look over a racehorse. On the plane, we hardly exchanged a word for fear of being recognized. I knew she didn't want any publicity upon becoming my fourth wife; neither did I.

Landing in Tijuana, we looked up one of the many marriage/divorce brokers. We filled out the license and presented our blood test results. The man looked up.

"William Dempsey, eh? Anyone ever tell you you look like Jack Dempsey?"

"Yes. He's my uncle and I've been told there's quite a resemblance."

"Well, whaddya know . . ."

The knot was tied and we went back to my home in Santa Monica.

In June the Manziel trial began in the old city of Jefferson, Texas. (It was the city upon which financier Jay Gould had placed a curse, causing it to become a ghost town, because Jefferson's townfolk had preferred water transportation to Gould's railroad and had not permitted it to come through town.)

The jury found in favor of the Manziel estate. I grinned at attorney Fred Erisman (a former judge of the 124th Judicial District of Texas) and tossed him my Rolex watch in appreciation of a job well done.

Shortly after we were married, I took Deanna and her daughter Barbara Lynn to Palm Springs, where one of the first people to spot us was Elsinore, who still had an eye out for me. Since no one knew I was married, Elsinore assumed Deanna was just a weekend date. Introducing her to Elsinore, I excused myself and went to make a few convenient telephone calls, leaving the two of them alone. At first Elsinore snubbed her, but Deanna handled her so deftly that by the time I returned they were chatting together like two magpies.

Luckily for us, no one was around when we settled in our suite. That night, whether due to anxiety or to something she had eaten, Deanna got terribly sick. We called the doctor around three-thirty in the morning. As he stepped through the door, I could tell he was sizing up what he thought was a sordid situation; he had "disgusting" written all over his face. I was sure he thought me despicable for shacking up with a woman and her innocent young child. Once Deanna had been cared for, I told him we were married and said I didn't want anyone in Palm Springs to know about it. He had trouble believing me, but eventually I convinced him.

Not wanting to stay away too long from my restaurant, and aware that Deanna wanted to keep an eye on her businesses and put her child back in school, we returned to New York. We moved into an eastside hotel while we considered where we wanted to live.

Shortly after returning to New York I had to go to Minneapolis on business and I asked Ernie Fliegel to make the necessary reservations. As he was writing "Mr. and Mrs. Jack Dempsey" on some hotel forms, a newspaperman peered over his shoulder and asked what was up—whereupon Ernie spilled the beans. The story hit the newspapers that night. I didn't care, I was used to it; but to Deanna it was a whole new world when she found herself besieged by questions. She learned, as she went along, which ones to answer and which ones to ignore.

Another friend to bite the dust a short while after me was Jimmy Durante, who finally decided to marry his Margie after a courtship lasting some twenty years. The wedding took place in the New York theater district's St. Malachy's Church.

Margie was a radiant bride that day and Jimmy fidgeted nonstop. After the ceremony, Jimmy was delayed by swarms of well-wishers and I suddenly found myself walking down the aisle with the bride—and getting smacked with a hail of rice—until Jimmy finally rescued Margie.

Funny thing about weddings: I had never been through a formal one like Durante's, but even as a married man they unnerved the hell out of me.

30

Jack Kearns Strikes Again

Most of my family had passed away over the years, leaving only my brother Joe and my sisters Elsie and Effie. By 1961 Effie was in her nineties and still living in Salt Lake. On one occasion Deanna and I stopped off in Salt Lake to visit her. We checked into the Hotel Utah, and that night Deanna sat up in bed with her eyes glued to the door.

"Go to sleep, Honey."

"I can't. I'm waiting for something to come through that door."

"What? Listen, shut off that light and go to sleep. You'll feel better in the morning."

At three o'clock I woke and saw that she was still awake.

"What's the matter? Don't you feel good?"

"I'm all right, but I have this feeling that something's going to happen."

"Forget about it and shut off that light, for Chrissakes."

At four o'clock someone pounded on the door, screaming "Fire!" Anyone with a heart condition would have died there and then. I looked at my wife, who was spooked and white as chalk, and told her to hurry. Within two minutes we were outside and the fire had been put out.

Returning to our room, I threw myself into bed and fell asleep almost immediately. Then I was reawakened by the press, who wanted to interview me. I struggled up, dressed and made my way downstairs, only to be asked to change to my bathrobe and muss up my hair, since it would look better. By the time I made it downstairs again, I looked as if I had been through not only a fire but an earthquake and a flood as well.

"Jack, can you tell us what was your toughest fight?"

I sighed and said, "Getting my wife out of the room without her makeup."

By the time I finally got to sleep it was already time for me to get up.

We traveled back and forth that year, but I began to spend more time in the restaurant since my bookings were no longer back to back. All sorts of people would come into the place: ladies seeking advice, new fighters wanting encouragement, and "sons." Through the years, at least twenty young men presented themselves to me as my long-lost sons. Some of them even carried albums of my clippings, which they insisted their dear mothers had collected, and photographs of themselves made up to look like me. It was incredible and pathetic. Some seemed to expect my denial; one or two got so inflamed that their anger bordered on the danger level. Unfortunately or fortunately, I had no son, and that was that.

One day Doc Kearns came into the restaurant and I invited him to sit down and have something to eat. Over a sandwich, he reminisced mistily about our good old days, when the three of us, Rickard, Doc and I, had turned a good thing into something great. Then he hit me for five hundred bucks to get to Florida. He had the shorts, he said, and he had turned to me knowing I wouldn't refuse him. I gave him the dough and, for the first time in all the years I had known him, I pitied him, which made me feel pretty awful.

That was to be the last time I saw Doc. On July 7, 1963, just before his eighty-first birthday, he passed away in his sleep, ending what had been a lifelong cat-and-mouse game. It didn't matter that I didn't see him very often; I always knew where he was and what he was saying. Now it was all over—along with a certain part of my life.

That year was a sad one for me as well as for the rest of the country. We all experienced shock and anguish over John F. Kennedy's assassination in Dallas. I didn't know him as well as I had known F.D.R., but I was stunned nevertheless. As had been the case approximately twenty years before, the United States was again involved in war, but this one was different: The undeclared Viet-Nam war was considered an official exercise in futility. Lyndon Baines Johnson was sworn in as President, and we watched as he grasped the reins of office. Draft calls were sounded across the country but, despite the drums' beating at a high pitch, the marchers were not in step with the tune as they had been in the second world war.

On January 8, 1964, a friend who worked for *Sports Illustrated* called me.

"Look, Jack. We're coming out with an issue that contains an article from Kearns's forthcoming book, which alleges that your gloves were loaded when you fought Willard for the title. It will be on the stands in a few days."

I put down the phone and hurriedly composed a letter to the magazine, with the help of my partner's son, Joe Amiel, an attorney, warning them that if they hit the stands with the story they'd have to face court action. They ignored my letter, preferring to publish rather than kill the story.

On January 13 *Sports Illustrated* hit the stands, reaching a readership of approximately nine million people.

Recommended to trial attorney Jerome Doyle, I asked him to represent me in a libel suit. The issue itself, as well as Kearns's allegations, I felt, were smearing me and damaging my good name. Doyle, after careful consideration, agreed to take me on. He soon learned that Kearns's publisher had sold certain chapters of the book to Time, Incorporated. When Doyle saw the original manuscript in the hands of the publisher, he realized that Time, Incorporated's people had edited the manuscript so that when it appeared in *Sports Illustrated* it seemed to conform to certain elements of a movie made in Toledo in 1919.

Colonel Eddie Eagan, who possessed a film of the Dempsey–Willard fight that was unlike the others, was called in by Doyle. His film showed the activity in Toledo before the fight, including shots of Rickard, of workmen hammering down the ropes and of people milling around and taking their seats. It also showed me having my gloves put on inside the ring.

The press got wind of my suit, and those who had been in Toledo in 1919 were on my side. In an article in the *Cleveland Plain Dealer* of February, 1964, Dallas Hanley (Jack) Robinson said *he* had the bandages in question. He had been in charge of a concession at the fight and afterwards, being an avid fight fan, he had come into my dressing room for a souvenir. Seeing my handlers unravel my bandages and throw them to the ground, young Robinson had picked them up and kept them until now in his sister's trunk.

An article around the same time in the *Cleveland Press* quoted an anonymous doctor who declared that plaster could have been applied to my bandages but the plaster would have taken five to ten minutes to set; for the plaster to be rock hard, I would have needed about five layers of it. He was very skeptical of Kearns's story, as were many others, including Louis B. Seltzer, editor of the *Cleveland Press*, who said, "I was sitting in the third row for the first two rounds before I had to come back to Cleveland with pictures. I didn't see anything amiss and I don't believe a word of it today."

Ed Bang, who was then sports editor of the *Cleveland News*, also rejected what Kearns had said:

> That rumor started right after the fight. It was started by the betting fraternity. I was sitting in one corner with Tex Rickard, who promoted the fight, and Beatrice Fairfax, a writer. Nobody I knew of ever saw any sign of plaster or anything else. I put it up to Jack later and he said, "You know me better than that." I followed him in all his fights. He never did anything out of the way.

My gloves, too, were produced by former bantamweight champion Pete Herman. Herman told *New Orleans States-Item* sports writer Art Burke:

> If Dempsey's hands had been taped with plaster of Paris, the gloves . . . would have been broken and every bone in Willard's face would have been broken too.

> Dempsey didn't have to resort to that sort of
> thing in 1919. He could have licked any fighter who
> ever lived on that day. He was in great condition.

He was right. It had taken me well over a decade to reach a
tired, older Willard, who had himself won the crown controver-
sially.

An avalanche of mail poured in from well wishers—and from
people in the plaster business who said that they had experimented
and had come to the conclusion that if I had had plaster of paris
inside my gloves, I would have broken my hands under the force
of a blow.

In April, 1964, the complaint was served and filed. It set forth
two causes of action, the first based on the bloody picture on the
magazine's cover and the headlines, DEMPSEY'S GLOVES WERE LOADED
and DOC KEARNS' OWN STORY OF THE BLOODY WILLARD FIGHT. Doyle
and his associates argued that the mere fact that the issue was on
the stands would cause the alleged libel to be seen and read at
face value, some people not even bothering to read the article itself.

The second cause of action concerned the contents of the article as well as the "Letter from the Publisher," which made comments on the story and suggested that "some readers might be
chilled by its revelations." The article itself was supposedly Kearns's
own tale of how he had soaked my bandages with water and plaster
of paris from a talcum can to insure his bet. In an insert interview
within the article, Willard was quoted as saying he was "dazed
from getting clobbered by those chunks of cement."

The people at Time, Incorporated, knew that "Kearns was a
self-admitted rogue and rascal" and therefore should have investi-
gated further before suggesting that I had acquired my title under
fraudulent circumstances.

They denied all charges, saying that "the general readership
did not know what loaded gloves were so they would only understand that Dempsey's gloves were loaded in the context of the cover
alone—not being anything more than a comment on a powerful
punch . . ."

I sued to prove that the cover and the inside story were both libelous, had damaged my reputation and name and caused me untold distress and loss of income, since they implied that I wasn't worthy of public acclaim or honor. My attorneys pointed out that "freedom of the press is not a license for profit at the expense of others."

Ultimately we didn't have to go to trial. We reached out of court an agreement that included a subsequent formal printed apology. From wherever he was, Jack Kearns had managed to give me one more good, swift kick in the butt. The man was not to be believed!

31

Birthday Party

When my personal turmoil had settled down, I received a call from Gene Tunney.

"Jack, could you help me?"

"Sure, Gene, what is it?"

"My son John is running for United States Congressman in Riverside, and I would very much appreciate it if you and Deanna would help us stump for him."

"Well, Gene, as a general rule I don't get involved in politics that don't concern me. But since it's you, well, it'll be my pleasure."

Before leaving for the west coast we saw more of Polly and Gene Tunney than we ever had before, while they filled me in on what was to be done for the campaign.

John was a nice young man, born the same year as my oldest daughter, Joanie. A Yale University graduate, he had gone on to the University of Virginia Law School, where he roomed with Teddy Kennedy, who subsequently became one of his closest friends. Gene had every right to be proud of John Varick Tunney.

We stumped hard for young Tunney, calling it a goodwill tour rather than a campaign. Separately and together we approached every prospective voter—and we in turn were besieged for autographs and bombarded with reminiscences. People even produced ticket stubs from our 1927 championship fight! And on September 26, Gene and I were given a public testimonial, a spaghetti dinner at Evans Park in Riverside, where films were shown of our famous long-count fight in which Gene retained the title.

John V. Tunney supported, among other things, the war on poverty and federal aid to education, two issues which I strongly supported as well. In October, L.B.J. visited Riverside, giving John an added boost. It was the first time since William Howard Taft that a President had visited Riverside.

Tunney won the election (as did L.B.J.), making me proud I had been of help. Attending his swearing-in ceremony at the House of Representatives, I couldn't help wondering what it would have been like to have had a son like John. Afterward, John thanked me profusely and sent me an album of the campaign and a pair of sterling silver donkey cufflinks. I wish that over the next ten years he'd found time to drop by to visit during his trips east.

Deanna and I also attended L.B.J.'s inaugural at the Mayflower Hotel in Washington, where I was buttonholed by a very distinguished gentleman who said, "Mr. Tunney. May I congratulate you on your fine son's winning the congressional seat."

I thanked him very much.

Shortly after Washington had meshed its gears again, I testified at a congressional hearing, along with Rocky Marciano and Gene Tunney, urging the creation of a federal commission to control boxing. Only five years before, I had appeared before Estes Kefauver's Senate Antitrust and Monopoly Subcommittee in favor of legislation creating a boxing czar. I felt then, as I do now, that federal control would clean up the undesirable elements in boxing through licensing trainers and promoters as well as regulating bouts. A referee, I said, should be given more responsibilities because, when all is said and done, he is the only one in a position really to see what's going on. In short, I was for a complete return to the Marquis of Queensberry rules.

After testifying in Washington I met Deanna in Los Angeles. We stayed for a while in the Hotel Miramar in Santa Monica (my daughter Barbara and my two grandchildren were occupying my house). One night the three of us and Meyer Littenberg, an attorney of mine at the time, were having dinner when talk rolled around to divorce, my daughter having been the latest victim.

As its pros and cons were discussed, Littenberg turned to Deanna and asked, "Where did you get divorced?"

"Tijuana."

He then turned to me and asked, "Jack, where did you two get married?"

"Same place."

Littenberg's jaw dropped. "I have news for you. You, Deanna, are not properly divorced, and therefore you two are not properly married."

"This is no time for jokes, Littenberg. Deanna's my wife and that's that. You don't know what you're talking about."

"On the contrary, Jack, I *do* know what I'm talking about. And I suggest you straighten this matter out—unless, of course, you prefer just to live together. Remember, Jack, the law is the law, no matter what you may think."

I didn't like what I had just heard and I told him to change the subject. One week later, a nervous Deanna and I consulted our New York attorney, Solon Kane, who confirmed what Littenberg had told us. Deanna and I then made plans for her to go to Reno for six weeks to establish residency for divorce. Because we didn't want publicity at this time, she checked into a local boarding house that was rather like the ones in which Doc and I had stayed in Long Branch. Staying at the boarding house had its advantages, our lawyer explained, as the landlady would establish and confirm Deanna's comings and goings more readily than a large hotel's ever-changing personnel.

I stayed away from her for about two weeks before I went to Reno, almost a madman because of the insecurity I still felt when it came to wives. We checked into a small Reno hotel within walking distance of the boarding house. Four weeks passed quickly and we returned to New York to cope with the problem of avoiding publicity all over again. But this wasn't for long; a friend of mine persuaded Herman Katz to marry us around midnight in his City Hall office.

On June 24, 1965, I turned seventy. That day no one wished me Happy Birthday but the newsmen. I dropped hints from the moment I woke up, but neither my wife nor my stepdaughter, Barbara Lynn, seemed to give a damn. Well, I thought, if they didn't care, neither did I. I called a few pals and tried to organize a gin rummy game for that night, but everyone was busy. Toward late afternoon, Dr. David Bloom called, begging me to accompany him to a black tie medical dinner. Anything to get out of the house. He picked me up in a taxi and said he had to stop and see a patient before going on to the dinner.

"That's okay with me. I'll wait in the cab."

"Jack, it would mean a great deal to my patient if you'd come up and say hello. What do you say?"

"All right."

We walked into a Fifth Avenue building where the doorman tipped his hat, grinning like a Cheshire Cat. Riding up in the elevator, I asked Bloom who his patient was. He said it was Bill Turner.

"Bill Turner! Why, I know Bill! What's the matter with him?"

"I can't go into it with you just yet. Wait'll you see him."

We rang the bell and the door slowly opened. I stepped inside—and suddenly everyone I knew was rushing up to wish me Happy Birthday. I spotted Deanna as she silently mouthed, "Aren't you surprised?" I'll say! Here I had thought she didn't care!

Among the eighty-five or so guests were my daughter Joanie; my stepdaughter, Barbara; Gene and Polly Tunney; Attorney General Louis Lefkowitz; my partner, Jack Amiel; Judge Nat Sobel; Judge John Sirica and his Lucy; Gordon and Vivian Fawcett; John Roosevelt and his soon-to-be-missus, Irene; Ed and Sylvia Sullivan; Bob Considine; Rube and Irma Goldberg; Earl and Rosemary Wilson; Carol Channing; Dave and Annabelle Margolis and many others I just can't recall.

It was the best birthday anyone could have asked for. In the middle of the party, the head man from Western Union arrived with a telegram from President Johnson, which Ed Sullivan gave to John Roosevelt to read out loud. I was very touched. The only thing I couldn't fathom was how my wife and Bill Turner had managed to arrange this celebration without my suspecting.

Just the thought of reaching seventy would have slowed a number of people into semi-retirement. But not me; I felt like sixty and was told I looked much younger. My hair was still jet black (thanks to a small bottle in my medicine chest) and my stomach fit neatly under my belt. The only thing that bothered me was an ache in my hip, but I knew that was nothing but the aftereffects of being thrown out of the ring onto typewriters catching up with me—a painful but honorable badge of my profession.

The following spring, I went home to Manassa for the first time in forty years. The people of Manassa had taken it upon themselves to renovate our old family log cabin, turning it into a museum and relocating it in a park named after me, all in conjunction with a San Luis Valley Tribute and Pioneer Day. My hosts, Mr. and Mrs. Harley Gilleland, were the greatest; they made me feel so much at home that I inadvertently stashed away a towel—which I used for many years before it dawned on me that it wasn't mine. (By then I was too shamefaced to send it back, imagining the good woman's reaction to my having snitched it, consciously or unconsciously.)

In Manassa they feasted me with a barbecue, and later I proudly rode through a parade, my stomach shot. Among the five thousand people present to greet their home-grown export were Eddie Eagan, a Colorado Hall of Famer like me; Maury Splain, a director of the Fraternal Order of Elks; Fred Dickerson of the Colorado Athletic Commission; Eddie Bohn, chairman of the Athletic Commission; the Chief of Police; and my pal, Duke Nally from Texas.

Word reached me from Los Angeles that Jess Willard had died. Poor Willard really hadn't had it easy, not being popular with the public. Through the years I have realized one thing: If a champion of anything, past or present, doesn't mingle with the masses, then he really can't expect public acclaim for very long. In April Jess Willard had been compelled to sell his house overlooking Pasadena and Glendale because of new freeway construction and moved to another with his beloved Hattie, for whom I'm sure life with Willard was far from easy. I had been able to help Willard on a few occasions, but in the end he really had only himself to blame for his failures. He was a fine family man, a man who might have been better off if only he could have brought his tenderness out from behind closed doors.

The terrible sixties were like no years I had ever known. Student protests, radical rallies, embassies burning, drug trafficking, hijackings, shoot 'em ups and casualties, all led to feelings of either outrage or apathy—there was no middle ground. And I thought I had seen it all.

An invitation to go to London offered relief in a chance to get away for a while, but I managed to encounter some anti-American sentiment over there. As a guest of the Anglo-American Sporting Club, I attended functions and appeared on television, where I had trouble understanding my own tongue. I made it a point to see my old pal, J. Paul Getty, who hadn't set foot on his native shores for years. Like a spectacular movie set, his Sutton Place estate was massive and beautiful, but, unlike a set, it housed the most magnificent art treasures I had ever seen, though something told me I was too ignorant to really appreciate what my eye was looking at. Paul was still Paul; he informed me that I was getting to be his oldest friend. Some time later he made me laugh, and at the same time want to cry, by modifying it to "his oldest living friend."

As the world spun, with the United States in domestic and international turmoil, President Johnson announced he would not run for reelection. His position had been a delicate one; no matter which way he leaned he got criticized, so he figured he'd be better off getting out. It was a time of wipe-outs and anguish as the slickly named Saturday Night Specials reappeared on the American scene, returned to the place they had held in the twenties and early thirties. Leaders of nations and movements were being scattered violently, and when we were least expecting it, the peaceful civil rights leader Martin Luther King, Jr. was gunned down, once more smearing America's hands with the blood of a stupid, senseless killing.

Internal dissent, disappointment and outrage were with us for quite a while, but by the late sixties and the early seventies the young people had managed to solder their weak and crumbling links together again. Luckily for me, my stepdaughter Barbara always informed me about what was going on. In her mind, there was no reason for me to identify entirely with my own generation when I could spread myself a bit thinner and understand hers as well.

The day Barbara invited her mother and me to attend her college graduation, I couldn't have been more pleased had she been of my own blood. My own daughters had given me, over the years, a good deal of joy—as well as seven beautiful granddaughters between them—but this one was part of a new, independent and enthusiastic breed that jumped their own hurdles on their way to wherever they were going.

Now that she was graduating college, I couldn't help recalling how it had been between us when we had first met. Naturally I had tried being nice to Barbara, despite my having outgrown children by that time, but from the outset she wouldn't have any part of me; it had been distrust and resentment at first sight. Brat. I believe the only thing that kept her in line at the time was that I was so much physically bigger than she—at least that's the impression she gave me.

For a while, after the three of us had moved in together, she wouldn't speak to me, as if I were a villain of sorts. One day I decided the time had come to straighten her out, so I invited her to accompany me somewhere. Amazingly, she agreed. Once in the car, I depressed the automatic door locks, imprisoning her until I finished saying what I had to say. I told her there was no use in fighting me because that was my business. I explained patiently that the love her mother had for me in no way interfered or encroached on mother love and the sooner Barbara got that straight, the better off we'd all be. I was trying my best to be like a father to her, but if she couldn't accept me on those terms, what about considering me her friend? She seemed to understand and mistily nodded her head, her little hand reaching for the door handle and, unfortunately, finding it locked, which caused her to burst into tears of exasperation and embarrassment.

When she had calmed down, she turned to me and stammered, "Um. You're grown-up and I know that you're . . . right, but, um . . . I guess I'm afraid of you."

I let that one sink in. Had that been the problem all along?

Had my own daughters been afraid of me as well? Something told me that this youngster's words had hit the nail squarely on the head. From that moment we were friends, and with the passing of years we developed a very special communication which I felt we both wanted and needed.

The college graduation ceremony itself was held outdoors, under a tremendous circus-like tent, with wooden chairs set up inside for the graduates and outside for parents and friends. Not wanting to cause a distraction, I sat in the rear, flanked by Deanna and my old pal Pete Shapiro, who had been through Barbara's trials and tribulations for many years.

I turned to Pete and asked, "Did you load the camera?"

"Camera? What camera?"

"Why, your camera. The one you use at the racetrack. Look around, everyone's snapping pictures and we're sittin' here soakin' up the sun!"

"Jack, I haven't got a camera with me. Jeez, you shoulda told me."

Well, we really couldn't blame ourselves; neither one of us had been through an experience like this before.

I tried paying attention to the speeches but got bored when I couldn't understand or always even hear them. As the graduates were congratulated, I was being asked to sign autographs by old-timers—and their kids, who were now parents themselves.

When it was all over, Barbara walked up to me and hugged me.

"Some ceremony. You know," I remarked, "we were pretty interested in what that guy was saying, weren't we, Deanna? Deanna? Pete?"

Barbara giggled and said, "You actually listened? You must be kidding, or you were just about the only parent here who paid any attention."

I felt a damn sight better.

When I approached my seventy-fifth birthday—three-quarters of a century old!—for the first time I became apprehensive of my age in terms of the years themselves. At seventy-five I should have been resting easy, but I wasn't so lucky. My daughter Joanie had obtained a divorce. Bringing my children up in the Catholic faith in the hope of eliminating the possibility of divorce certainly hadn't worked out very well.

The week of my birthday, Madison Square Garden inaugurated its Hall of Fame, to which I was the first in my field to be elected, followed by eighty-eight others in various fields. (As a sign of the times, the Hall of Fame is no longer.) In addition to that honor, New York Mayor John V. Lindsay presented me with a bronze medallion of the city of New York, in City Hall, before a swarm of pressmen. Like Madison Square Garden's Hall of Fame, John Lindsay is no longer in office.

On June 17, 1970, the night of the Jerry Quarry–Mac Foster fight, 15,915 people sang Happy Birthday to me in the Garden. Before the scheduled fight, I had been led into a darkened ring while two giant screens showed highlights of my fights with Willard, Firpo and Tunney (the long count). When the lights were turned on, there I was, alone in the ring for the first and only time in my life, as everyone seemed to stand up at once. It was very moving and, sensing that my wife was crying, I refused to look her way.

In the weeks before my publicized appearance I received letters from all over, from people who had shaken my hand, from people who had shaken the hand that had shaken mine and from pillars of society and industry who confessed like schoolboys that I had always been their hero.

Joe Frazier presented me with an oil portrait of myself, while Gene Tunney, Georges Carpentier, Jack Sharkey, Joey Giardello, George Chuvalo, José Torres, Emile Griffith, Ben Jeby, Dick Tiger, Sandy Saddler, Lou Salica, Petey Scalzo and Ismael Laguna looked on.

The place was jam-packed, and I heard one p.r. man remark, "Too bad his birthday doesn't come more often."

It certainly was a night to remember. It moved me—and at the same time saddened me, for I knew that this would probably be my last big occasion of public acclaim.

On March 8, 1971, at 10:30 P.M., just before the Clay–Frazier fight (and before Clay became Muhammad Ali), announcer Johnny Addie introduced celebrities in the audience but overlooked me, causing a clamor and a "We Want Dempsey" chant to reverberate through the Garden. Addie, embarrassed, looked around and called me into the ring, but the emotional damage had inadvertently been done; I realized then that one prominent member of the old guard was no longer quite so prominent. But I didn't mind; after all, how long could a person keep that spotlight in focus before the bulb had to be changed?

Still, I wasn't to be sold short. Late one night, riding home in a taxi that had stopped at a red light, I saw two young punks running for the cab from both sides. The cabby was frozen with fear as they flung the doors open, so I took care of the situation by swiftly belting one with a right and the other with a left hook, flattening them both.

In a way I felt sorry for them, having to hustle what they thought was the perfect victim—a nicely dressed older gentleman who would have forked over his money immediately rather than risk a fight. They were young, no more than nineteen or twenty, but given a few boring but active years on the streets, they could age and harden mighty fast. These were the kids that boxing would have helped, by rerouting their hostility and aggression until they developed a sensible defensive or offensive skill with pride instead of vengeance.

My restaurant was just about thirty-seven years old, twenty-three of which had been in partnership with Jack Amiel, when Broadway began to deteriorate. Peep shows, pimps, hookers and massage parlors mushroomed all over the place. Gone was Lindy's and those who had made it famous. Gone were the clumps of tourists, scared away with tales of muggers and pickpockets, and gone were the profits that used to roll in.

Broadway had become just another street, but because both of us had been around it so long, we vowed to stay open as long as we could, or until the eight years remaining in our lease expired. But it never came to that; Amiel and I were notified that we had to get out by the Inch Corporation, our new landlords, who had taken over the leasing 1619 Broadway Realty Company for nonpayment of rent.

In court we inquired about the Inch Corporation, only to be told by a barrage of lawyers that they were not at liberty to discuss the identity of their principals—which in turn sparked our curiosity as well as that of the press. Calling the Corporation's office at 25 Broadway, we invariably got an answering service, which annoyed us even more. We were being asked for double the rent while the landlords wouldn't even identify themselves. Soon one rumor led to another. Among the more credible ones was that the property belonged to the Royal Family in England. Naturally, it couldn't be proved; investigations led fruitlessly to Italy, Panama and back.

At one point the case was dismissed because plaintiff had neglected to give us a thirty-day notice. Taking advantage of a breather from our trying and exhausting days in court, Deanna and I went to London as guests of Jack Solomons and the World Sporting Club, where I was to be honored along with my old friend Georges Carpentier. It was a swell affair, though I couldn't unwind for thinking about what was going on back home. Even Georges sensed there was something troubling me despite my denials. I had been through so many lawsuits and aggravations that denying their existence was easier than acknowledging them. I was tired of fighting, but I wouldn't give up—that was defeat. Realizing this, my stepdaughter jumped in and vowed to fight for me tooth and nail. I tried to dissuade her, to tell her that if people didn't want you to know something it was better not to probe, but she was adamant.

Upon our return to New York to fight once more for what was mine, Barbara informed us that she was off to London. Once settled, she did some independent research with the help of friends. Finding very little, she marched into the *Daily Express* newsroom and publicly announced that she was about to write a letter to the Queen. Hastily and happily provided with pen and paper, she wrote, asking point blank: "Has the Royal Family any connection with the firm that is putting my stepfather out of business?" The next day she made the front page and the U.P.I. wires as well. Somewhere, someone had taught her well. Needless to say, she never quite received the answer she wanted; she did, however, receive a curt negative reply, which she promptly framed.

In New York our case looked grim. Because everyone had so much to say, I sat in court and said nothing while my heart was breaking apart. It was sad to hear my partner shout theatrically, "Why, they'll have to drag me out by my heels before I get out!" The press was more than sympathetic to us, but no one could ever know how much it was destroying me inside. My restaurant had been a gathering place for sports writers, songwriters, two Presidents, music publishers, actors, actresses and, most important, my friends. Now it was about to be sucked down the drain.

As time wore on, I realized that while Judge Harry Davis was a sort of referee, and the court a kind of makeshift ring, I had no gloves with which to fight. They were breaking my spirit by breaking my lease. Sitting in my restaurant when not in court, I knew that the patient had but a short time left to live. Sure, the pulse was still present, but the face and personality had changed dramatically. It was as if my getting old was in direct violation of the briskly moving wheels of change.

We reached the point where there was just no use in continuing the fight. Our water pipes burst and a portion of our ceiling collapsed, forcing us to call it quits.

In a way, closing night was like opening night, except that it was Deanna by my side instead of Hannah; Amiel instead of Amron; the press watching the comings and goings instead of my father— and it was a noisy wake rather than a celebration. That closing night, the closing of a part of my life, damn near killed me. Even a disgruntled dishwasher suffered, smashing five windows with a monkey wrench in fear of not getting paid. He raced down Broadway but was caught and had to face criminal charges the next day.

Hundreds of friends turned out to say good-bye to the place and to me, making its shuttering even more pathetic as I tried cheering up those who had come to cheer me. I went to retrieve some precious photographs and found that most were missing; people grabbed everything. A few days before, I had donated my James Montgomery Flagg mural to the Smithsonian in Washington, but the colorful montage on the wall had to be destroyed just like the restaurant itself. It was the toughest fight of my life and I lost it; there was no chance for a comeback or a rematch.

The year 1975 found me a somewhat different man. My restaurant had been taken away, my youth was gone and my eightieth birthday loomed before me. I still felt I had much to do, but the years, like galloping horses, had slowed me down to the point that I annoyed myself—that is, when others weren't annoying me by exclaiming, "My God! *eighty years old?* Who'd ever believe it?" or writing to Sunday supplements to ask if I were still alive. Far from being dead, I resolved to remain as active as I could, to try in my own way to recapture what by now was long lost—though I still saw a close facsimile of the man that once was.

Even New York, my town, is no longer what it was; it is the only place in the world that lives for its present. Everyone I knew who painted this town is gone now. Looking back on a full life with all its ups and downs, I wouldn't change it for anything. Five wars, fifteen Presidents, the advent of the automobile, the airplane, motion pictures, radio, television, political assassinations—and an unbelievable landing on the moon. I lived it my way, and if I were asked, I would do it all over again.

Index

Acord, Art, 164
Actors Equity Association, 182, 228
Adams, Annette, 128
Addie, Johnny, 306
Adlon Hotel, Berlin, 149, 175
Ahern, Goldie, 241, 242
Alaskan, The, 167, 168
All Good Marines, 133
All's Swell on the Ocean, 164
Ambers, Lew, 257
American Burlesques, Barney Gerard's, 90–92
American-Russian Eagle Club, 222
Amiel, Jack, 271, 300, 306, 308
Amiel, Joe, 293
Amos 'n' Andy, 235
Amron, Jake, 245, 246, 248, 261, 263, 271, 308
Ancestry, 1, 2
Anderson, Andre, 44, 45
Anglo-American Sporting Club, 302
Aquitania, 148
Arbuckle, Fatty, 164
Archer, Ray, 106, 115, 120
Arch Street Theatre, 94
Astor, Mrs. Vincent, 218
Atlantic City, New Jersey, 140, 156, 157, 158, 244
Aubrey, Dorothy, 279
Auerbach, Al, 67
Auguste, Estelle Harmon Spencer, 275
Autry, Gene, 264

Baer, Bugs, 114

Baer, Max, 234, 237, 238, 239, 240, 243, 269
Baker, Mrs. Raymond T., 154
Bang, Ed, 294
Banky, Vilma, 164
Barbara Hotel, 155, 165, 172, 190, 207, 222
Barbour, W. Warren, 100, 117, 250
Barry, Dave, 217, 218, 219
Barrymore, Ethel, 113
Barrymore, John, 164, 168, 195
Baruch, Bernard, 145
Basquette, Lena, 234, 235
Bautzer, Greg, 280
Beery, Wallace, 234
Belasco, David, 182, 183, 184, 185, 218
Bellows, George, 161, 245
Belmont Hotel, 147, 193, 211
Benac, Gaston, 143
Benjamin, Joe, 148, 161, 174, 218, 226, 227, 235, 282
Benton Harbor, Michigan, 135
Berle, Milton, 161
Berlin, Germany, 149, 174, 175
Berlin, Irving, 218
Bernstein, Willie, 284
Beverly Hills, California, 133
Biddle, Major A. J. Drexel, 100, 115, 118
Biddle Bible Class, 100
Big Fight, The, 182, 183
Big Wheel, The, 269
Billingsley, Sherman, 236
Billy Gerard's American Burlesques, 90–92
Biltmore Hotel, 248

311

Bingham Canyon, Utah, 19
Bohn, Eddie, 301
Bond, Joe, 62, 63, 67
Boston Bearcat, 38, 43, 44, 268
Bow, Clara, 164
Boxing Blade, Milwaukee, 153
Boxing Managers' Guild Dinner, 271, 272
Boyle's Thirty Acres, 140, 142
Braddock, Jimmy, 243
Brand, Harry, 267
Branston, Eddie, 170
Brennan, Bill, 76, 80, 138, 139, 155
Brenon, Herbert, 167
Brix, Lou, 218
Broadway Saint, 167
Bronson, Jimmy, 218
Brooks, Louie, 245
Broun, Heywood, 184, 185
Brower, George, 179
Brown, Bill, 142
Brown, May, 75, 80
Brown, Ned, 114
Brown, Warren, 68, 141, 147
Brown Palace Hotel, 267
Brunton, Robert C., 125
Brunton Studios, 132, 133
Buckley, Johnny, 212, 213
Buffalo, New York, 77
Buffalo Bill's Wild West Show, 98, 100
Burg, Kopelin, 200
Burke, Art, 294
Burke, Marty, 89, 90, 91, 210, 216
Butler Rolls-Royce Agency, 165

Campbell, Anamas, 32
Capone, Al, 217, 225
Carey, Harry, 164
Carey, William F., 225
Carlyle, Thomas, 13
Carnera, Primo, 237, 243
Carpentier, Georges, 104, 139–147, 156, 160, 282, 283, 305, 307
Castor, 174, 175, 176
Cates, Maxine. *See* Dempsey, Maxine Cates
Cessna, Miriam, 248, 249
Chaney, Lon, 125, 164
Channing, Carol, 300
Chapeau Rouge, 186
Chaplin, Charlie, 133, 164, 168, 222
Chapman, Hannah Lyle, 230
Chapman, John, 224
Chasen's, 284
Chicago, Illinois, 73, 74, 75, 214, 215, 217, 220, 231, 233, 274, 276, 281
Chicago Daily News, 109

Chicago Stadium, 233
Chicago Tribune, 114, 127
  Sunday, 196, 197
Childs Restaurants, 235, 236
Christian, George, 32
Chuvalo, George, 305
Cincinnati, Ohio, 124
Civic Auditorium, San Francisco, 85
Clark, Wilbur, 278, 279, 280
Clay-Frazier fight, 305, 306
Clements, B. E., 216
Clendenning, John H., 131
Cleveland News, 294
Cleveland Plain Dealer, 294
Cleveland Press, 294
Cobb, Irvin S., 145
Coffroth, James W., 222
Cohan, George M., 145, 218, 255
Collins, Mike, 152, 153
Cologne, Germany, 174
Colony, 186
Colorado State Senate, 93
Columbo, Russ, 238, 239
Come-on Charley, 167
Conejos River, Colorado, 5
Connolly, One-Eyed, 154, 218
Considine, Bob, 267, 300
Continental Hotel, 131
Contracts, 26, 46, 47, 100, 150, 163, 216, 245
Cook County Jail, 274, 275
Copacabana, 265
Copelin, George, 33, 34
Coq Rouge, 186
Corbett, James J., 133, 142, 180
Corum, Bill, 95
Cotton Club, 186
County Kildare, Ireland, 1
Cox, James M., 99, 100, 115, 251
Creede, Colorado, 8
Cripple Creek, Colorado, 21, 32, 35, 55
Crocker, Harry, 222
Cugat, Xavier, 229
Curley, Jack, 83, 84, 96, 122, 140
Curly, 91, 92

Damita, Lily, 222
Daniels, Bebe, 132
Daredevil Jack, 124–127, 131, 236
Davenport, Iowa, 231
Davies, Marion, 164, 191
Davis, Edward Mike, 281
Davis, Harry, 308
Dawson, Jim, 98
Dayton, Ohio, 248, 249
Day with Jack Dempsey, A, 140

Dead or Alive, 133
DeForest, Jimmy, 84, 103, 108, 114, 115, 117, 155, 162
Delmonico's, 186
Democratic National Convention, 163
Dempsey, Andrew (grandfather), 1, 4
Dempsey, Barbara (daughter), 244, 254, 258, 260–262, 266, 276–279, 284, 288
Dempsey, Barbara Lynn (stepdaughter), 289, 298, 300, 302–304, 307, 308
Dempsey, Bernie (brother), 16, 17, 19, 32–35, 55, 56, 115, 116, 119, 129
Dempsey, Bruce (brother), 8, 62, 63
Dempsey, Deanna (wife), 286–291, 297–300, 304, 307, 308
Dempsey, Effie (sister), 291
Dempsey, Elsie (sister), 8, 17, 291
Dempsey, Estelle Taylor (wife), 167–179, 181–185, 188–190, 194, 195, 197, 198, 200, 202, 204–207, 209, 211, 213–217, 222, 223, 226–232, 239, 259, 265
Dempsey, Florence (sister), 8
Dempsey, Hannah Williams (wife), 236, 238, 248, 252–256, 258–261, 276, 288, 308
Dempsey, Harry. *See* Dempsey, Jack
Dempsey, Hyrum (father), 1, 74, 110, 129, 153, 165, 204, 212, 216, 230, 242, 246, 268
  character, 4, 6
  religion, 3
  teacher, 3
  westward move, 4
Dempsey, Jack
  ancestry, 1, 2
  birth, 6
  boyhood jobs, 15
  business ventures, 147
  contracts, 26, 46, 47, 100, 150, 163, 216, 245
  DeVry Institute, 281
  enlistment, 256
  family life, 11
  first fight lessons, 16, 17
  First Lieutenant, Coast Guard, 256
  first marriage, 49
  fourth marriage, 289
  goal, 23
  Harry, 17
  indictment and trial, 127–131
  Jack, 17
  Jack the Giant Killer, 77
  Kid Blackie, 23, 31, 33, 34
  last professional fight, 254
  libel suit, 293–296

Manassa Jack, 45
Manassa Mauler, 45
Maneater, 77
miner, 19–22, 27, 28
nose operation, 173
realtors license, 206
restaurant business, 245, 255, 271, 278, 306, 307, 308, 309
school, 10, 14
second marriage, 169–232
third marriage, 239–251
This Is Your Life!, 282
training, 38, 45, 76, 84, 86, 102, 103, 105, 106, 109, 135, 138, 140, 153, 198, 208, 209, 211, 215
Dempsey, Jack, the Nonpareil, 17
Dempsey, Joan (daughter), 241, 242, 244, 254, 258, 260–262, 266, 276–279, 284, 300, 305
Dempsey, Joe (brother), 124, 210, 279, 282
Dempsey, Johnny (brother), 16, 37, 74, 124, 212
Dempsey, Mary Celia S. (mother), 74, 124, 129, 130, 155, 204, 212, 230, 240, 241, 259, 261
  character, 6, 7, 12
  illness, 8
  marriage, 2
  religion, 3
  restaurant, 12, 13
Dempsey, Maxine Cates (wife), 40, 48, 49, 54, 56, 57, 63, 64, 66, 74, 82, 84, 126, 127–131
Dempsey, William Harrison. *See* Dempsey, Jack
Dempsey-Anderson fight, 44, 45
Dempsey-Boston Bearcat fight, 38
Dempsey-Brennan fights, 81, 139
Dempsey-Carpentier fight, 140–147
Dempsey-Firpo fight, 155–162, 305
Dempsey-Fulton fight, 84, 85
Dempsey-Gibbons fight, 154, 155
Dempsey-Gunboat Smith fight, 69
Dempsey-Johnson fight, 46, 47
Dempsey-Kearns Corporation, 174
  dissolved, 207
Dempsey-Levinsky (Battling) fight, 88
Dempsey-Levinsky (Kingfish) fight, 233
Dempsey-Meehan fight, 85
Dempsey-Sharkey fight, 212–215
Dempsey-Smith fight, 90
Dempsey-Tunney fights, 283
  controversy, 219, 220
  first, 179, 198, 200, 201, 205
  second, 214, 218, 305

Dempsey-Vanderbilt Hotel, 248, 261
Dempsey-Willard fight, 114–121, 122, 293, 305
  arrangements for, 92–100
Dempsey-Wills fight, 150, 151, 192
Denver, Colorado, 8, 10, 72, 267
Denver and Rio Grande Railroad, 9, 13
Denver Post, The, 28, 42, 72, 73, 75, 101
Deschamps, Marcel, 140, 141, 146
DeVry, Bill, 282
DeVry brothers. *See* DeVry Technical Institute
DeVry Technical Institute, 281
Diamond, "Legs," 186
Diamond Horseshoe, 265
Dickerson, Fred, 301
DiMaggio, Joe, 269
Dinty Moore's, 235
Dix, Richard, 222
Dom Hotel, 174
Don Juan, 168, 195
Dooling, Maurice T., 129, 130
Dorgan, Ike, 96, 152
Dougherty, Jack, 167
Dougherty, Jim, 136, 142
Downey, Jack, 32
Downing, Hardy, 31, 32, 39
Doyle, Jerome, 293, 295
Dreamland Pavilion, 70
Drennen, Cody, 87
Driscoll, Arthur, 193, 194, 211, 228, 259
Duffy, Billy, 218
Dunn, Harvey, 167
Durante, Jimmy, 290
Durante, Margie (Mrs. Jimmy), 290

Eagan, Eddie, 101, 154, 293, 301
Earp, Wyatt, 70, 71, 114
Eddie Cantor's Purple Heart circuit, 261
Edge, Bob, 256
Edgewater Beach Hotel, 215
Edgren, Bob, 97, 114, 142, 210, 218
Edwards, Ralph, 282
Einstein, Izzy, 187
Eisenhower, Dwight D., 242
El Fay Club, 186
El Morocco, 186, 235, 265
Ely, Nevada, 126
Emeryville, California, 68
Encyclopaedia Britannica, 244
Ensenada Bay, Baja California, 228
Erisman, Fred, 289
Ertle, Harry, 142

Fairbanks, Douglas, 132, 133, 147, 148, 177, 218

Fairbanks, Douglas, Jr., 148
Fairfax, Beatrice, 294
Fairmont Athletic Club, 44
Farley, James A., 179, 192, 214, 218
Farnsworth, Bill, 83, 98, 152, 172
Farrell, Marty, 64, 67
Fawcett, Gordon, 300
Fawcett, Vivian (Mrs. Gordon), 300
Federal Boxing Control, 298
Federal League Ball Park, 84
Fight and Win serials, 163
Fight crowds, 38
Fighters' Jubilee, 37
Fight films, transportation of, 250
Fighting techniques, 26, 38
Fink, Lou, 212, 218
Firpo, Luis Angel, 155, 156, 160–162, 282, 283
Fitzgerald, Tommy, 128, 129
Fitzsimmons, Bob, 114
Fitzsimmons, Floyd, 135, 136, 180, 225, 226
Flagg, James Montgomery, 261, 308
Fleischer, Nat, 42, 45, 115, 146, 218, 225, 254
Fliegel, Ernie, 246, 247, 264, 289, 290
Florey, George, 281, 282
Floto, Otto, 28–30, 73, 101, 102, 114, 116, 142
Flournoy, Frank, 100, 152
Flynn, Ed, 179
Flynn, Jim, 55, 59, 63, 77
Flynn, Leo P., 80, 81, 210, 211–213, 215, 218
Fool There Was, A, 168
Ford, Henry, 145
Fowler, Agnes Hubbard (Mrs. Gene), 48
Fowler, Gene, 42, 47, 48, 98, 103, 120, 132, 143, 144, 156, 157, 172, 174, 176, 180, 185, 189, 203, 218, 224, 255, 262, 265, 272
Fox, William, 164, 167
Fox Studios. *See* Twentieth Century Fox Studios
Frayne, Eddie, 172
Frazier, Joe, 305
Frederick, Pauline, 195
Fulton, Fred, 81, 83–85, 91, 282

Gabriel, Gilbert W., 183, 184
Gallagher, Anne, 262
Gallagher, Johnny, 161
Gallico, Paul, 157–159, 218
Gans, Joe, 94
Getty, J. Paul, 159, 160, 302
Getz, George F., 214

Giardello, Joey, 305
Gibbons, Tommy, 151–155, 179
Gibson, Billy, 44, 80, 192, 218
Gibson, Hoot, 164
Gilleland, Mr. and Mrs. Harley, 301
Gish, Dorothy, 164
Gish, Lillian, 164
Gleeson, Edgar "Scoop," 58, 59, 102, 116, 206, 218
Godfrey, George, 179
Goldberg, Irma (Mrs. Rube), 300
Goldberg, Rube, 70, 71, 98, 114, 180, 300
Golden Cycle Mine, 33
Goldfield, Nevada, 35
Goldman, Harry, 260
Goodfriend, Jake, 35
Good Neighbor Policy, 5
Gorilla controversy, 244
Gould, Jay, 145, 289
Graham, Frank, 140
Grand Central Station, 42
Grand Junction, Colorado, 28
Grand Junction Hotel, 29
Granlund, Nils T., 236
Great Falls, Montana, 153
Great Lakes Naval Training Station, 88, 89, 130
Great Northern Hotel, 261, 278
Greenspun, Hank, 269, 270, 278
Griffith, Emile, 305
Grupp's 116th Street Gym, 45
Guinan, Texas, 186
Gunnison Tunnel, 13, 14
Guys and Dolls, 280

Hague, Frank, 140
Hall, Arthur G., 257
Hal Roach Studios, 132
Hannagan, Steve, 226
Hanfsraengl, Putzy, 239
Happy Morticians Club, 185
Hard drugs, 37
Harlem Sporting Club, 46
Harris, Sam H., 182
Harrison, New Jersey, 84
Harrison, William Henry, 6
Hatfield, "Devil" Anse, 1
Hatfields, the, 1
    cousin Don, 153
Hayes, Teddy, 67, 88, 89, 125, 127, 128, 131, 140–142, 147, 148, 157, 162–165, 167–173, 188, 189, 212, 213, 234, 235
Hazen, Melvin, 241
Hearn, Eddie, 125
Hearst, William Randolph, 191

Hearst's Milk Fund, 243
Heinon, Jack, 89
Hemple, Jack, 115
Henaghan, Red, 231
Herman, Pete, 294
Hicks, Leonard, 175
Hiroshima, 263
Hitler, Adolf, 239, 240, 251, 255
Hobart, George V., 167
Hobo jungles, 24, 25
Hodges, Maxine, 163
Hoff, Boo Boo, 216
Hoffman, Ancil, 234, 238, 243
Hollywood, California, 124, 125, 131, 132, 134, 155, 163–165, 168, 176, 177, 206, 212, 236, 282
Hollywood Hospital, 206, 207
Hooray for What!, 253
Hoover, Herbert, 228
Hoover, J. Edgar, 236
Hope, Bob, 274
Hotel Edison, 271
Hotel Iroquois, 77
Hotel Navarro, 240–242, 259
Hotel Utah, 24, 291
Hotsy Totsy Club, 186
Houdini, Harry, 137
Howard, Andrea Leeds, 284
Howard, Bob, 284
Howard Manor Hotel, 284
Hubbard, Agnes. *See* Fowler, Agnes Hubbard
Hudnut, Richard, 195
Hughes, Howard, 279, 280
Humphrey, Hubert H., 264
Humphreys, Joe, 146, 218, 243
Hunchback of Notre Dame, The, 164
Hylan, John F., 158

Igoe, Hype, 98, 114, 156, 161, 190, 194, 207, 218
Inch Corporation, 306, 307
International News Service, 161

Jack Dempsey's Special Label Whiskey, 247, 248
Jacobs, Mike, 141, 160, 216, 243
Jamaica Kid, 84, 105, 109, 110, 157
Jeby, Ben, 305
Jefferson, Texas, 289
Jeffries, Jim, 92, 93, 142, 156, 216
Jeffries-Johnson fight, 92, 93, 150
Jenkins, Lew, 258
Jerry Quarry-Mac Foster fight, 305
Jerry the Greek, 143, 157, 194, 198, 199, 200, 202, 205, 207–210, 215, 218, 247

Johnson, Edwin, 250
Johnson, Jack, 92, 93, 106, 108, 119, 122, 139, 243
Johnson, Jim, 84
Johnson, John Lester, 46, 47
Johnson, Lyndon Baines, 264, 293, 298, 300, 302
Johnson, Mayor, 152, 153
Johnson-Jeffries fight, 92, 93
Johnston, Charley, 264
Johnston, Jimmy, 43, 114
John the Barber, 46, 47, 49–52, 82, 83
Jolson, Al, 70, 145
Jones, Buck, 164
Jones, Tom, 122
Juarez, Mexico, 131

Kahn, Otto, 238
Kahn, Roger Wolfe, 238
Kane, Eddie, 152
Kane, Walter, 279
Kanner, Jack, 48
Kaplan, Max, 91, 108
Katz, Herman, 299
Kaufman, S. Jay, 245
Kearns, Jack, 26, 39, 62–100, 104–112, 114–120, 123, 124, 126–144, 147–151, 153–159, 161–174, 178, 188–190, 195, 197, 198, 200, 201, 207, 212, 218, 236, 269, 271–273, 292–296
Keaton, Buster, 137
Keeler, Ruby, 186
Kefauver, Estes, 298
Kelly, Emmett, Sr., 273
Kelly, Mark, 172
Kelly, Shipwreck, 210
Kelly, W. E., 256
Kennedy, Edgar, 125, 126
Kennedy, Edward (Ted), 297
Kennedy, John F., 130
Kennedy, John F., Jr., 292
Kenny Institute, 262
Kenton, Erle C., 164
Kerr, Deborah, 280
Kid Blackie. *See* Dempsey, Jack
Kid Hancock, 31, 32
Kid Howard, 76
Kiernan, John, 218
Kilgallen, Jim, 200
Kilpatrick, John Reed, 249
King, Martin Luther, Jr., 302
Koch, Arnold, 258, 260

Laemmle, Carl, Sr., 163, 164
La Falaise de la Coudray, Marquis de, 222
La Hiffs, 235

Laguna, Ismael, 305
Lake Swannanga, New Jersey, 23
Lakeview, Utah, 14, 15
LaMarr, Barbara, 167
Langford, Sam, 38, 46
Lardner, Ring, 114, 140, 185, 204, 218
Latin Quarter, 265
Lavin, Jack, 107
Laughlin Park, Hollywood, 176
Lawrence, Jack, 161
Leadville, Colorado, 8
Leeds, Andrea. *See* Howard, Andrea Leeds
Lefkowitz, Louis, 300
Lehman, J. Irving, 152
Lehr, W. H., 267, 268
Leon and Eddie's, 235
Levinsky, Battling, 86–88, 139, 200
Levinsky, Kingfish, 232, 234
Levinsky, Leaping Lena, 234
Lewin, Murray, 245
Lewis, Albert, 182
Liberty Line, 229
Life of a 19th Century Gladiator, 8
Lincoln Fields Track, 215
Lindbergh, Charles A., 210
Lindsay, John V., 305
Littenberg, Meyer, 298, 299
Lloyd, Harold, 132, 164
Locklear, Lieutenant, 116
Lodge, Farmer, 159
Logan County, West Virginia, 1
London, England, 88, 89, 148, 302, 307
Long, Baron, 206, 222
Long Branch, New Jersey, 84
Los Angeles, California, 155, 160, 214, 229, 279, 288
Los Angeles Examiner, 230
Lothario, 177
Louis, Joe, 243, 268, 269
Loy, Myrna, 237
Lundeen, Ernest, 250
Luther, Uncle Tom, 157, 211
Lutrell, Cowboy, 254
Luvadis, Jerry. *See* Jerry the Greek
Lyall, Jim, 209
Lyman, Abe, 236
Lyon, Charles, 142
Lyons, Wild Bill, 93, 252

McAllister, Bob, 68
McArdle, Tom, 44
MacArthur, Charles, 120
McAuliffe, Jack, 155
McCabe, Bill, 192
McCormack, John, 222

McCoy, Bibber, 257
McCoys, the, 1
MacFarland, A. J., 239
McGrath, J. Howard, 270
McGraw, John, 93
Machris, Elsinore, 284, 289
Mackay, Clarence H., 218
McKiernan, Mrs. (Kearns's mother), 64–67
McNab, Gavin, 128–130
McNamee, Graham, 218
McPartland, Dorothy, 239, 255, 259
McPartland, Jimmy, 239
Madden, Owney, 186, 236
Madison Square Garden, New York, 163, 189, 192, 225, 245, 273, 305
Majestic Theatre, 182, 183
Malloy, Andy, 26, 27
Malone, Jock, 115
Manassa, Colorado, 5, 8, 301
Manassa Jack. *See* Dempsey, Jack
Manassa Mauler. *See* Dempsey, Jack
Manhattan, Kansas, 42
Manhattan Beach Training Station, 257
Manhattan Hotel, 285
Manhattan Madness, 176
Mann, Nathan, 257
Manziel, Bobby, 281, 282, 289
Mara, Tim, 216
Marciano, Rocky, 298
Margolis, Annabelle (Mrs. Dave), 284, 300
Margolis, Dave, 248, 249, 284, 300
Marshall, Ellye, 269
Martin, Dr. Harry, 235, 266
Masterson, Bat, 114, 122
Maxim, Joey, 269, 273
Maxim's, 39
Mayer, Louis B., 237
Mayo Brothers, 223
Medicine shows, 15
Meehan, Willie, 58, 67, 68, 85
Meighan, Thomas, 167
Menjou, Adolphe, 164
Menke, Frank, 161
Merrill, Slick, 35
Mexico City, Mexico, 177
Miami, Florida, 223, 225, 248
Miami Daily News, 276
Mike Romanoff's, 284
Miles, Nelson, 114
Miller, Charley, 68
Miller, Dave, 217
Milwaukee Arena, 81
Miske, Billy, 83, 135, 136
Mission Baseball Park, 68
Mr. Broadway, 237

Mix, Tom, 115, 154, 164, 190, 191, 200, 218
Mizpah Hotel, 36
Mocambo, 284
Moffett, Admiral, 88
Moir, Harry, 225, 226
Molumby, Loy, 152
Monaghan, Tommy, 276
Monaghan, Walter, 99, 107, 114, 115, 119
Montana, Bull, 125, 126, 190
Montrose, Colorado, 12, 14, 25
Mooney, Spike, 257
Moore, Colleen, 222
Moore, Lee, 175, 176
Moran, Frank, 50, 52, 53, 139
Mormon religion, 3
Morning Telegraph, 114
Morris, Carl, 52, 53, 70, 71, 77–79, 89, 96
Morrison Hotel, 74, 75, 175
Muhammad Ali, 306
Muldoon, William, 114, 151, 179, 192, 193
Mullen, Jim, 74
Mullins, Paddy, 150, 151, 178
Murray, Charlie, 77–79
Murray, Mae, 154
Murray, Utah, 55

Nally, Duke, 301
National Sports Committee, 251
N.B.C. Studios, 282
Negri, Pola, 196
Nelson, Oscar Matthew, 109, 113
Nesbit, Evelyn, 138
Neutral Corner Rule, 162
Newman, Ray, 159
New Orleans, Louisiana, 96
New Orleans States-Item, 294
New York, New York, 39–41, 93–100, 109, 140, 178, 180, 185, 186, 211, 214, 226, 235, 236, 238, 245, 308, 309
New York American, 43, 98, 172
New York *Daily News*, 157, 158, 159
New York Evening Journal, 98, 161, 196
New York Globe, 181
New York *Graphic*, 181
New York Heart Association, 273
New York Mirror, 245
New York Press, 42
New York State Athletic Commission, 178, 179, 180, 191
New York Times, 98, 145, 162
New York Tribune, 122
New York World, 210
Normile, Gene, 173, 176, 178, 192–194, 197–199, 201–203, 206, 207, 210, 211, 222, 226, 227, 245

Northern Bar Saloon, 93–95
Norton, Al, 57, 59, 68
Nugent, Dick, 79

Oakland, California, 57, 62, 64, 68
O'Day, Jack, 164
O'Donnell, Jim, 127
Ogden, Utah, 38
Ohio Ministerial Association, 100
Ohio State Legislature, 101
Ojai, California, 209
Oland, Warner, 190
Old Kickapoo, 206
O'Loughlin, Agnes, 227
O'Neill, Buck, 196
O'Neill, Ike, 114, 119
O'Rourke, Tex, 118
Oval Room, White House, 252
Overland Club, 102
Ovey, Ed, 164

Palm Springs, California, 284, 289
Pantages, Alexander, 137
Pantages vaudeville circuit, 124, 137, 235, 279
Paradise Restaurant, 236
Paramount Studios, 167, 168
Paris, France, 148, 149, 174, 175
   Le Bourget, 210
Parker, Dr. Painless, 116
Parsons, Louella, 132, 164, 168, 173, 188, 197, 198, 200, 235, 266, 267
Paterson, Big Boy, 216
Pathé, 124, 125, 127, 164
Patterson, Joseph, 159
Patterson, Mortimer B., 260
Peabody, Kenneth, 168, 169
Pearl Harbor, Hawaii, 255
Pecord, Ollie, 100, 115–118
Pegler, Westbrook, 203, 218
Pelakoff, Moses, 254
Peterson, Ned, 258
Phantom of the Opera, The, 164
Phelan, John, 193
Philadelphia, Pennsylvania, 52, 86, 87, 198, 199, 205
Philadelphia Centennial, 194
Pickfair, 133
Pickford, Mary, 128, 133, 164
Playa Ensenada, 228, 229
Police Gazette, 16
Polo Grounds, New York, 152, 160
Pope, Frankie, 203
Preston, John W., 129
Price, Jack, 39–42, 44–46
Price, Jim, 42

Price, Utah, 32
Prizefighter and the Lady, The, 237
Provo, Utah, 14, 282
Pueblo, Colorado, 53, 54
Purdy, Eddie, 233
Pyle, Ernie, 262

Quimby, Fred C., 124

Rabagliati, Alberto, 177
Racine, Wisconsin, 76
Rambova, Natacha, 195, 197
Red Cross, 53, 82, 83, 84, 87, 89, 101, 123
Reid, Wally, 212
Reisler, John. *See* John the Barber
Reno, Nevada, 32, 36, 37, 229, 231, 232, 234, 235, 238, 239, 299
Rice, Grantland (Grannie), 95, 98, 114, 122, 123, 127, 153, 185, 218
Richman, Harry, 186
Rickard, Edith Mae (Mrs. Tex), 163
Rickard, Maxine (Mrs. Tex), 224, 225
Rickard, Tex, 35, 76, 92–100, 102, 105, 110, 111, 113–115, 119, 131, 135, 139–143, 147, 150, 155, 156, 157, 160–163, 173, 179, 182, 183, 188–194, 197, 198, 200, 201, 205, 206, 208–214, 216, 221, 223–225, 273, 292, 294
Riders of the Purple Sage, 190
Riding and Hunt Club, 241
Ringling, John, 131, 141, 152, 218, 273
Ringling Brothers Barnum & Bailey Circus, 273
Rio Grande Eating House, 13, 14
Rio Grande Railroad, 5
Roberts, Race Horse, 209
Robinson, Dallas Hanley (Jack), 294
Robinson, "Spike," 125
Roche, Billy, 43, 44
Rockefeller, John D., 145
Rogers, Will, 164, 216
Rooney, Mickey, 269
Roosevelt, Franklin Delano, 213, 235, 251, 252, 263
Roosevelt, John, 300
Roosevelt, Theodore, Jr., 145
Royal Family (English), 307
Runyon, Damon, 39, 42–45, 98, 99, 103, 115, 116, 141, 148, 153, 162, 172, 174, 176, 189, 190, 216, 218, 236, 255, 273
Ruppert, Jake, 83, 245
Russell, Dr. Joseph L., 216
Ruth, Babe, 207, 208, 216, 267, 269

Ryan, John, 107, 108

Sacco and Vanzetti, 210
Sacks, Leonard, 211, 230, 231, 245
Saddler, Sandy, 305
St. Patrick's Cathedral, 255
St. Paul, Minnesota, 83
Salica, Louis, 260, 305
Salt Lake City, Utah, 23, 31, 32, 35, 39,
    45, 54, 56, 73, 124, 128, 146, 155,
    195, 239, 241, 291
Sampson, Sam, 152, 153
San Diego, California, 169, 229
San Francisco, California, 64, 68, 85, 128,
    206
  draft board, 89, 130
  draft evasion trial, 129–131
San Francisco Bulletin, 58, 116
San Francisco Call, 141
San Francisco Examiner, 68, 69
San Joaquin Valley, California, 222
San Luis Valley, Colorado, 5
San Luis Valley Tribune and Pioneer Day,
    301
San Remo, 244, 245
San Simeon, California, 191
Santa Monica, California, 278, 289
Saratoga Springs, New York, 157, 193, 194
Sardi's, 235, 287
Sargent School of Dramatic Arts, 167
Scalzo, Petey, 305
Scarsdale, New York, 258
Schenck, Joe, 206, 266
Schmeling, Max, 174, 230, 238, 269
Scott, Joseph, 232
Sedgwick, Josie, 125
Seeman, Billy, 180, 181
Sells-Floto Circus, 28, 124
Seltzer, Louis B., 294
Senate Antitrust and Monopoly Subcom-
    mittee, 298
Sennett, Jimmy, 181
Servo, Marty, 257
Shade, Dave, 216
Shapiro, Pete, 304
Sharkey, Jack, 210, 211, 213, 305
Sharkey, Tom, 114
Sharkey-Stribling fight, 223, 225
Sheehy, Mother, 75, 80
Shelby, Montana, 151–155
Shor, Toots, 186, 236, 265, 266
Simmons, Jean, 280
Simpson, 67
Sinatra, Frank, 266
Sirica, John J., 241, 242, 264, 266, 274,
    300

Sirica, Lucy Camalier (Mrs. John J.), 274,
    300
1619 Broadway Realty Company, 307
Smith, Edward H., 265
Smith, Ethel, 266
Smith, Gunboat, 46, 49, 50, 68, 69, 70, 90
Smith, Harry B., 114
Smith, Homer, 76, 77
Smith, Moe, 187
Smithsonian Institution, 309
Smoot, Mary Celia. *See* Dempsey, Mary
    Celia S.
Smoot, Reed, 2
Sobel, Nat, 300
Soldier Field, Chicago, 214, 217
Solomons, Jack, 307
Soper's Ranch, 209
Splain, Maury, 301
Spirit of St. Louis, 210
Spokane, Washington, 230
Sports Illustrated, 293
Stage Door Canteen, 255
Steamboat Springs, Colorado, 10
Steinman, Harold, 234
Stevenson, Hayden, 164
Steward, G. U., 257
Stockdale, Carl, 125
Stone, Lewis, 168
Stork Club, 235, 236, 239, 265, 287
Stubbs, Roy, 282
Sudenberg, Johnny, 35–37, 278, 282
Sullivan, Ed, 181, 182, 255, 300
Sullivan, John L., 7, 8, 25, 180
Sullivan, Sylvia (Mrs. Ed), 300
Sun Shipyard, Philadelphia, 87, 127
Sutherland, Eddie, 222
Swanson, Gloria, 222

Tacoma Shipyards, Washington, 60
Talmadge, Norma, 164
Tammen, H. H., 28, 72
Tate, Bill, 105, 106, 115, 116
Taylor, Estelle. *See* Dempsey, Estelle
    Taylor
Tepp, David, 260
Thalberg, Irving, 163
Thatcher, Addison Q., 99, 100
Thaw, Harry K., 138
This Is Your Life!, 282
Thomas, Charles W., 128
Thomas, James, 48
Thompson, Kay, 253
300 Club, New York, 186
Tiger, Dick, 305
Tijuana, Mexico, 288
Tijuana Jockey Club, 222

Time, 244
Time, Incorporated, 293, 295
Tobin, Henry, 198
Toledo, Ohio, 99–105, 108, 113, 293, 294
Toledo Athletic Club, 99
Tonopah, Nevada, 35, 36, 278
Toots Shor's, 287
Torres, José, 305
Tortorich, 96
Training, 38, 45, 76, 84, 86, 102, 103, 105,
    106, 109, 135, 138, 140, 153, 198,
    208, 209, 211, 215
Treat Hotel, 85
Trent, Mike, 198–200, 202, 203
Truman, Harry S., 263
Tunney, Gene, 44, 139, 178, 179, 188–192,
    197, 198, 200–203, 205, 209, 210,
    212–221, 240, 241, 244, 249, 297,
    298, 300, 305
Tunney, John Varick, 297, 298
Tunney, Polly (Mrs. Gene), 300
Turkey in the Straw, 2
Turner, Bill, 300
Twentieth Century Fox Studios, 164, 177,
    190, 266
Twentieth Century Sporting Club, 243
"21," 186, 235
Twyman, Harvey, 262

Uncle Tom Luther's, 157, 160, 211
Uncompahgre, Colorado, 8, 10
Underwood, George, 140, 191, 218
United States Coast Guard, 256, 257, 264
United States District Attorney, 128
United States Federal Court, San
    Francisco, 129
United States Navy, 88
Universal Detective Agency, 258
Universal Studios, Hollywood, 163, 167,
    169, 195

Valentino, Rudolph, 83, 164, 177, 195,
    196, 197
Van Doren, Mamie, 284
Van Dyke, W. S., 125, 126, 236, 237
Van Kelton Tennis Courts, 138
Vaudeville, 90–92, 101, 137
Velez, Lupe, 176, 209, 226, 232
Vietnam War, 293

Walcott, Jersey Joe, 268
Walker, Beany, 115
Walker, Frank, 153
Walker, H. W., 116
Walker, Jimmy, 145, 180, 181, 235
Walker, Mickey, 168, 169, 172, 201
Wall, Jack, 182
Walsh, George, 168
Walsh, Herbert, F., 257
Wanger, Walter, 168
War loan drive, 264, 265
Warner Brothers, 195
Waxman, Max, 245–248, 251, 255, 256
Wentz, Ray, 14
Western Avenue, Hollywood, 155
Westward move, 4, 5
While New York Sleeps, 167
White, Andrew, 146
White, Bill, 265
White, Stanford, 138
Willard, Hattie (Mrs. Jess), 301
Willard, Jess, 53, 58, 72, 73, 75, 80, 84–86,
    91, 93–99, 103–120, 122, 155, 212,
    237, 247, 248, 295, 301
William Fox Studio. *See* Twentieth
    Century Fox Studios
Williams, Hannah. *See* Dempsey, Hannah
    Williams
Wills, Harry, 106, 150, 151, 178, 179, 188,
    191, 210
Wilmington, Delaware, 167, 211, 213
Wilshire Apartments, 155, 165, 190, 207
Wilson, Earl, 300
Wilson, Gus, 200, 209
Wilson, Rosemary (Mrs. Earl), 300
Winchell, Walter, 161, 186, 190, 218, 236,
    255
Windsor, Fred, 54–60, 116
Winn, Matt, 215
Winnipeg, Canada, 246
Woodall, Benny, 258–260
Woods, Fred, 25, 26
World Sporting Club, 307
World War I, 53, 87, 88
World War II, 255–263
Wynn, Ed, 235, 253

Yankee Stadium, New York, 191, 192, 269

Zanzibar, 265